Table of Cor

Introduction	
Breakfast	14
Apple Oatmeal	14
French Toast Pudding	14
Breakfast Quiche	15
Pot Pancake	15
Monkey Bread	16
Morning Muffins	16
Soy Yogurt	17
Coconut Yogurt with Berries	17
Breakfast Potatoes	18
Rice with Maple Syrup	18
Acorn Squash Oats	19
Miso Oat Porridge	19
Buckwheat with Pecans	20
Rice Pudding	20
Tapioca Pudding	21
Soaked Quinoa	21
Raspberry Pancake Bites	22
Chia Pudding	22
Breakfast Grits	23
Falafel	23
Coconut Cut Oats	24
Mini Breakfast Carrot Cakes	24
White Couscous with Syrup	25
Baked Oatmeal Cake	25
Breakfast Banana Bread	26
Cashew Yogurt with Pomegranate Seeds	26
Granola Bars	27
Idli	27
Banana Pancakes	28
Tofu Scramble	28
Breakfast Hash	29
FlapJacks	29
Chocolate Morning Bars	30
Breakfast Cookies	30
Stuffed Sweet Potato	31
Superfood Cookies	31
Brown Rice Congee	32
Potato Chaat	32

Almond Milk Cocktail ... 33
Banana Rolls ... 33
Breakfast Bowl ... 34
Tofu Omelet ... 34
Tapioca Porridge ... 35
Zucchini Frittata ... 35
Apple Cream of Wheat ... 36
Oatmeal Muffins ... 36
Tempeh Bowl ... 37
Tender Tofu Cubes ... 37
Potato Pancakes ... 38
Avocado Sandwiches ... 38

Burgers and Patties ... 39
Quinoa Patties ... 39
Broccoli Patties ... 40
Cauliflower Potato Burgers ... 40
Sweet Potato Burgers ... 41
Potato Patties ... 41
Lentil Burger ... 42
Black Beans Burger ... 42
Mushroom Burger ... 43
Seitan Burger ... 43
Spinach Patties ... 44
Tempeh Burger ... 44
Pumpkin Burger ... 45
Apple Patties ... 45
Butternut Squash Burger ... 46
Chickpea Burger ... 46
Mexican Style Burger ... 47
Jalapeno Burger ... 47
Beet Burger ... 48
Portobello Burgers ... 48
Green Burgers ... 49
Onion Patties ... 49
Zucchini Patties ... 50
Carrot Patties ... 50
Artichoke Burger ... 51
Spicy Kale Burger ... 51
Wild Rice Burger ... 52
Sun Dried Tomato Patties ... 52
Eggplant Burger ... 53
Tofu Burger ... 53
Cabbage Patties ... 54
Corn Burger ... 54
Banana Patties ... 55

Spaghetti Patties 55
Sweet Pepper Patties 56
Green Peas Burger 56
Oatmeal Patties 57
Amaranth Burger 57
Turnip Patties 58
Celery Patties 58
Farro Burger 59
Yam Patties 59
Barley Burger 60
Red Kidney Beans Burger 60
Bok Choy Patties 61
Semolina-Cilantro Patties 61
Cranberry Patties 62
Sweet Pear Patties 62
Mashed White Potato Patties 63
Leek Patties 63
Asparagus Burger 64

Side Dishes 65
Glazed Bok Choy 65
Pumpkin Puree 65
Lemon Potatoes 66
Quinoa with Basil and Lemongrass 66
Tender Yellow Couscous 66
Mashed Potato 67
Vermicelli Bowl 67
Broccoli Rice 67
Sweet Potato Mash 68
Red Cabbage with Apples 68
Garlic Spaghetti Squash 68
Baked Potato 69
Vegan Applesauce 69
Mexican Rice 69
Polenta 70
Pasta Marinara 70
Butter Corn 70
Artichoke Petals 71
Beets 71
Tender Sweet Peppers 71
Spiced Okra 72
Sweet Baby Carrots 72
Soft Kale 72
Cauliflower Rice 73
Barley 73
Creamed Corn 73

Mac'n Cheese 74
Green Beans with Nuts... 74
Potato Salad.. 75
Cilantro Brussels Sprouts 75
Mushroom Risotto 76
Ratatouille 76
Pineapple Rice.. 77
Mongolian Stir Fry... 77
Mushroom "Bacon" 77
Crushed Baby Potatoes.. 78
Bang Bang Broccoli 78
Tikka Masala with Cauliflower 79
Vegetable En Papillote... 79
Brown Rice 80
Fragrant Bulgur 80
Baked Apples 80
Scalloped Potatoes 81
Glazed White Onions 81
Spicy Garlic 81
Pasta and Green Peas Side Dish.. 82
Almond Milk Millet... 82
Stir Fried Kale 82
Zoodles 83
Buckwheat.. 83
Grains and Pasta 84
Japgokbap 84
Proso Millet.. 84
Sweet Rice 84
Basmati Rague 85
Arborio Rice... 85
Vanilla Rice Pudding... 86
Oatmeal with Tender Onions.. 86
Cayenne Pepper Corn 87
PopCorn 87
Teff in Tomato Paste 87
Amaranth Banana Porridge 88
Basic Amaranth Recipe.. 88
Multi-Grain Porridge... 88
Green Buckwheat... 89
Balsamic Rice Noodles 89
Rosemary Creamed Polenta.. 90
Pasta Puttanesca 90
Pasta Fagioli 91
Mushroom Tetrazzini 91
Arrabiatta Pasta 92

Bolognese 92
Italian Style Pasta 93
Tomato Spaghetti 93
Tofu Spaghetti 94
Pumpkin Mac and Cheese 94
Basil Pasta 95
Buckwheat Pasta with Mushroom Sauce 95
Classic Wheat Berries 95
Freekeh Tacos 96
Quinoa and Freekeh Mix 96
Sorgotto 97
Tuscan Sorghum 97
Rye Berries 98
Soba Noodles with Curry Tofu 98
Mac with Artichokes 99
Pesto Pasta 99
Curry Rice 100
Taco Pasta 100
Caprese Pasta 101
Pizza Pasta 101
Pasta Alfredo 102
Penne Rigate 102
Dill Orzo 103
Tomato Farfalle with Arugula 103
Buckwheat Groats 104
Creamy Spelt Berries 104
Bulgur Salad 104
Vegan Quinoa Pilaf 105
Rice Garden Salad 105
Lemon Pasta 106
Beans and Lentils 107
Baked Beans 107
Mexican Pinto Beans 107
Vegan Black Beans 108
Lentil Radish Salad 108
Lebanese Lemon and Beans Salad 109
Lentil Tacos 109
Red Kidney Beans Burrito 110
Lentil Meatballs 110
Black Beans Chili 111
Burrito Bowl 111
Cowboy Caviar 112
Chipotle Chili with Hot Sauce 112
Vaquero Beans Chili with Tempeh 113
Creamy Kidney Beans 113

Spicy Tacos with Beans 114
Edamame Dip 114
Zoodles with Lentils 115
Buffalo Chickpea..115
Mung Beans Croquettes 115
Pinto Beans Quinoa Salad 116
Beanballs 116
Lentil Stew with Spinach...117
Bean Loaf...117
Bean Enchiladas 118
Rice and Beans Bowl..118
Frijoles Negros 119
Bean Casserole 119
Spaghetti Squash Bean Bowl...120
Red Beans Cauliflower Rice..120
Stuffed Sweet Potato with Beans 121
Curry White Beans...121
Kidney Beans Koftas with Mushrooms...122
Stuffed Peppers with Kidney Beans 122
Chickpea Shakshuka 123
Buddha Bowl...123
Chickpea Curry...124
Chickpea Salad..124
Buffalo Chickpea..125
Edamame Toast 125
Lentils Shepherd's Pie 126
Lentil Bolognese...126
Lentil Loaf 127
Lentil Chili...127
Sloppy Lentils 128
Masala Lentils 128
Lentil Ragout...129
Lentil Mash 129
Red Lentil Dal 130
Lentil Tomato Salad...130
Cabbage Rolls with Lentils...131
Soup and Stews..132
Wild Rice Soup...132
Pumpkin Cream Soup 132
Classic Vegetable Soup..133
Cauliflower Soup...133
Noodle Soup 134
Potato Chowder with Corn 134
Leek Soup..135
French Onion Soup..135

Potato Cream Soup...136
Quinoa Tomato Soup 136
Lentil Soup..137
Butternut Squash Ginger Soup 137
Minestrone 138
Carrot Soup...138
Kale and Sweet Potato Soup 139
Beta Carotene Booster Soup...139
Beet Soup 140
Anti-Inflammatory Soup..140
Creamy Tomato Soup 141
Taco Soup..141
Chickpea Soup 142
Cabbage Detox Soup..142
Spinach and Lentils Soup...143
Tuscan Soup..143
Broccoli Soup..144
Tortilla Soup 144
Mushroom Cream Soup...145
Penne Pasta Soup 145
Winter Stew 146
Vegan "Beef" Stew 146
Egyptian Stew...147
Moroccan Stew 147
Peas and Carrot Stew 148
Mediterranean Vegan Stew 148
Sweet Potato Stew 149
Kuru Fasulye...149
Rainbow Stew 150
Irish Stew 150
Fennel Soup 151
African Stew 151
Thai Curry Soup...152
Garden Stew 152
Tom Yum Soup...153
Coconut Cream Soup 153
Hot Pepper Chickpea Stew 154
Summer Stew..154
Texas Stew 155
Soybean Stew..155
Iranian Stew 156
Ratsherrenpfanne 156
Main Dishes... 157
Greek Style Stewed Artichokes 157
Turkish Green Beans..157

7

Nutritious Lasagna	158
Vegan Butter "Chicken"	158
Jackfruit Curry	159
Asian Steamed Dumplings	159
Portobello Roast	160
Posole	160
Lentil Gumbo	161
Chana Masala with Spinach	161
Potato Tamales	162
Saag Tofu with Spinach	162
Tofu Matar	163
Tso's Tofu	163
Tofu Cubes in Peanut Sauce	164
Tempeh	164
Tempeh Tajine	165
Aloo Gobi	165
Korma	166
Cassoulet	166
Stuffed Eggplants	167
Herbed Cauliflower Head	167
Potato Cakes with Filling	168
Norwegian Style Balls	168
Teriyaki Tofu	169
Broccoli Gnocchi	169
Hash Brown Omelette	170
Mushroom "Pulled Pork"	170
Chipotle Fajitas	171
Bibimbap	171
Mushroom Bourguignon	172
Vegetable Gnocchi	172
Cashew Cheese	173
Popcorn Cauliflower	173
Lentil Steak	174
Ravioli	174
Vegan Pepperoni	175
Vegan Sausages	175
Deli Slices	176
Mushroom Pie	176
Stuffed Spinach Shells	177
Pumpkin Risotto	177
Strudel	178
Tempeh Ribs	178
Rainbow Vegetable Pie	179
Stuffed Mini Pumpkins	179
Nut Loaf	180

Fragrant Spring Onions ... 180
Beet Steaks ... 181
Stuffed Figs ... 181
Snacks and Appetizers ... 182
    Boiled Peanuts ... 182
    Tempeh Potato Wraps ... 182
    Tofu Wraps ... 183
    Pumpkin Hummus ... 183
    Roasted Nuts ... 184
    Spicy Edamame Snack ... 184
    Vegan Nuggets ... 185
    Crunchwrap Supreme ... 185
    Spring Rolls ... 186
    Delicious Lettuce Wraps ... 186
    Garlic Toasts ... 187
    Quinoa Sandwich ... 187
    Crispy Chickpea ... 187
    Turkish Vegan Borek ... 188
    Vegan Jerky ... 188
    Carrot "Dogs" ... 188
    Gyros ... 189
    Herbed Tomato ... 189
    Lentils Crackers ... 190
    Eggplant Rolls ... 190
    Mushroom Bruschetta ... 191
    BBQ Cauliflower Florets ... 191
    Asparagus Pastries ... 192
    Cocktail Balls ... 192
    Arugula Puffs ... 193
    Beetroot Fold-Overs ... 193
    Sweet Apple Wedges ... 194
    Candied Pecans ... 194
    Buffalo Brussels Sprouts ... 195
    Mushroom Pate ... 195
    Cardamom Pineapple Sticks ... 196
    Appetizer Quinoa Balls ... 196
    Tofu Strips ... 197
    Chickpea Slices ... 197
    Crunchy Oyster Mushrooms ... 198
    Jackfruit Coated Bites ... 198
    Sofritas Tofu ... 199
    Garlic Pumpkin Seeds ... 199
    Flatbread ... 199
    Polenta Fries ... 200
    Green Croquettes ... 200

    Cigar Borek 201
    Flaked Clusters 201
    Chickpea Crackers 202
    Eggplant Fries 202
    Crunchy Artichoke Hearts 203
    Scallion Pancakes 203
    Mushroom Arancini 204
    Coated Heart of Palm 204
    Sweet Tofu Cubes 205

Sauces and Fillings 206
    Vegan Gravy 206
    Samosa Filling 206
    Cacao Spread 207
    Mexican Rice Filling 207
    Cauliflower Sauce 208
    Vegan French Sauce 208
    Pumpkin Butter 209
    Cranberry Sauce 209
    Spinach Dip 209
    Red Kidney Beans Sauce 210
    Cayenne Pepper Filling 210
    Vegan Cheese Sauce 211
    Beetroot Garlic Filling 211
    Avocado Pesto 212
    Pear Filling 212
    Mushroom Sauce 212
    White Bean Sauce 213
    Caramel Pumpkin Sauce 213
    Ravioli Sauce 213
    Queso Sauce 214
    Basil Cream Sauce 214
    Creamy Green Peas Filling 214
    Tomato Sauce 215
    Alfredo Sauce 215
    Spaghetti Sauce 216
    Marinara Sauce 216
    Tomato Bean Pate 217
    Mint Filling 217
    Artichoke Sandwich Filling 217
    Caramel Sauce for Vegetables 218
    Spinach Sauce 218
    Coconut Filling 218
    Ginger Sauce 219
    Tahini Sauce with Orange Juice 219
    Sriracha Sauce 219

Chimichurri Sauce 220
Guacamole with Broccoli 220
Miso Butter 221
Vegan Buffalo Dip 221
Oregano Onion Dip 221
Baba Ganoush 222
Chili Sauce 222
Walnut Sauce 222
Green Sauce 223
Herbed Lemon Sauce 223
Roasted Pepper Salsa 224
Arugula Hummus 224
Edamole 225
Pizza Sauce 225
Garlic Dip 225
Desserts 226
Black Beans Cookies 226
Bean Cookie Dough 226
Navy Beans Biscuits 227
Chickpea Chocolate Hummus 227
White Beans Blondies 228
Cranberry Cake 228
Apple Crumble 229
Gajar Halwa 229
Chocolate Cake 230
Pumpkin Muffins 230
Vanilla Custard 231
Vanilla Caramel Cream 231
Strawberry Gummies 231
Carrot Cake 232
Pumpkin Spice Pie 233
Lemon Curd 233
Brownies 234
Dulce de Leche 234
Cheesecake 235
Flan Mini Cakes 235
Creme Brulee 236
Maple Syrup Apples 236
Pear Pudding 236
Rhubarb Bars 237
Pumpkin Pudding 237
Sweet Potato Pie 238
Soda Cake 238
Poached Peaches 239
Date Bars 239

Banana Cream Tart 240
Cookie Cake 240
Chocolate Pudding 241
Chia Seeds Cookies...241
Orange-Pineapple Cake 242
Almond Cookies...242
Gingerbread Pie..243
Apple Upside Down Cake 243
Snickerdoodle Bars 244
Walnut Sweets 244
Cinnamon Swirls 245
Turmeric Loaf 245
Semolina Halwa..246
Pecan Pie 246
Warm Aromatic Lassi..247
Toffee...247
Pear Compote..247
Cream Pie Pudding..248
Banana Cake..248
Carambola in Chai Syrup...249
Semolina Pudding with Mango..249
Conclusion... 250
Recipe Index 251

Introduction

Nowadays veganism is one of the most popular trends all over the world. Thousands of people prefer to refuse animal products and follow a natural lifestyle. A vegan diet has started its history since the 1944 year and in five years later Leslie J Cross suggested to get the definition for veganism. He supported the idea of the emancipation of animals from the human's exploitation. During the years the definition of veganism had been modified and now it became the lifestyle which supports respectful attitude to animals and nature in general.

Veganism is the type of vegetarianism which implies the restriction of meat, poultry, seafood, and dairy products. What do vegans eat? The vegan diet is very diverse. There are a million recipes that can satisfy the most demanded tastes. Cakes, pastries, pies, stews, curries – each of this meal is included in a vegan diet. There is only one condition: every meal should be cooked from plant-based ingredients. Vegans get all the vital vitamins, minerals, and proteins from vegetables, fruits, grains, nuts, and seeds. The right combination of ingredients and cooking technology makes vegan meals delicious and useful. There is a huge range of vegan food. For instance, there are vegan ice cream, burritos, cheese, burgers, mayonnaise, etc. If you become a vegan it doesn't mean you will avoid all your favorite food. Veganism involves eating such regular non-vegan food as lettuce, pasta, chips, bread, and different sauces.

People make a solution to become vegans for many reasons. Anyways this lifestyle has a range of advantages for everyone! First of all plant-based diet (vegan diet) allows the body to receive enough amount of iron, folic acid, magnesium, vitamins C and B1 that are vital for our organism. In the same time during a vegan diet, it is impossible to consume a high amount of saturated fats and cholesterol.

Veganism helps to decrease such dangerous diseases as stroke, Type 2 diabetes, obesity, colon and prostate cancer, Hypertension, and Ischemic heart disease. The diet is indicated for people of any age. However, to avoid the lack of nutrient deficiencies such way of eating requires special attention to your daily meal ratio.

In this book, you will find various recipes for any occasion. There is no need to come up with what to cook. The cookbook includes breakfast recipes, side dishes, recipes of burgers, patties, snack, appetizers, beans and lentils meals, sauces, grains, pasta, and delicious desserts! Everything you need is the inspiration and desire to cook masterpieces!

Breakfast

Apple Oatmeal
Prep time: 5 minutes | Cooking time: 20 minutes | Servings: 2

Ingredients:
- 1 cup cut oats
- 2 teaspoon coconut oil
- 1 cup apples, chopped
- 2 ½ cup water
- 3 tablespoon brown sugar
- 1 teaspoon vanilla extract
- ½ teaspoon ground cinnamon

Directions:
Press the Saute mode on your instant pot. Place the coconut oil, apples, brown sugar, vanilla extract, and ground cinnamon in the instant pot. Add cut oats and stir. Saute the mixture for 4-5 minutes. Stir it from time to time. Then add water and mix it up. Close the lid and press Manual mode (High pressure). Cook the oatmeal for 13 minutes on High. Then make quick pressure release. Mix up the meal well before serving.

Nutrition value/serving: calories 236, fat 6.2, fiber 5, carbs 42.9, protein 6.2

French Toast Pudding
Prep time: 10 minutes | Cooking time: 16 minutes | Servings: 5

Ingredients:
- 4 bananas, chopped
- 1 cup almond milk
- 4 slices vegan French bread
- 2 tablespoons maple syrup
- 1 teaspoon vanilla extract
- 1 tablespoon almond butter
- 1 teaspoon ground cinnamon
- ¼ teaspoon ground cloves
- 1 cup water, for cooking

Directions:
Pour water in the instant pot. Chop the bread and place it in the round pan. Blend together maple syrup, chopped bananas, vanilla extract, ground cinnamon, and ground cloves until smooth. Pour the liquid over the bread. Cover the pan with the foil and secure the edges well. Transfer the pan in the instant pot and close the lid. Set the manual mode and cook pudding on High for 16 minutes. Then make quick pressure release. Open the lid and remove foil from the pan. Add almond butter and stir gently.

Nutrition value/serving: calories 387, fat 14.5, fiber 5.3, carbs 59.6, protein 8.9

Breakfast Quiche
Prep time: 15 minutes | Cooking time: 25 minutes | Servings: 2

Ingredients:
- 10 oz firm tofu
- 1 cup spinach
- 1 oz mushrooms, chopped
- ½ teaspoon turmeric
- ½ teaspoon salt
- 1 teaspoon coconut oil
- ½ teaspoon ground cumin
- ¼ cup fresh dill, chopped
- 1 cup water, for cooking

Directions:
Chop tofu and put in the blender. Add spinach, mushrooms, turmeric, salt, coconut oil, ground cumin, dill, and blend the mixture until smooth. Pour water in the instant pot. When the tofu mixture is done – pour it in the pan and flatten gently. Place the pan in the instant pot (in water) and cover with foil. Make the medium hole in the foil and close the lid. Cook the quiche for 25 minutes on High (Manual mode). Then make a quick pressure release. Chill the quiche for 10 minutes before serving.

Nutrition value/serving: calories 144, fat 8.7, fiber 2.8, carbs 7.4, protein 13.8

Pot Pancake
Prep time: 10 minutes | Cooking time: 50 minutes | Servings: 5

Ingredients:
- 1 cup all-purpose flour
- 1 teaspoon baking powder
- 1 teaspoon lemon juice
- 1/3 cup almond milk
- 1 teaspoon vanilla extract
- 1 teaspoon almond butter
- 5 teaspoon maple syrup

Directions:
Whisk together all-purpose flour, baking powder, lemon juice, almond milk, and vanilla extract. When the mixture is homogenous and smooth let it rest for 10 minutes. Meanwhile, set the Saute mode and toss almond butter inside the instant pot. Melt it. Pour the flour mixture in the instant pot and flatten it gently to get the shape of a pancake. Set the Manual mode (Low Pressure) and close the lid. Cook the pancake for 50 minutes. Check if the pancake is cooked with the help of the toothpick. Transfer it on the plate. Pour it over with the maple syrup.

Nutrition value/serving: calories 99, fat 5.6, fiber 0.9, carbs 11.2, protein 1.7

Monkey Bread

Prep time: 15 minutes | *Cooking time:* 40 minutes | *Servings:* 4

Ingredients:
- 3 refrigerated biscuits
- 3 tablespoon brown sugar
- 1 teaspoon vanilla extract
- 4 tablespoon coconut oil
- 2 tablespoons maple syrup
- Cooking spray

Directions:
Chop the biscuits into medium pieces. Spray the instant pot with the cooking spray from inside. Then transfer the chopped biscuits in the instant pot and sprinkle with brown sugar. Add maple syrup and coconut oil. Stir the mixture well. Close the lid and set Manual mode (High pressure). Cook monkey bread for 40 minutes. Then make quick pressure release and chill the meal for 5 minutes.

Nutrition value/serving: calories 219, fat 14.4, fiber 0.3, carbs 22.2, protein 1.2

Morning Muffins

Prep time: 10 minutes | *Cooking time:* 10 minutes | *Servings:* 5

Ingredients:
- 1 banana, chopped
- 1 teaspoon vanilla extract
- 1 tablespoon cocoa powder
- 4 tablespoon flax meal
- 4 teaspoon almond butter
- 3 teaspoon white sugar
- 2 tablespoons almond milk
- ½ teaspoon baking powder
- 1 cup water, for cooking

Directions:
Blend chopped banana until smooth and transfer it in the mixing bowl. Add vanilla extract, cocoa powder, flax meal, almond butter, white sugar, almond milk, and baking powder. Mix up the mixture and place it in the muffin molds. Fill ½ part of every muffin mold. Pour water in the instant pot and set the rack. Place the muffins on the rack and close the lid. Cook the muffins for 10 minutes on Manual mode (High pressure). After this, make quick pressure release. Chill the muffins for 3-4 minutes before serving.

Nutrition value/serving: calories 152, fat 10.9, fiber 4, carbs 13.1, protein 4.5

Soy Yogurt

Prep time: 10 minutes | *Cooking time:* 11 hours | *Servings:* 6

Ingredients:

- 2 cups of soy milk
- 2 probiotic capsules
- 1 cup strawberries, chopped

Directions:

Pour 1 ½ cup of soy milk in the big jar. Mix up together remaining soy milk with probiotic capsules and whisk well. Then mix up together all soy milk and stir. After this, pour it in the yogurt jars and insert in the instant pot. Set the "Yogurt" mode and close the lid. Cook yogurt for 11 hours. When the time is over – place the yogurt in the fridge to chill and to start the process of probiotic development. Add strawberries directly before serving.

Nutrition value/serving: calories 52, fat 1.5, fiber 1, carbs 7, protein 2.8

Coconut Yogurt with Berries

Prep time: 10 minutes | *Cooking time:* 4 hours | *Servings:* 4

Ingredients:

- ¾ cup blueberries
- ¾ cup blackberries
- 1 teaspoon chia seeds
- 1 cup of coconut milk
- 1 tablespoon coconut yogurt
- 2 tablespoons white sugar

Directions:

Pour coconut milk in the instant pot bowl. Set yogurt mode and adjust the setting to get "to boil". Cook the coconut milk until it reaches 100F. Use the cooking thermometer for this step. Then add coconut yogurt and stir it until homogenous. Close the lid and leave on the yogurt mode for 3-4 hours. When the time is over – you will get a thick creamy mixture. Transfer it on the cheesecloth and squeeze gently. Then place the yogurt in the yogurt jars. Before serving add chia seeds, blackberries, and blueberries.

Nutrition value/serving: calories 198, fat 15.1, fiber 4, carbs 16.8, protein 2.3

Breakfast Potatoes

Prep time: 10 minutes | Cooking time: 21minutes | Servings: 4

Ingredients:
- 4 potatoes, peeled
- 1 tablespoon coconut oil
- ½ teaspoon dried cilantro
- 1 teaspoon salt
- ½ teaspoon ground black pepper
- 1 teaspoon dried parsley
- 1 teaspoon dried dill
- ¼ cup of water
- 1 red pepper, chopped
- 1 white onion, chopped

Directions:

Chop potatoes and place in the instant pot. Add coconut oil, dried cilantro, salt, ground black pepper, dried parsley, and dill. Stir the ingredients, set Saute mode and cook it for 6 minutes. Stir time to time. Then add red pepper and white onion. Stir. Add water and close the lid. Set the Manual mode (Low pressure) and cook potatoes for 15 minutes or until the potatoes are tender.

Nutrition value/serving: calories 198, fat 3.7, fiber 6.2, carbs 38.6, protein 4.3

Rice with Maple Syrup

Prep time: 8 minutes | Cooking time: 15 minutes | Servings: 5

Ingredients:
- 1 cup of rice
- 2 cups almond milk
- 1 teaspoon vanilla extract
- ¼ cup maple syrup
- 1 teaspoon almond butter

Directions:

Place rice in the instant pot. Add almond milk and vanilla extract. Stir gently and close the lid. Set the "Rice" mode and cook rice for 15 minutes. Then add almond butter and maple syrup. Stir it.

Nutrition value/serving: calories 419, fat 25, fiber 2.9, carbs 46.2, protein 5.5

Acorn Squash Oats

Prep time: 10 minutes | Cooking time: 10 minutes | Servings: 2

Ingredients:
- 1 acorn squash, halved
- 1 cup oatmeal
- 1 tablespoon chocolate
- 1 cup hot water
- 1 tablespoon maple syrup
- 1 teaspoon ground cinnamon
- 1 teaspoon creamed coconut milk
- 1 cup water, for cooking

Directions:
Pour water in the instant pot and set the steamer basket. Put acorn squash halves inside and close the lid. Set the manual mode and cook the vegetable for 5 minutes on High. Then make quick pressure release. Meanwhile, mix up together oatmeal and hot water in the bowl. Close the lid and leave it for 10 minutes. When the acorn squash halves are cooked – place them in the serving plate. Melt the chocolate. Mix up together cooked oatmeal and creamed coconut milk together. Transfer it inside the squash halves. Then sprinkle with melted chocolate, maple syrup, and ground cinnamon.

Nutrition value/serving: calories 306, fat 4.9, fiber 9.2, carbs 62.1, protein 7.7

Miso Oat Porridge

Prep time: 30 minutes | Cooking time: 4 minutes | Servings: 4

Ingredients:
- 1 cup Steel cut oats
- 1 teaspoon miso paste
- 1 tablespoon tahini
- ½ avocado, peeled
- ½ teaspoon nutritional yeast
- 2 cups almond milk
- ½ teaspoon chives, chopped

Directions:
Mix up together almond milk, nutritional yeast, and tahini. Then pour the liquid in the instant pot bowl. Add steel cut oats and stir gently. Close the lid. Cool the oats on High Pressure for 4 minutes. Then allow natural pressure release for 25 minutes. Meanwhile, mash the avocado well. Add miso paste and chives. Stir until smooth. Transfer the cooked oats in the bowl and add avocado mash. Stir carefully.

Nutrition value/serving: calories 394, fat 36.4, fiber 5.9, carbs 16.9, protein 5.7

Buckwheat with Pecans

Prep time: 20 minutes | Cooking time: 5 minutes | Servings: 6

Ingredients:
- 2 cups buckwheat
- ¼ cup pecans, chopped
- 1 tablespoon raisins, chopped
- 1 teaspoon vanilla extract
- 4 tablespoon maple syrup
- 2 cups of water
- 2 cups of coconut milk

Directions:
Place buckwheat in the instant pot. Add vanilla extract, water, and coconut milk. Close the lid and set Manual mode (High pressure). Cook the buckwheat for 5 minutes. Then allow the natural pressure release for 20 minutes. Add raisins, maple syrup, and chopped pecans in the buckwheat and stir well before serving.

Nutrition value/serving: calories 468, fat 26, fiber 8.2, carbs 56.2, protein 10.1

Rice Pudding

Prep time: 20 minutes | Cooking time: 8 minutes | Servings: 4

Ingredients:
- 1 ½ cup of rice
- 3 cups of rice milk
- 1 tablespoon all-purpose flour
- 2 tablespoon sugar
- ¼ teaspoon turmeric
- 1 teaspoon vanilla extract

Directions:
In the mixing bowl combine together ½ cup of rice milk and all-purpose flour. Add sugar, turmeric, and vanilla extract. Then pour it in the instant pot bowl. Add rice, sugar, and remaining rice milk. Stir gently. Close the lid and set the Manual mode (High pressure). Cook the rice pudding for 8 minutes. Then allow natural pressure release for 20 minutes. Open the lid and stir the rice pudding – it should have a soft but thick texture.

Nutrition value/serving: calories 376, fat 2, fiber 1, carbs 81.8, protein 5.5

Tapioca Pudding

Prep time: 10 minutes | Cooking time: 10 minutes | Servings: 5

Ingredients:
- ½ cup tapioca
- 3 cups of coconut milk
- 3 tablespoon brown sugar
- ½ teaspoon ground cinnamon
- 1 teaspoon cornstarch
- 1 teaspoon almond butter

Directions:
Combine together coconut milk and cornstarch. Whisk the mixture until smooth. Then pour the liquid in the instant pot. Add tapioca, brown sugar, ground cinnamon, and almond butter. Stir it. Close the lid and cook pudding on Manual mode (High pressure) for 10 minutes. Then make quick pressure release and open the lid. Stir the pudding well. Close the lid and let it chill till the room temperature before serving.

Nutrition value/serving: calories 428, fat 36.1, fiber 3.8, carbs 28, protein 4

Soaked Quinoa

Prep time: 6 hours | Cooking time: 4 minutes | Servings: 4

Ingredients:
- 2 cups of water
- 1 cup vegetable stock
- 1 cup quinoa
- ½ tablespoon apple cider vinegar
- ½ teaspoon salt
- 1 teaspoon almond butter

Directions:
Combine together quinoa, apple cider vinegar, and water in the bowl and let it stay for 8 hours. Then drain the water and strain quinoa. Transfer quinoa in the instant pot and add vegetable stock, salt, and almond butter. Close the lid and cook on Manual mode (High pressure) for 4 minutes. Make a quick pressure release and stir the cooked quinoa.

Nutrition value/serving: calories 184, fat 4.9, fiber 3.6, carbs 28.5, protein 7.1

Raspberry Pancake Bites
Prep time: 10 minutes | *Cooking time:* 9 minutes | *Servings:* 6

Ingredients:
- 1 cup all-purpose flour
- 1 teaspoon vanilla extract
- 1/3 cup raspberries
- 1/3 cup rice milk
- 1 teaspoon baking powder
- ½ tablespoon lemon juice
- 1 tablespoon coconut shred
- 2 tablespoon sugar

Directions:
In the mixing bowl mix up together all-purpose flour, baking powder, and coconut shred. Add sugar, lemon juice, rice milk, and vanilla extract. Use the hand mixer to make the smooth mass. Add raspberries and mix it up with the help of the spoon. Fill ½ part of every egg molds with batter and transfer in the instant pot. Close the lid and cook bites on Manual mode (High pressure) for 9 minutes. Then make quick pressure release.

Nutrition value/serving: calories 120, fat 1.8, fiber 1.4, carbs 23.3, protein 2.4

Chia Pudding
Prep time: 10 minutes | *Cooking time:* 5 minutes | *Servings:* 2

Ingredients:
- ½ cup chia seeds
- 1 tablespoon sugar
- 1 tablespoon Maple syrup
- 1 cup almond milk
- ½ teaspoon vanilla extract
- 1 banana, sliced

Directions:
Pour almond milk in the instant pot. Add maple syrup, vanilla extract, and sugar. Stir gently. Close the lid and cook on Manual mode (High pressure) for 5 minutes. Then make quick pressure release. Chill the liquid till the room temperature and transfer in the jars. Add sliced banana and chia seeds. Mix up gently. Close the jar lids and transfer the pudding in the fridge. The pudding is cooked in 1 hour.

Nutrition value/serving: calories 575, fat 41.1, fiber 17.9, carbs 49.8, protein 10

Breakfast Grits
Prep time: 8 minutes | Cooking time: 9 minutes | Servings: 3

Ingredients:
- 1 cup stone ground grits
- 1 tablespoon coconut oil
- ½ teaspoon salt
- 1.5 cup almond milk
- 1 teaspoon almond butter
- 4 oz tofu, grinded

Directions:
Set saute mode and put coconut oil inside instant pot. When the oil is hot – add grits and salt. Stir gently and cook for 2 minutes. After this, add grilled tofu, almond butter, and almond milk. Mix it up. Close the lid and set Manual mode (High pressure) for 9 minutes. Then make quick pressure release and mix up the cooked grits.

Nutrition value/serving: calories 410, fat 38.2, fiber 4.2, carbs 16, protein 7.9

Falafel
Prep time: 10 minutes | Cooking time: 10 minutes | Servings: 2

Ingredients:
- 7 oz chickpea, cooked
- 2 tablespoon almond flour
- 1 teaspoon tahini paste
- 1 teaspoon ground cumin
- ¼ teaspoon salt
- 1 oz fresh cilantro, chopped
- 1 teaspoon minced garlic
- ½ teaspoon onion powder
- 1 tablespoon olive oil

Directions:
Place the chickpea, almond flour, tahini paste, ground cumin, salt, cilantro, minced garlic, and onion powder in the blender. Blend the mixture until you get a smooth texture. Then make the medium balls and press them gently with the help of hands. Preheat the instant pot on Saute mode. Add olive oil. Then place falafel in the instant pot and cook it for 4-5 minutes from each side or until the meal gets a light brown color.

Nutrition value/serving: calories 304, fat 14.3, fiber 10.5, carbs 34.3, protein 13.1

Coconut Cut Oats
Prep time: 25 minutes | *Cooking time:* 6 minutes | *Servings:* 2

Ingredients:
- 1 cup of coconut milk
- ½ cup steel cut oats
- 1 tablespoon coconut shred
- 1 tablespoon brown sugar
- 1 tablespoon creamed coconut milk

Directions:
Pour coconut milk in the instant pot bowl. Add steel cut oats, coconut shred, and brown sugar. Stir gently and close the lid. Cook the oats on Manual mode (High pressure) for 6 minutes. After this, make natural pressure release for 20 minutes. Transfer the cooked oats in the serving bowls and add creamed coconut milk. Stir well. Add more sugar if desired.

Nutrition value/serving: calories 433, fat 34.9, fiber 7.7, carbs 29.2, protein 6.2

Mini Breakfast Carrot Cakes
Prep time: 15 minutes | *Cooking time:* 12 minutes | *Servings:* 6

Ingredients:
- 2 carrots, grated
- 1 banana, mashed
- 4 tablespoon brown sugar
- 1 cup all-purpose flour
- 1 teaspoon vanilla extract
- 1 ½ cup of rice milk
- 1 teaspoon baking powder
- 2 tablespoon flax meal
- 1 tablespoon pumpkin seeds
- 1 teaspoon coconut oil
- 1 cup water, for cooking

Directions:
In the mixing bowl mix up together grated carrot and mashed banana. Add brown sugar and vanilla extract. Then add flour, baking powder, and flax meal. Mix up the mixture until smooth and add rice milk. Mix it up again. Brush the mini cake molds with coconut oil and pour the carrot mixture inside them. Pour water in the instant pot and set the steamer trivet. Place the molds on the trivet and cover with foil. Secure the edges and make medium holes on the foil with the help of a toothpick. Close the lid and set Manual mode (High pressure). Cook the cakes for 12 minutes. Then make quick pressure release for 10 minutes. Remove the foil from the cakes and chill them till the room temperature.

Nutrition value/serving: calories 182, fat 3, fiber 2.3, carbs 35.9, protein 3.5

White Couscous with Syrup
Prep time: 10 minutes | Cooking time: 6 minutes | Servings: 4

Ingredients:
- 1/3 cup maple syrup
- 1/3 teaspoon ground cinnamon
- 1 cup white couscous
- 1 teaspoon almond butter
- 2 cups of water

Directions:
Pour water in the instant pot. Add almond butter and couscous. Close the lid and cook on Manual mode (High pressure) for 6 minutes. Then make quick pressure release and transfer cooked couscous in the bowl. Add maple syrup and ground cinnamon and stir well.

Nutrition value/serving: calories 252, fat 2.6, fiber 2.7, carbs 52, protein 6.4

Baked Oatmeal Cake
Prep time: 10minutes | Cooking time: 25minutes | Servings: 6

Ingredients:
- 1 cup oatmeal
- ½ cup blackberries
- 3 tablespoon all-purpose flour
- 2 tablespoons honey
- 1 teaspoon almond butter
- ½ cup of rice milk
- ½ tablespoon flax meal
- 1 tablespoon ground nutmeg

Directions:
Mash the blackberries and mix them up with the oatmeal, all purpose flour, almond butter, and rice milk. Add flax meal and ground nutmeg. Mix up the mixture until you get a smooth texture. Then pour the mixture in the non-sticky springform pan. Flatten the surface of the cake well with the help of the spatula. Cover the cake with the foil and secure the edges. Pin the foil with the help of the toothpick and insert in the instant pot. Close the lid and cook the cake on Manual mode (High pressure) for 25 minutes. Then make quick pressure release. Chill the cake till the room temperature before slicing.

Nutrition value/serving: calories 127, fat 3.3, fiber 2.8, carbs 22.5, protein 3.2

Breakfast Banana Bread

Prep time: 10 minutes | Cooking time: 40 minutes | Servings: 8

Ingredients:
- ¼ cup flax meal
- ½ cup of water
- 3 bananas, peeled
- 3 tablespoon applesauce
- 4 tablespoon brown sugar
- 1 teaspoon vanilla extract
- 1 teaspoon ground cinnamon
- ½ teaspoon ground nutmeg
- 3 cups all-purpose flour
- ¼ cup pecans, chopped
- 3 tablespoon soy milk
- 1 cup water, for cooking

Directions:

Combine together all the liquid ingredients in the mixing bowl. Then take a separate mixing bowl and mix up together flax meal, ground cinnamon, nutmeg, flour, and stir well. Mash the bananas and add in the flour mixture too. After this, add liquid mixture and mix it up with the help of the hand mixer. Add chopped pecans and stir with the help of the spoon. Spray the bread mold with the cooking spray and pour the banana batter inside. Flatten it gently with the help of a spatula. Pour water in the instant pot and insert steamer rack. Place the bread on the rack and cover it with foil. Close the instant pot lid and set Manual mode (High pressure). Cook the bread for 40 minutes. Then make the quick pressure release for 10 minutes. Chill the bread and remove it from the mold. Slice it.

Nutrition value/serving: calories 287, fat 5.8, fiber 4.3, carbs 53.4, protein 6.9

Cashew Yogurt with Pomegranate Seeds

Prep time: 10 minute | Cooking time: 12 hour | Servings: 4

Ingredients:
- 3 oz pomegranate seeds
- 2 cup cashews, soaked
- ½ cup almond yogurt
- 1 tablespoon honey
- 1 cup of water

Directions:

Blend together cashews and water until smooth and soft. Then add almond yogurt and pulse it for 30 seconds more. Transfer the mixture in the instant pot and close the lid. Set the Yogurt mode and cook it for 12 hours. When the time is over – mix up the yogurt and honey. Place the cooked yogurt in the serving bowls and sprinkle with pomegranate seeds.

Nutrition value/serving: calories 446, fat 32.9, fiber 2.5, carbs 32.7, protein 11.2

Granola Bars
Prep time: 10minutes | Cooking time: 5 minutes | Servings: 6

Ingredients:
- 3 tablespoon almond butter
- 1/3 cup maple syrup
- 1 tablespoon honey
- 3 cups quick oats
- 2 tablespoon raisins
- 1 teaspoon vanilla extract
- ¼ cup walnuts, crushed

Directions:
Set Saute instant pot mode and place almond butter, maple syrup, and honey inside. Cook it for 2-3 minutes until the mixture is homogenous. After this, add quick oats, raisins, vanilla extract, and walnuts. Mix up the mixture well and transfer in the glass mold. Flatten it well and cut into the bars. Leave the granola bars in the mold and chill it in the fridge for at least 30 minutes or until solid.

Nutrition value/serving: calories 304, fat 10.3, fiber 5.4, carbs 46.8, protein 8.4

Idli
Prep time: 5 minutes | Cooking time: 14 minutes | Servings: 2

Ingredients:
- ½ cup idli batter
- ¼ cup of water
- 1 teaspoon olive oil

Directions:
Pour water in the instant pot. Then grease the idli molds with olive oil and transfer the idli stans in the instant pot. Pour idli batter in every mold and close the lid. Cook the meal on High (Pressure mode) for 14 minutes. Then make quick pressure release.

Nutrition value/serving: calories 79, fat 2.3, fiber 3, carbs 12, protein 3

Banana Pancakes

Prep time: 10 minutes | Cooking time: 8 minutes | Servings: 6

Ingredients:
- 3 bananas, peeled
- 1 teaspoon vanilla extract
- 1 cup all-purpose flour
- 1 tablespoon white sugar
- 1 teaspoon baking powder
- 1 teaspoon apple cider vinegar
- ½ cup of rice milk
- 1 cup water, for cooking
- Cooking spray

Directions:
Mash bananas and mix them up with the flour and rice milk. Add vanilla extract, white sugar, baking powder, and apple cider vinegar. With the help of the hand whisker, stir the mixture until smooth. Spray the pancake molds with the cooking spray. Pour water in the instant pot bowl and insert rack. Pour the pancake batter in the molds and transfer in the instant pot. Close the lid and set manual mode (High pressure). Cook the pancakes for 8 minutes. Then make quick pressure release. The cooked pancakes should be soft but not liquid.

Nutrition value/serving: calories 150, fat 0.7, fiber 2.1, carbs 33.9, protein 2.8

Tofu Scramble

Prep time: 8 minutes | Cooking time: 15 minutes | Servings: 3

Ingredients:
- 8 oz firm tofu
- 1 sweet pepper, chopped
- 1 tomato, chopped
- ¼ onion, diced
- 1 teaspoon Italian seasoning
- 1 teaspoon tomato paste
- 1 teaspoon olive oil
- ¼ cup vegetable broth
- 1 teaspoon salt

Directions:
Set Saute mode and pour olive oil inside instant pot bowl. Add chopped pepper, tomato, and diced onion. Stir gently and sprinkle with Italian seasoning and salt. Saute the vegetables for 5 minutes. Stir time to time. Meanwhile, scramble tofu with the help of a fork. Add tofu in the instant pot bowl. Stir gently. Then add vegetable broth and close the lid. Saute the meal for 10 minutes.

Nutrition value/serving: calories 96, fat 5.4, fiber 1.7, carbs 6.5, protein 7.4

Breakfast Hash
Prep time: 10 minutes | Cooking time: 25 minutes | Servings: 5

Ingredients:
- 1 cup mushroom, chopped
- 1 zucchini, chopped
- 2 red potatoes, chopped
- 1 red sweet pepper, chopped
- 1/3 cup vegetable broth
- 1 teaspoon salt
- 1 tablespoon fresh dill, chopped
- ½ teaspoon ground black pepper
- 1/3 cup pinto beans, canned
- 1 tablespoon fresh parsley, chopped
- 1 tablespoon olive oil

Directions:
Preheat instant pot on Saute mode for 5 minutes. Pour olive oil and add zucchini and potatoes. Sprinkle the vegetables with salt and ground black pepper and close the lid. Saute the ingredients for 5 minutes. Then add mushrooms and sweet pepper. Add dill and parsley. Then add pinto beans and vegetable broth. Mix up the hash and close the lid. Cook the meal for 20 minutes on Saute mode.

Nutrition value/serving: calories 126, fat 0.6, fiber 4.5, carbs 25.8, protein 6

Flap Jacks
Prep time: 58 minutes | Cooking time: 15 minutes | Servings: 4

Ingredients:
- 1 cup oats
- 1 tablespoon golden syrup
- 2 tablespoon almond butter
- ½ teaspoon vanilla extract
- 1 tablespoon brown sugar
- ½ cup water, for cooking

Directions:
Place oats golden syrup, almond butter, vanilla extract, and sugar in the instant pot bowl. Stir gently and cook for 8 minutes on Saute mode. Stir the mixture from time to time. Then transfer the mixture into the instant pot baking trivet and flatten well. Pour water in the instant pot and insert rack. Place the baking trivet on the rack and close the lid. Cook the meal on Manual mode (High pressure) for 7 minutes. Then make quick pressure release, chill the meal well and cut into the bars.

Nutrition value/serving: calories 151, fat 5.8, fiber 2.9, carbs 21.5, protein 4.4

Chocolate Morning Bars
Prep time: 10 minutes | Cooking time: 13 minutes | Servings: 6

Ingredients:
- ¼ cup chocolate drops
- ½ cup all-purpose flour
- ½ teaspoon baking soda
- 1 tablespoon lime juice
- 2 tablespoon sugar
- 2 tablespoon almond butter
- 2 tablespoon creamed coconut milk
- ½ cup of water

Directions:
In the mixing bowl mix up together flour and baking soda. Add lime juice, sugar, almond butter, and creamed coconut milk. Start to knead the dough. When the dough is tender but not homogenous – add chocolate drops. Keep kneading dough until it is soft and non-sticky. Roll up the dough with the help of the rolling pin and cut into the medium bars. Line the instant pot baking pan with baking paper and put dough bars. Insert rack in the instant pot bowl and add water. Put the baking pan in the rack and close the lid. Set manual mode (high pressure) and cook the bars for 13 minutes. The time of cooking depends on the bars thickness.

Nutrition value/serving: calories 130, fat 5.3, fiber 3.7, carbs 19.1, protein 2.8

Breakfast Cookies
Prep time: 10 minutes | Cooking time: 10 minutes | Servings: 5

Ingredients:
- ¼ cup walnuts, crushed
- ¼ cup dried cranberries
- ¾ cup almonds, chopped
- 5 tablespoon aquafaba
- 1 cup wheat flour
- 2 tablespoon coconut oil
- ¼ cup maple syrup

Directions:
In the mixing bowl mix up together coconut oil, maple syrup, and aquafaba. Gradually start to add wheat flour. When the mixture is homogenous, add walnuts and dried cranberries. Stir it until the dough is smooth. Make the log from the dough and cut it into equal pieces. Roll the cookies into balls and press them gently. Place the cookies in the lined with baking paper pan and transfer in the instant pot. Close the lid and cook the cookies on Manual mode (High pressure) for 10 minutes. Make a quick pressure release. Store the cookies in a closed glass jar up to 10 days.

Nutrition value/serving: calories 303, fat 16.5, fiber 3.1, carbs 33.8, protein 7.1

Stuffed Sweet Potato

Prep time: 10 minutes | Cooking time: 30 minutes | Servings: 2

Ingredients:
- 2 sweet potatoes
- ½ cup spinach, chopped
- 4 oz leek, chopped
- 1 tablespoon olive oil
- 3 oz tempeh, chopped
- ½ teaspoon salt
- ½ teaspoon smoked paprika
- 1 teaspoon sesame seeds
- 2 teaspoons almond butter
- 1 cup of water, for cooking

Directions:

Pour water in the instant pot bowl and insert the trivet. Place the sweet potatoes on the trivet and close the lid. Cook the vegetables for 20 minutes on High. Use the quick pressure release. Meanwhile, mix up together spinach, leek, olive oil, tempeh, salt, smoked paprika, sesame seeds, and almond butter. When the sweet potatoes are cooked – remove them from the instant pot. Clean the instant pot bowl and transfer the vegetable mixture inside. Cook them on saute mode for 8 minutes. Stir them from time to time. Meanwhile, cut the sweet potatoes into halves and scoop ½ part of all flesh. Add the sweet potato flesh in the instant pot. Stir the ingredients until homogenous. Fill the sweet potato halves with the mixture.

Nutrition value/serving: calories 288, fat 21.6, fiber 3.2, carbs 16.2, protein 12.7

Superfood Cookies

Prep time: 15 minutes | Cooking time: 6 minutes | Servings: 4

Ingredients:
- ½ cup oats
- 1 tablespoon pumpkin seeds, chopped
- 1 tablespoon sunflower seeds
- 1 tablespoon almonds, chopped
- 1 tablespoon cranberries
- ½ teaspoon ground nutmeg
- 3 tablespoon aquafaba
- 1 tablespoon almond flour
- ¼ cup golden syrup
- Cooking spray

Directions:

In the mixing bowl mix up together all the ingredients except cooking spray. Then with the help of 2 spoons make medium size balls and place them on the instant pot baking trivet. Spray the cookies with cooking spray and place in the instant pot. Set manual mode (High pressure) and close the lid. Cook the cookies for 6 minutes. Then make low pressure release for 10 minutes. Chill the cookies till the room temperature.

Nutrition value/serving: calories 124, fat 2.9, fiber 1.5, carbs 24, protein 2.4

Brown Rice Congee

Prep time: 20 minutes | *Cooking time:* 25 minutes | *Servings:* 4

Ingredients:
- ½ cup of brown rice
- ½ cup basmati rice
- 4 cups mushroom broth
- 1 teaspoon Pink salt
- 4 tablespoon quinoa
- 1 teaspoon turmeric
- ½ teaspoon smoked paprika

Directions:
Put all the ingredients in the instant pot bowl and stir gently. Close the lid and set High pressure on Manual mode. Cook the meal for 25 minutes and then make the quick pressure release for 15 minutes. Stir rice congee carefully and transfer into the serving plates.

Nutrition value/serving: calories 222, fat 1.5, fiber 2.1, carbs 45.9, protein 5

Potato Chaat

Prep time: 10 minutes | *Cooking time:* 43 minutes | *Servings:* 5

Ingredients:
- 3 russet potatoes, peeled, chopped
- 1 tablespoon olive oil
- ½ tablespoon garam masala
- ½ teaspoon ground cumin
- ½ teaspoon dried basil
- ½ teaspoon dried oregano
- ½ teaspoon garlic powder
- 1 zucchini, chopped
- 1 carrot, peeled, chopped
- 1 sweet red pepper, chopped
- ¼ teaspoon ground cinnamon
- ½ cup of water
- 1 cup collards, chopped

Directions:
Put potatoes in the instant pot bowl and add olive oil and garam masala. Mix up potatoes with the help of a spatula and cook on Saute mode for 5 minutes. Meanwhile, in the mixing bowl combine together ground cumin, basil, oregano, garlic powder, and ground cinnamon. Add the spices in the instant pot bowl and mix up. Then add chopped carrot and zucchini. Cook it for 2 minutes more. Pour water in the instant pot bowl and add collards. Close the lid and cook the meal on Saute mode for 35 minutes.

Nutrition value/serving: calories 136, fat 3.2, fiber 4.6, carbs 25.3, protein 3.3

Almond Milk Cocktail

Prep time: 10 minutes | *Cooking time:* 3 minutes | *Servings:* 4

Ingredients:
- 2 cups almonds
- 4 cups of water
- 2 tablespoons honey
- ½ teaspoon ground cinnamon
- 4 teaspoon walnuts, chopped

Directions:
Place the almonds in the instant pot bowl and add 1 cup of water. Close the lid and cook almonds on Manual mode (High pressure) for 3 minutes. Then make quick pressure release. Strain the almonds and transfer them in the blender. Add all remaining water and blend the mixture until smooth and white color. Then strain the liquid to get almond milk. Mix up together almond milk, chopped walnuts, and honey. Pour the cocktail in the glasses and sprinkle with cinnamon.

Nutrition value/serving: calories 324, fat 25.3, fiber 6.3, carbs 19.3, protein 10.7

Banana Rolls

Prep time: 25 minutes | *Cooking time:* 25 minutes | *Servings:* 4

Ingredients:
- ½ teaspoon yeast
- 1/3 cup warm water
- 1 cup wheat flour
- ½ teaspoon salt
- 3 tablespoon white sugar
- 2 bananas, mashed
- 1 teaspoon vanilla extract
- 1 tablespoon brown sugar
- 1 tablespoon olive oil

Directions:
Mix up together warm water, yeast, and ½ cup of wheat flour. Add white sugar and stir the mixture until smooth. Leave it for 10 minutes. Then add salt, vanilla extract, and all remaining flour. Knead soft and non-sticky dough. Leave the dough for 10 minutes to rest in the warm place. Meanwhile, mix up together brown sugar and mashed bananas. Roll up the dough and spread it with mashed banana mixture. Roll it and cut into the buns. Brush the instant pot bowl with a ½ tablespoon of olive oil. Place the rolls in the instant pot and brush with remaining olive oil. Close the lid and set manual mode (High pressure). Cook rolls for 25 minutes. Then make quick pressure release. The time of cooking depends on rolls size.

Nutrition value/serving: calories 243, fat 4, fiber 2.5, carbs 48.9, protein 4.1

Breakfast Bowl

Prep time: 10 minutes | Cooking time: 14 minutes | Servings: 3

Ingredients:
- ½ cup quinoa, soaked
- 1 ½ cup almond milk
- 1 tablespoon coconut shred
- 2 teaspoon honey
- 1 teaspoon vanilla extract
- ½ teaspoon ground cinnamon
- 1 tablespoon hemp seeds

Directions:
Place quinoa and almond milk in the instant pot bowl. Add vanilla extract and stir gently. Close the lid and set Rice mode. Cook quinoa for 14 minutes (Low pressure). Transfer cooked quinoa in the big bowl and add honey, coconut shred, and ground cinnamon. Add hemp seeds and mix up the mixture well. Transfer hot quinoa into the serving bowls.

Nutrition value/serving: calories 459, fat 35.4, fiber 5.7, carbs 30.8, protein 8.8

Tofu Omelet

Prep time: 10 minutes | Cooking time: 8 minutes | Servings: 3

Ingredients:
- 8 oz firm tofu
- ¾ cup aquafaba
- 1 tablespoon chickpea flour
- 1 tablespoon cornflour
- ¼ cup almond milk
- 1 tablespoon wheat flour
- ½ teaspoon salt
- ¾ teaspoon turmeric
- ½ teaspoon dried basil
- 1 teaspoon olive oil
- 1 tablespoon fresh parsley, chopped

Directions:
In the blender mix up together firm tofu, aquafaba, chickpea flour, cornflour, almond milk, wheat flour, salt, and turmeric. Blend the mixture until you get a smooth yellow liquid that looks like an omelet. Brush the instant pot bowl with the olive oil from inside and pour tofu mixture. Add parsley and dried basil and stir gently. Close the lid and cook the omelet on Manual mode (High pressure) and cook it for 8 minutes. Then make quick pressure release.

Nutrition value/serving: calories 148, fat 9.9, fiber 2.3, carbs 9.2, protein 8

Tapioca Porridge

Prep time: 5 minutes | Cooking time: 17 minutes | Servings: 4

Ingredients:
- ½ cup tapioca pearls
- 1 tablespoon tapioca flour
- 2 cups almond milk
- 1 tablespoon honey

Directions:

In the instant pot, mix up together tapioca pearls, tapioca flour, and almond milk. Close the lid and cook on High for 17 minutes. Then allow natural pressure release for 10 minutes. Open the lid and add honey. Stir the porridge until homogenous. Transfer the cooked porridge in the serving bowls

Nutrition value/serving: calories 366, fat 28.6, fiber 2.8, carbs 29.5, protein 2.8

Zucchini Frittata

Prep time: 7 minutes | Cooking time: 12 minutes | Servings: 5

Ingredients:
- 6 oz firm tofu
- 1 zucchini
- 1 red onion, diced
- ¼ cup almond milk
- 1 teaspoon salt
- 1 teaspoon ground black pepper
- 2 tablespoons wheat flour
- ½ teaspoon olive oil

Directions:

Grate zucchini and scramble tofu. Mix up together zucchini, tofu, onion, and almond milk. Add salt, ground black pepper, and wheat flour. Mix up the mixture until homogenous. Brush the instant pot bowl with olive oil from inside. Then transfer zucchini mixture in it. Flatten it with the help of a spatula. Close the lid and set Manual mode (High pressure). Cook frittata for 12 minutes. Then allow natural pressure release for 10 minutes. The frittata should be served warm.

Nutrition value/serving: calories 83, fat 4.9, fiber 1.7, carbs 7.3, protein 4.1

Apple Cream of Wheat
Prep time: 8 minutes | *Cooking time:* 7 hours | *Servings:* 3

Ingredients:
- ½ cup cream of wheat
- 2 ½ cup almond milk
- 4 teaspoon sugar
- ½ teaspoon ground cinnamon
- 1 granny smith apple

Directions:
Put cream of wheat and almond milk in the instant pot bowl. Add sugar and cinnamon. Mix up gently. Close the lid. Set the Rice mode (Low pressure) and cook the meal for 7 hours. When the cream of wheat is cooked – slice the apple. Place the cream of wheat in the bowls and garnish with apple.

Nutrition value/serving: calories 469, fat 36.2, fiber 5.4, carbs 36.7, protein 5.8

Oatmeal Muffins
Prep time: 10 minutes | *Cooking time:* 8 minutes | *Servings:* 6

Ingredients:
- 1 cup quick oats
- 2 tablespoon white sugar
- 1 teaspoon vanilla extract
- ¼ cup wheat flour
- 1 teaspoon almond butter
- 2 tablespoon coconut milk
- 1 oz walnuts, chopped
- Cooking spray

Directions:
In the mixing bowl combine together dry ingredients: white sugar, quick oats, wheat flour, and chopped walnuts. Mix up the mixture well and add almond butter, vanilla extract, and coconut milk. Stir the mixture with the help of a spoon Spray muffin molds with the cooking spray. Scoop the oat mixture in the molds and press gently. Cover the molds with foil and pin it with the help of a toothpick. Transfer it in the instant pot bowl and close the lid. Cook muffins on High (Manual mode) for 8 minutes. Use quick pressure release.

Nutrition value/serving: calories 145, fat 6.4, fiber 2.2, carbs 18.6, protein 4.2

Tempeh Bowl

Prep time: 10 minutes | Cooking time: 11 minutes | Servings: 5

Ingredients:
- ½ cup potatoes, chopped
- 1 cup spinach, chopped
- ½ cup of water
- 1 teaspoon Italian seasoning
- 1 teaspoon sriracha
- 1 tablespoon soy sauce
- 1 teaspoon minced garlic
- 1 teaspoon salt
- 8 oz tempeh, chopped
- ½ cup kale, chopped
- 1 teaspoon nutritional yeast

Directions:
In the mixing bowl mix up together salt, Italian seasoning, and chopped potato. Insert the steamer rack in the instant pot bowl. Place the potatoes and water in the bottom of the instant pot bowl. Then take round instant pot pan and place tempeh inside. Add sriracha, soy sauce, and minced garlic. Mix it up. Then add kale and spinach. Sprinkle the greens with nutritional yeast and cover with foil. Make the pins in the foil with the help of a knife or toothpick. Place the pan on the steamer rack and close the instant pot lid. Cook the meal for 11 minutes on Manual mode (High pressure). Then make quick pressure release. Place the meal in the bowls by layers: the layer of potatoes, then greens, and then tempeh.

Nutrition value/serving: calories 111, fat 5.3, fiber 0.8, carbs 8.6, protein 9.6

Tender Tofu Cubes

Prep time: 10 minutes | Cooking time: 15 minutes | Servings: 4

Ingredients:
- 15 oz firm tofu, cubed
- 1 teaspoon curry powder
- ½ teaspoon salt
- 1 teaspoon garlic powder
- ½ onion, diced
- 1 teaspoon smoked paprika
- 1 teaspoon almond butter
- 1 cup of coconut yogurt

Directions:
Preheat instant pot bowl on Saute mode. When it shows "hot" toss almond butter inside. Melt it and add diced onion, garlic powder, salt, curry powder, and smoked paprika. Stir the ingredients and saute for 2 minutes on Saute mode. Then add firm tofu cubes and mix up well. Close the lid and set Manual mode (High pressure) Cook tofu for 2 minutes and then use natural pressure release for 10 minutes. Open the lid and add coconut yogurt. Mix up the meal very well. Place meal in the bowls and serve when it reaches room temperature.

Nutrition value/serving: calories 185, fat 10.3, fiber 2.3, carbs 12.2, protein 13.5

Potato Pancakes
Prep time: 8 minutes | Cooking time: 15 minutes | Servings: 4

Ingredients:
- 3 potatoes, peeled
- 2 tablespoon wheat flour
- 1 teaspoon cornstarch
- 1 teaspoon salt
- ½ teaspoon ground black pepper
- 1 tablespoon chives
- 1 teaspoon fresh dill, chopped
- 1 tablespoon olive oil

Directions:
Grate potatoes and mix them up with wheat flour, cornstarch, salt. Ground black pepper, chives, and fresh dill. Separate the mixture into 4 parts. Preheat instant pot bowl till it shows "hot", and pour olive oil inside. Place the first part of grated potato mixture in the instant pot bowl and flatten it to make the shape of a pancake. Cook it on Saute mode for 4 minutes from each side or until "pancake" is light brown. Repeat the same steps with all remaining grated potato mixture.

Nutrition value/serving: calories 159, fat 3.7, fiber 4.1, carbs 29, protein 3.2

Avocado Sandwiches
Prep time: 10 minutes | Cooking time: 6 minutes | Servings: 2

Ingredients:
- 4 vegan bread slices
- 1 avocado, peeled
- 1 teaspoon minced garlic
- 1 tomato, chopped
- 1 tablespoon coconut oil
- 1 tablespoon chives, chopped
- 1 teaspoon smoked paprika

Directions:
Mash the avocado with the help of fork and transfer in the blender. Add minced garlic, chopped tomato, chives, and smoked paprika. Blend the mixture until smooth. Then spread each bread slice with avocado mixture and make sandwiches. Preheat the instant pot until it shows "Hot". Place the coconut oil inside instant pot bowl and add avocado sandwiches. Set Saute mode and cook them for 3 minutes from each side. Cooked sandwiches should have a light crunchy texture.

Nutrition value/serving: calories 326, fat 27.3, fiber 8.1, carbs 20.6, protein 4.2

Burgers and Patties

Quinoa Patties

Prep time: 10 minutes | *Cooking time:* 25 minutes | *Servings:* 4

Ingredients:
- ½ cup panko bread crumbs
- ½ cup quinoa, soaked
- 1 oz peas, frozen
- 1 cup of water
- 1 teaspoon salt
- 1 teaspoon dried dill
- 1 teaspoon dried basil
- ½ teaspoon smoked paprika
- ½ teaspoon ground black pepper
- ½ jalapeno pepper
- 1 potato, grated
- ¾ cup almond milk
- 1 teaspoon olive oil

Directions:
Place quinoa, water, and green peas in the instant pot bowl. Add salt, dried dill, basil, smoked paprika, ground black pepper, and grated potato. Mix up the mixture gently with the help of a wooden spatula and close the lid. Set Manual mode (High pressure) and cook ingredients for 4 minutes. Then allow natural pressure release for 15 minutes. Transfer the cooked ingredients in the blender and add almond milk. Blend the mixture until it will have got puree texture. Then make the medium patties with the help of fingertips. Coat them in the panko bread crumbs. Preheat instant pot and pour olive oil inside. Place patties and set Saute mode. Cook them for 2 minutes from each side or until they have a golden brown color.

Nutrition value/serving: calories 286, fat 14, fiber 4.6, carbs 34.9, protein 7.2

Broccoli Patties

Prep time: 10 minutes | Cooking time: 5minutes | Servings: 6

Ingredients:
- 1-pound broccoli florets
- 3 tablespoon wheat flour
- 1 teaspoon salt
- 1 tablespoon fresh dill, chopped
- 1 potato, peeled
- 1 teaspoon sriracha sauce
- ½ red onion, grated
- 1 teaspoon olive oil
- 1 cup water, for cooking

Directions:
Pour water in the instant pot bowl and insert steamer rack. Place broccoli and potato on the steamer rack and close the lid. Cook the vegetables on Manual mode (High pressure) for 3 minutes. Then allow natural pressure release for 5 minutes. Transfer broccoli and potato to the blender together with salt, fresh dill, sriracha sauce, grated onion, and blend for 2 minutes or until smooth. Then make the medium patties from the mixture and coat them in the wheat flour. Freeze the patties for 5-10 minutes in the freezer. Meanwhile, preheat instant pot and brush it with olive oil from inside. Place the frozen patties in the instant pot and close the lid. Cook the meal on High for 2 minutes (quick pressure release).

Nutrition value/serving: calories 79, fat 1.7, fiber 3, carbs 14.2, protein 3.3

Cauliflower Potato Burgers

Prep time: 15 minutes | Cooking time: 7 minutes | Servings: 2

Ingredients:
- 7 oz cauliflower rice
- ¼ cup mashed potato
- 1 tablespoon almond flour
- 1 teaspoon salt
- 1 teaspoon white pepper
- 1 tablespoon coconut yogurt
- 1 tablespoon bread crumbs
- ½ cup water, for cooking

Directions:
In the mixing bowl combine together cauliflower rice and mashed potato. Add almond flour, salt, white pepper, and coconut yogurt. Then wear gloves and make medium size burgers from the mixture. Sprinkle every burger with bread crumbs and wrap in the foil. Pour water in the instant pot bowl and insert steamer rack. Place wrapped burgers on the steamer rack and close the lid. Cook the meal on High (Manual mode) for 7 minutes. Then allow natural pressure release for 10 minutes.

Nutrition value/serving: calories 163, fat 9, fiber 4.8, carbs 17, protein 6.6

Sweet Potato Burgers

Prep time: 10 minutes | Cooking time: 20 minutes | Servings: 2

Ingredients:
- 1 sweet potato
- ½ onion, diced
- 1 teaspoon chives
- ½ teaspoon salt
- 1 teaspoon cayenne pepper
- 3 tablespoon flax meal
- ½ cup kale
- 1 teaspoon olive oil
- ½ cup water, for cooking

Directions:

Pour water in the instant pot and insert steamer rack. Place sweet potato on the steamer rack and close the lid. Cook the vegetables on Manual mode (High pressure) for 15 minutes (quick pressure release). Meanwhile, place onion, chives, and kale in the blender. Blend until smooth. Transfer the blended mixture in the mixing bowl. When the sweet potato is cooked – cut it into halves and scoop all the flesh into the kale mixture. Mix it up carefully with the help of the fork. Add flax meal, salt, and cayenne pepper. Stir well. With the help of the fingertips make medium burgers. Clean the instant pot bowl and put olive oil inside. Preheat for 2-3 minutes on Saute mode. Then add burgers and cook them for 2 minutes from each side on Saute mode.

Nutrition value/serving: calories 139, fat 6.4, fiber 6, carbs 19.7, protein 4.3

Potato Patties

Prep time: 10 minutes | Cooking time: 15 minutes | Servings: 4

Ingredients:
- 3 russet potatoes, peeled
- 3 tablespoon aquafaba
- ½ teaspoon salt
- 1 teaspoon almond butter
- ½ teaspoon smoked paprika
- ¼ teaspoon chili flakes
- 2 tablespoon wheat flour

Directions:

With the help of the hand mixer, whisk aquafaba until you get soft peaks. Then grate potatoes and combine them together with aquafaba in the mixing bowl. Add salt, smoked paprika, chili flakes, and wheat flour. Mix it up carefully. Preheat the instant pot on Saute mode for 4 minutes. Add almond butter and melt it. Then with the help of the spoon make medium patties; press them little with the help of hand palms and put in the hot almond butter. Cook the patties for 3 minutes then flip into another side. Cook the patties for 4 minutes more.

Nutrition value/serving: calories 150, fat 2.5, fiber 4.4, carbs 29, protein 4

Lentil Burger

Prep time: 20 minutes | Cooking time: 26 minutes | Servings: 7

Ingredients:
- 1 cup lentils, soaked overnight
- 1 cup of water
- ½ carrot, peeled
- 1 teaspoon cayenne pepper
- 4 tablespoon wheat flour
- 1 teaspoon salt
- 1 teaspoon olive oil
- 1 tablespoon dried dill

Directions:

Put lentils to the Instant pot together with water, carrot, salt, and cayenne pepper. Close the lid and set Manual mode (High pressure). Cook the ingredients for 25 minutes and allow natural pressure release for 10 minutes. Transfer the cooked ingredients in the blender and blend until smooth. Add wheat flour and dried dill. Mix it up until smooth. If the mixture is liquid – add more flour. Make the burgers and place them together with the olive oil in the instant pot. Set Manual mode (High pressure) for 1 minutes (quick pressure release). It is recommended to serve burgers warm.

Nutrition value/serving: calories 122, fat 1.1, fiber 8.7, carbs 20.7, protein 7.7

Black Beans Burger

Prep time: 15 minutes | Cooking time: 5 minutes | Servings: 5

Ingredients:
- 1 cup black beans, cooked
- 2 tablespoon bread crumbs
- 1 teaspoon salt
- ¼ cup sweet corn, cooked
- 1 teaspoon turmeric
- 1 tablespoon fresh parsley, chopped
- ½ yellow sweet pepper, chopped
- ½ cup of water

Directions:

Mash the black beans until you get puree and combine together with salt, sweet corn, turmeric, parsley, and sweet pepper. Mix it up carefully with the help of a spoon. Add bread crumbs and stir again. Pour water in the instant pot bowl and insert steamer rack. Make the burgers from the black bean mixture and freeze them for 30 minutes. Then wrap every burger in the foil and place on the steamer rack. Close the lid and cook on Manual mode (High pressure) for 5 minutes. Then allow natural pressure release for 5 minutes. Remove the foil from the burgers and transfer on the plate. Garnish burgers with lettuce leaves if desired.

Nutrition value/serving: calories 155, fat 0.9, fiber 6.5, carbs 28.8, protein 9.2

Mushroom Burger

Prep time: 10 minutes | Cooking time: 14 minutes | Servings: 4

Ingredients:
- 2 cups mushrooms, chopped
- 1 onion, diced
- ½ cup silken tofu
- ½ teaspoon salt
- ½ teaspoon chili flakes
- 1 tablespoon dried parsley
- 1 teaspoon dried dill
- 3 tablespoon flax meal
- ½ teaspoon olive oil

Directions:
Put mushrooms in the blender and grind. Then transfer the vegetables to the instant pot together with onion, and olive oil. Stir gently and close the lid. Cook ingredients on Saute mode for 10 minutes. Meanwhile, mash silken tofu until you get a puree. Mix it up with salt, chili flakes, dried parsley, and dried dill. Add flax meal and pulse for 10 seconds. When the mushroom mixture is cooked transfer it in the bowl and combines together with the silken tofu. Stir well. Make the burgers. Line the instant pot pan with baking paper and place burgers on it. Close the lid and meal for 4 minutes on High. Then use quick pressure release. Chill the burgers till the room temperature before serving.

Nutrition value/serving: calories 47, fat 2.6, fiber 2.5, carbs 5.4, protein 2.6

Seitan Burger

Prep time: 10 minutes | Cooking time: 2 minutes | Servings: 1

Ingredients:
- 1 burger bun
- 1 teaspoon mustard
- 1 teaspoon soy sauce
- 1 seitan steak
- 1 teaspoon onion powder
- 1 teaspoon olive oil
- 1 tablespoon apple cider vinegar

Directions:
Make sauce for seitan steak: mix up together soy sauce, onion powder, olive oil, and apple cider vinegar. Brush seitan steak with sauce from each side and place in the instant pot. Close the lid and cook on Manual mode (High pressure) for 2 minutes (quick pressure release). Meanwhile, cut burger bun into halves and spread with mustard. Place seitan steak on the one half of burger bun and cover with the second one.

Nutrition value/serving: calories 303, fat 8.8, fiber 2.8, carbs 24.9, protein 26.8

Spinach Patties
Prep time: 10 minutes | Cooking time: 10 minutes | Servings: 7

Ingredients:
- 3 cups spinach, chopped
- 2 tablespoon coconut shred
- 4 tablespoon panko bread crumbs
- 1 teaspoon salt
- ½ teaspoon chili flakes
- 2 tablespoon flax meal
- 6 tablespoon hot water
- 1 teaspoon olive oil
- 1 tablespoon coconut yogurt

Directions:
In the mixing bowl mix up together flax meal and hot water. Whisk the mixture. Then add coconut shred, panko bread crumbs, spinach, chili flakes, coconut yogurt, and salt. Mix up the mixture until homogenous. Set the Saute mode in Instant pot and preheat it until shows "Hot". Then brush instant bowl with olive oil from inside. Make patties from the spinach mixture with the help of 2 spoons and place them in the instant pot. Saute them for 10 minutes. You can flip the patties during cooking if desired.

Nutrition value/serving: calories 47, fat 2.9, fiber 1.3, carbs 4.5, protein 1.5

Tempeh Burger
Prep time: 15 minutes | Cooking time: 11minutes | Servings: 5

Ingredients:
- 10 oz tempeh
- 1 carrot, peeled
- 4 tablespoon oatmeal
- ¼ teaspoon minced garlic
- 1 teaspoon onion powder
- ½ teaspoon salt
- 2 oz black beans, canned
- 1 tablespoon tomato sauce
- 1 teaspoon golden syrup
- ½ cup water, for cooking

Directions:
Cut tempeh into the chunks and place on the steamer rack. Pour water in the instant pot and insert steamer rack with tempeh. Close the lid and cook on Manual mode (High pressure) for 7 minutes. Then use quick pressure release. Meanwhile, chop carrot and place in the food processor. Add minced garlic, oatmeal onion powder, salt, canned beans, tomato sauce, and golden syrup. Blend the mixture for 2-3 minutes. Then add cooked tempeh and keep blending for 1 minute more. The final mixture texture shouldn't be too smooth. Use the burger mold and make burgers. Freeze them until solid. Then wrap every burger in foil or use non-sticky paper and place in the cleaned instant pot bowl. Cook the burgers on High (Manual mode) for 4 minutes. Then allow natural pressure release for 10 minutes.

Nutrition value/serving: calories 175, fat 6.6, fiber 2.5, carbs 18, protein 13.7

Pumpkin Burger

Prep time: 10 minutes | Cooking time: 3 minutes | Servings: 2

Ingredients:
- 2 hamburger buns
- 1 tablespoon pumpkin seeds
- 1 tablespoon pumpkin powder
- 3 tablespoon pumpkin puree
- 2 tablespoon bread crumbs
- ½ teaspoon chili flakes
- 1 teaspoon turmeric
- 1 tablespoon flax meal
- 3 tablespoons hot water

Directions:
In the mixing bowl combine together flax meal and hot water. Whisk the mixture and add pumpkin powder, pumpkin puree, bread crumbs, chili flakes, and turmeric. Mix up the mixture. Add pumpkin seeds. With the help of the burger mold, make 2 burgers. Place them in the instant pot bowl and close the lid. Set Manual mode (High pressure) and cook for 3 minutes. Then use quick pressure release and open the lid. Fill the burger buns with pumpkin burgers.

Nutrition value/serving: calories 197, fat 5.6, fiber 3.3, carbs 30.5, protein 7.2

Apple Patties

Prep time: 10 minutes | Cooking time: 6 minutes | Servings: 4

Ingredients:
- 2 granny smith apples
- 3 tablespoon wheat flour
- ½ teaspoon baking powder
- 1 tablespoon sugar
- 1 teaspoon vanilla extract
- 1 teaspoon olive oil

Directions:
Wash the apple and grate them and transfer in the mixing bowl. Add wheat flour, baking powder, sugar, and vanilla extract. With the help of the spoon mix up the mixture until homogenous. Let it rest. Meanwhile, set Saute mode and preheat the instant pot. Pour olive oil in the instant pot. With the help of the spoon make patties from the apple mixture and put it into the instant pot. Saute the patties for 3 minutes from each side or till they are golden brown.

Nutrition value/serving: calories 104, fat 1.4, fiber 2.9, carbs 23.3, protein 0.9

Butternut Squash Burger

Prep time: 10 minutes | *Cooking time:* 15 minutes | *Servings:* 4

Ingredients:
- 10 oz butternut squash, boiled
- ¼ cup chickpea, cooked
- 1 tablespoon fresh parsley, chopped
- 1/3 cup quinoa, soaked
- 1 cup vegetable broth
- 3 tablespoons flax meal
- 2 tablespoons wheat flour
- 1 teaspoon salt
- 1 teaspoon smoked paprika
- 1 teaspoon ground black pepper
- 1 teaspoon minced garlic
- 1 tablespoon olive oil

Directions:

Pour vegetable broth in the instant pot. Add quinoa and close the lid. Cook it on Manual mode (High pressure) for 8 minutes. Use the quick pressure release. Meanwhile, in the mixing bowl combine together chickpea, parsley, flax meal, wheat flour, salt, smoked paprika, ground black pepper, butternut squash, and minced garlic. Add cooked quinoa and mix up the mixture well with the help of the fingertips. Then make four burgers and place them in the instant pot. Add olive oil and Saute them for 5 minutes. Then flip burgers onto another side and cook them for 2 minutes more.

Nutrition value/serving: calories 210, fat 7.6, fiber 6.6, carbs 30.6, protein 8.1

Chickpea Burger

Prep time: 10 minutes | *Cooking time:* 13 minutes | *Servings:* 5

Ingredients:
- 1 ½ cup chickpea, soaked
- 5 cups of water
- 1 bay leaf
- 1 teaspoon ground cumin
- ½ teaspoon coriander
- 1 teaspoon onion powder
- 1/3 teaspoon garlic powder
- 1 teaspoon chili flakes

Directions:

Place chickpea to the instant pot together with water. Add bay leaf. Close the lid, set Manual mode (High pressure) and cook for 15 minutes. Make a quick pressure release. Meanwhile, in the mixing bowl mix up together ground cumin, ground coriander, onion powder, garlic powder, and chili flakes. When the chickpeas are cooked strain them and remove bay leaf. Add chickpeas in the spice bowl and mash gently with the help of the spoon. Stir the mixture. Make the medium size burgers and sprinkle them with olive oil. Wrap the burgers in the foil. Place them in the instant pot and close the lid. Set Manual mode (High pressure) and cook for 3 minutes. Then allow natural pressure release for 10 minutes. Remove the burgers from the foil.

Nutrition value/serving: calories 223, fat 3.7, fiber 10.6, carbs 37.3, protein 11.8

Mexican Style Burger

Prep time: 10 minutes | Cooking time: 10 minutes | Servings: 8

Ingredients:

- 1 cup black beans, cooked
- 1/3 cup lentils, cooked
- 1 tablespoon fresh cilantro, chopped
- ¾ cup corn, frozen
- ½ teaspoon salt
- 1 tablespoon flax meal
- 3 tablespoons hot water
- 1 teaspoon smoked paprika
- ½ teaspoon minced garlic
- 1 teaspoon onion powder
- 2 bell peppers, chopped
- 1 teaspoon canola oil
- 2 tablespoon almond flour

Directions:

Mash black beans and lentil until you get a puree. In the separate bowl whisk together flax meal and hot water. Add the mixture in the mashed beans. Then add cilantro, corn, salt, smoked paprika, minced garlic, onion powder, and chopped pepper. Add almond flour. With the help of the spoon mix up together burger mixture. Make burgers with the help of the fingertips. Preheat the instant pot on Saute mode. When it shows "hot" add canola oil. Then add burgers and cook them for 2 minutes. Then flip onto another side and close the lid. Saute the burgers for 8 minutes.

Nutrition value/serving: calories 184, fat 5.1, fiber 8, carbs 27.1, protein 9.8

Jalapeno Burger

Prep time: 15 minutes | Cooking time: 3 minutes | Servings: 4

Ingredients:

- ½ cup brown rice, cooked
- ¼ cup silken tofu
- ½ teaspoon cayenne pepper
- ¾ cup pickled jalapeno pepper, chopped
- 3 tablespoon flax meal
- ¼ teaspoon minced garlic
- 1 teaspoon salt
- 1 tablespoon oatmeal, grinded
- 1 tablespoon coconut milk

Directions:

Mash silken tofu with the help of a fork and combine it together with brown rice, cayenne pepper, and chopped jalapeno. Add minced garlic and flax meal. Stir the mixture gently. After this, add salt, oatmeal, and coconut milk. Mix up the burger mixture with the help of the spoon until homogenous. Make the burgers from the mixture and wrap them in the foil. Insert steamer rack in the instant pot and place wrapped burgers on it. Close the lid and set Manual mode (High pressure). Cook the burgers for 3 minutes. Then use quick pressure release. Remove the burgers from foil and transfer on the serving plates. Garnish with lettuce if desired.

Nutrition value/serving: calories 135, fat 4, fiber 3.1, carbs 22, protein 4.1

Beet Burger

Prep time: 15 minutes | Cooking time: 15 minutes | Servings: 8

Ingredients:
- 1 cup beetroot, grated
- 1 carrot, peeled, grated
- 1 zucchini, grated
- 1 red onion, diced
- 2 tablespoons olive oil
- ½ cup chickpea, cooked
- 1 teaspoon tahini paste
- 3 tablespoon lemon juice
- 2 tablespoons chives, chopped
- 1 teaspoon ground cumin
- 8 burger buns
- 1 avocado, peeled

Directions:

Pour 1 tablespoon of olive oil in the instant pot. Add beetroot, carrot, zucchini, and red onion. Sprinkle the vegetables with ground cumin and stir well. Close the lid and saute for 10 minutes. Meanwhile, in the blender mix up together chickpea, tahini paste, and lemon juice. Blend the mixture until smooth and transfer in the big mixing bowl. Then add cooked vegetable and stir well. Make the medium size burgers. Pour remaining olive oil in the instant pot. Add burgers and cook them on Saute mode for 2 minutes from each side. Meanwhile, slice avocado and place it into the burger buns. Add cooked burger into the buns and serve them warm.

Nutrition value/serving: calories 295, fat 10.7, fiber 8.2, carbs 42.1, protein 11

Portobello Burgers

Prep time: 10 minutes | Cooking time: 20 minutes | Servings: 4

Ingredients:
- 4 portobello mushroom hats
- 1 big onion, sliced
- 1 tablespoon soy sauce
- 1 teaspoon sriracha
- 1 teaspoon ground black pepper
- 1 teaspoon salt
- 1 teaspoon almond butter
- 4 burger buns
- 1 tablespoon mustard
- 1 tablespoon vegan mayo

Directions:

Mix up together soy sauce, sriracha, ground black pepper, and salt. Then rub the mushroom hats with this mixture and place in the instant pot. Add almond butter and sliced onion. Close the lid and cook on Saute mode for 20 minutes. Meanwhile, cut the burger buns into halves. Mix up together mustard and mayo. Spread the buns with this mixture. Fill the burger buns with the hot cooked mushrooms and onion.

Nutrition value/serving: calories 226, fat 5, fiber 5.8, carbs 36.4, protein 12.3

Green Burgers

Prep time: 15minutes | Cooking time: 3 minutes | Servings: 3

Ingredients:
- ½ cup green peas, cooked
- 1 tablespoon flax meal
- 3 tablespoons hot water
- ¼ teaspoon ground nutmeg
- 1 tablespoon fresh coriander
- 1 cup fresh basil
- ½ cup kale
- ¼ cup fresh parsley
- 1 avocado, peeled
- 2 tablespoons rice flour

Directions:
Blend together basil, kale, parsley, and coriander until smooth. Then transfer the mixture in the big mixing bowl and add green peas. Stir the mixture with the help of the fork. Mash the green peas little bit. After this, in the separated bowl whisk together flax meal and hot water. Add liquid into the green mixture. Mash avocado and add it in the burger mixture too. After this, add ground nutmeg and stir it. With the help of the hand palms, make the burgers and place them in the instant pot. Close the lid and set Manual mode – High pressure. Cook the burgers for 3 minutes. Then use quick pressure release. The burgers are recommended to serve hot.

Nutrition value/serving: calories 201, fat 14.3, fiber 7.1, carbs 17, protein 4.2

Onion Patties

Prep time: 10 minutes | Cooking time: 6minutes | Servings: 4

Ingredients:
- 3 yellow onions, peeled, diced
- 4 tablespoons wheat flour
- ¾ cup of coconut milk
- ½ teaspoon baking powder
- 1 teaspoon garlic powder
- 1 teaspoon turmeric
- 1 tablespoon sesame oil

Directions:
Mix up together diced onions, wheat flour, and coconut milk. Add garlic powder and turmeric. Mix up the mixture with the help of the spoon. Set Saute mode and pour sesame oil in the instant pot. Preheat it until hot. With the help of the spoon pour onion patties in the instant pot and cook them for 3 minutes from each side.

Nutrition value/serving: calories 266, fat 19.1, fiber 4.2, carbs 23.1, protein 3.9

Zucchini Patties
Prep time: 10 minutes | *Cooking time:* 5 minutes | *Servings:* 2

Ingredients:
- 1 zucchini, grated
- ½ teaspoon ground black pepper
- 1 teaspoon smoked paprika
- ¼ teaspoon turmeric
- 1 teaspoon salt
- 3 tablespoon flax meal
- 1 teaspoon sesame seeds
- ¼ cup white rice, boiled

Directions:
In the big mixing bowl combine together grated zucchini, ground black pepper, smoked paprika, and turmeric. Add salt, flax meal, sesame seeds, and boiled rice. Mix up the mixture with the help of the spoon. Then make the medium size patties and freeze them for 20 minutes in the freezer. Wrap the frozen patties in the foil and place on the steamer rack. Insert rack in the instant pot and close the lid. Cook patties for 5 minutes on High (Manual mode) and then use quick pressure release. Remove the foil from the patties.

Nutrition value/serving: calories 159, fat 5, fiber 5.2, carbs 26.2, protein 5.6

Carrot Patties
Prep time: 10 minutes | *Cooking time:* 8 minutes | *Servings:* 4

Ingredients:
- 1 cup chickpea, cooked
- 2 carrots, grated
- 1 tablespoon fresh cilantro
- 1 tablespoon tahini paste
- ½ teaspoon miso paste
- 1 teaspoon salt
- ½ teaspoon chili flakes
- 1 teaspoon olive oil

Directions:
Blend the chickpea and cilantro until smooth and transfer the mass in the bowl. Add grated carrot, tahini and miso paste, salt, and chili flakes. Mix up the mixture with the help of the spoon. Wet your hands and make medium size patties. Press them gently. Preheat olive oil in the instant pot on Saute mode. Put the patties in the hot oil and saute them for 4 minutes from each side.

Nutrition value/serving: calories 228, fat 6.3, fiber 9.9, carbs 34.3, protein 10.6

Artichoke Burger

Prep time: 5 minutes | *Cooking time:* 13 minutes | *Servings:* 6

Ingredients:

- 1-pound artichoke hearts, canned
- 1 cup of water
- ½ cup brown rice, cooked
- 1 tablespoon fresh dill, chopped
- ¼ cup cashew
- 1 teaspoon lemon zest
- ½ yellow onion, diced
- 1 teaspoon almond butter
- 1 teaspoon olive oil
- 3 tablespoon rolled oats

Directions:

Chop artichoke hearts and transfer in the mixing bowl. In the food, processor, grind rolled oats and cashew. Combine together rolled oats, cashew, chopped artichoke hearts, brown rice, dill, and lemon zest. Saute the diced onion together with almond butter in the instant pot for 5 minutes. Stir time to time. Then add sauteed onion in the artichoke mixture and stir well. You have to get smooth and soft artichoke dough. Make the burgers from the mixture and place in the instant pot. Add olive oil and close the lid. Saute the meal for 8 minutes. You can flip the burgers onto another side after 4 minutes of cooking if you like a crunchy crust.

Nutrition value/serving: calories 163, fat 5.7, fiber 5.6, carbs 25.3, protein 5.7

Spicy Kale Burger

Prep time: 10 minutes | *Cooking time:* 12 minutes | *Servings:* 3

Ingredients:

- ½ teaspoon cayenne pepper
- ¼ teaspoon chili flakes
- ¼ teaspoon white pepper
- 1 teaspoon turmeric
- ½ teaspoon garlic powder
- 1 green pepper, diced
- 1 white onion, diced
- 1 cup kale, chopped
- 4 tablespoons bread crumbs
- 2 tablespoons olive oil
- ½ teaspoon salt
- 2 tablespoon flax meal
- 6 tablespoons hot water

Directions:

Preheat instant pot on Saute mode. Add 1 tablespoon of olive oil, diced green pepper, salt, onion, and kale. Stir the vegetables and close the lid. Saute them for 5 minutes. Meanwhile, whisk together hot water and flax meal. Add garlic powder, turmeric, chili flakes, and cayenne pepper. Then add sauteed kale mixture and bread crumbs. Mix up it with the help of the spoon and make medium size burgers. Clean the instant pot bowl and preheat it on Saute mode again. Add remaining olive oil and burgers. Close the lid and cook them for 7 minutes on Saute mode.

Nutrition value/serving: calories 175, fat 11.7, fiber 3.9, carbs 16.5, protein 3.8

Wild Rice Burger

Prep time: 20 minutes | *Cooking time:* 10 minutes | *Servings:* 6

Ingredients:
- 2 cup wild rice, cooked
- ½ cup panko bread crumbs
- 1 tablespoon water
- 1 teaspoon salt
- 1 teaspoon cayenne pepper
- 1 tablespoon almond butter

Directions:
Mix up together wild rice, water, panko bread crumbs, and cayenne pepper. Then make medium size burgers and place them in the freezer for 15-20 minutes. Meanwhile, preheat instant pot on Saute mode and add almond butter. Melt it. Put frozen burgers in the instant pot and saute them for 5 minutes then flip onto another side and cook for 5 minutes more.

Nutrition value/serving: calories 243, fat 2.6, fiber 4.1, carbs 47.1, protein 9.7

Sun Dried Tomato Patties

Prep time: 10 minutes | *Cooking time:* 10 minutes | *Servings:* 2

Ingredients:
- ¼ cup sun-dried tomatoes
- ¼ cup fresh parsley
- ½ cup chickpea, cooked
- 1 teaspoon salt
- 2 tablespoons tahini paste
- ¼ teaspoon minced garlic
- 1 tablespoon water
- 1 teaspoon olive oil

Directions:
In the food processor carefully blend sun-dried tomatoes, chickpea, salt, fresh parsley, and minced garlic. Transfer the mixture in the bowl and mix it up with tahini paste and water. Make the patties and place them in the instant pot. Add olive oil and close the lid. Set Saute mode and cook for 10 minutes.

Nutrition value/serving: calories 299, fat 13.5, fiber 10.6, carbs 35, protein 12.6

Eggplant Burger

Prep time: 10 minutes | *Cooking time:* 25 minutes | *Servings:* 6

Ingredients:
- 2 eggplants, trimmed
- ½ cup bread crumbs
- ½ cup Swiss chard
- 1 teaspoon salt
- ½ onion, diced
- 3 tablespoons flax meal
- 9 tablespoons hot water
- 1 teaspoon ground black pepper
- 1 tablespoon chives, chopped
- 1 tablespoon olive oil

Directions:
Chop the eggplants into small cubes and place in the instant pot. Add olive oil, diced onion, salt, and ground black pepper. Mix it up and close the lid. Cook the vegetables on Saute mode for 25 minutes. Chop Swiss chard and place in the food processor. Add sauteed vegetables, chives and bread crumbs. In the separated bowl whisk together hot water and flax meal. Add the liquid in the food processor too. Blend the mixture until it smooth and homogenous. Then make medium size burgers. The burgers can be served immediately or have to be frozen and reheated before serving.

Nutrition value/serving: calories 122, fat 4.4, fiber 8.2, carbs 19.4, protein 4

Tofu Burger

Prep time: 15 minutes | *Cooking time:* 10 minutes | *Servings:* 4

Ingredients:
- 1 red bell pepper, diced
- ½ yellow onion, diced
- 4 tablespoons bread crumbs
- 7 oz firm tofu
- 1 tablespoon flax meal
- 3 tablespoons hot water
- 1 carrot, grated
- ½ teaspoon minced garlic
- 1 tablespoon olive oil

Directions:
In the big mixing bowl scramble firm tofu with the help of the fingertips. Add chopped bell pepper, onion, bread crumbs, and grated carrot. Then add minced garlic and mix the mixture up. In the separated bowl whisk together hot water and flax meal. Add the liquid in the tofu mixture and stir well. Make the medium burgers and place them on the baking paper. Freeze the burgers. Brush the instant pot bowl with olive oil. Place the burgers in the instant pot and close the lid. Set the Manual mode (High pressure) and cook the meal for 8 minutes. Allow natural pressure release for 10 minutes.

Nutrition value/serving: calories 121, fat 6.7 fiber 2.3, carbs 11.4, protein 5.9

Cabbage Patties
Prep time: 15 minutes | Cooking time: 10 minutes | Servings: 2

Ingredients:
- 11 oz white cabbage, shredded
- 3 tablespoons coconut yogurt
- 1 teaspoon salt
- ½ teaspoon turmeric
- ½ teaspoon dried dill
- 1 teaspoon dried parsley
- 1 teaspoon olive oil
- 4 tablespoons wheat flour
- 2 tablespoons bread crumbs

Directions:
Put white cabbage in the big bowl and add salt. Mix up well and leave it for 5 minutes or until cabbage starts to give juice. Then add turmeric, dried dill, dried parsley, wheat flour, and bread crumbs. Add coconut yogurt and mix up the mass well. Preheat instant pot on Saute mode and add olive oil. Use 2 spoons to make medium size patties from cabbage mixture. Transfer the patties in the preheated instant pot bowl and close the lid. Saute them for 5 minutes. Then open the lid and flip the patties onto another side and cook for 5 minutes more. The cooked patties should have a tender texture.

Nutrition value/serving: calories 167, fat 3.8, fiber 4.8, carbs 29.5, protein 5.3

Corn Burger
Prep time: 15 minutes | Cooking time: 7 minutes | Servings: 2

Ingredients:
- 1 cup pinto beans, cooked
- ½ cup chickpea, cooked
- 4 oz firm tofu
- 1 cup sweet corn kernels
- 1 teaspoon salt
- 1 teaspoon chili flakes
- 1 tablespoon almond yogurt
- 1 teaspoon panko bread crumbs
- ½ cup water, for cooking

Directions:
In the food processor blend together pinto beans and chickpea until smooth. Transfer the mixture in the mixing bowl and add chili flakes and salt. Stir well. In the separated bowl scramble firm tofu and mix it up with panko bread crumbs and almond yogurt. Chop corn kernels. Then make 5 balls from the bean mixture. Make 5 balls from tofu mixture. Fill the bean balls with tofu balls and press them gently to get the shape of a burger. Coat the burgers in chopped corn. Pour water in the instant pot and insert instant pot pan inside. Place burgers in the instant pot pan and close the lid. Set Manual mode (High pressure) and cook burgers for 7 minutes. Then make quick pressure release.

Nutrition value/serving: calories 253, fat 3.1, fiber 10.3, carbs 43.4, protein 15

Banana Patties

Prep time: 10 minutes | *Cooking time:* 5 minutes | *Servings:* 3

Ingredients:
- 3 bananas, peeled, chopped
- 4 tablespoons wheat flour
- 2 tablespoons flax meal
- 1 teaspoon vanilla extract
- ¼ teaspoon ground cinnamon
- ½ teaspoon sunflower oil
- 1 teaspoon Truvia

Directions:
Mash bananas well with the help of the fork. Add wheat flour and flax meal. After this, add vanilla extract, ground cinnamon, and Truvia. Mix up the mixture until smooth and non-sticky. Add more wheat flour if needed. Then make medium size patties. Brush the instant pot bowl with sunflower oil and insert patties inside. Set Manual mode (High pressure) and close the lid. Cook patties for 5 minutes then use quick pressure release.

Nutrition value/serving: calories 174, fat 2.9, fiber 4.8, carbs 37.1, protein 3.4

Spaghetti Patties

Prep time: 10 minutes | *Cooking time:* 10 minutes | *Servings:* 6

Ingredients:
- 5 tablespoons wheat flour
- 2 tablespoons coconut milk
- 1 tablespoon chives, chopped
- 1 cup whole-wheat spaghetti, cooked
- 1 teaspoon olive oil
- ½ teaspoon salt
- 1 teaspoon flax meal

Directions:
Chop spaghetti roughly. Whisk together flour, flax meal, and coconut milk. Add chopped spaghetti, chives, and salt. Mix up the batter. Preheat instant pot on Saute mode. When it is hot, add olive oil. With the help of the spoon place patties in the instant pot. Close the lid and saute them for 10 minutes. When the patties are light brown – they are cooked.

Nutrition value/serving: calories 73, fat 2.3, fiber 1.5, carbs 11.6, protein 2.1

Sweet Pepper Patties

Prep time: 10 minutes | Cooking time: 5 minutes | Servings: 2

Ingredients:
- 1 green bell pepper
- 1 red bell pepper
- 1 tablespoon bread crumbs
- 1 tablespoon flax meal
- 3 tablespoon hot water
- 1 teaspoon salt
- 1 teaspoon curry powder
- 2 tablespoons wheat flour

Directions:
Grind the peppers and transfer in the mixing bowl. Add bread crumbs, flax meal, hot water, salt, curry powder, and wheat flour/ Mix up the mixture until smooth and non-sticky. With the help of the fingertips make medium size patties and wrap them in the foil. Place the patties in the instant pot and close the lid. Cook them on Manual mode (High pressure) for 5 minutes. Use quick pressure release.

Nutrition value/serving: calories 84, fat 1.9, fiber 3.7, carbs 15.5, protein 3.2

Green Peas Burger

Prep time: 10 minutes | Cooking time: 10 minutes | Servings: 4

Ingredients:
- 1 cup green peas, cooked
- ¼ cup chickpea, cooked
- 1 teaspoon olive oil
- ½ onion, diced
- 3 tablespoons bread crumbs
- ½ teaspoon salt
- ½ teaspoon cayenne pepper
- 1 tablespoon fresh coriander leaves, chopped

Directions:
Place green peas and chickpea in the food processor. Pulse the ingredients for 3-4 times. Transfer the mixture in the mixing bowl and add diced onion, bread crumbs, salt, coriander leaves, and cayenne pepper. Mix up the mixture and make burgers. Brush instant pot with the olive oil from inside and place burgers. Close the lid and set Saute mode. Cook burgers for 10 minutes.

Nutrition value/serving: calories 111, fat 2.4, fiber 4.6, carbs 17.9, protein 5.2

Oatmeal Patties

Prep time: 10 minutes | Cooking time: 12 minutes | Servings: 6

Ingredients:
- 1 cup quick oats
- 1/3 cup broccoli, chopped
- ½ carrot, chopped
- 3 tablespoons flax meal
- 8 tablespoon hot water
- 1 teaspoon ground black pepper
- ½ teaspoon ground nutmeg
- ½ teaspoon salt
- ¼ cup panko bread crumbs
- 1 teaspoon sesame oil

Directions:
Put broccoli and carrot in the food processor and blend until smooth. In the mixing bowl combine together flax meal and hot water. Add blended vegetables, quick oats, ground black pepper, salt, and bread crumbs. Mix up the patties mixture well. With the help of the fingertips make patties. Sprinkle instant pot bowl with sesame oil and add patties. Close the lid and cook them on Saute mode for 12 minutes.

Nutrition value/serving: calories 97, fat 3.2, fiber 3, carbs 14.6, protein 3.4

Amaranth Burger

Prep time: 10 minutes | Cooking time: 7 minutes | Servings: 4

Ingredients:
- ½ cup amaranth
- 1 cup of water
- 1 teaspoon salt
- 1 cup pinto beans, cooked
- 2 tablespoon bread crumbs
- 1 teaspoon chili flakes
- 3 tablespoons rice flour
- 1 tablespoon dried basil
- 1 teaspoon avocado oil

Directions:
Place amaranth and water in the instant pot. Add salt and close the lid. Cook the ingredients on High (Manual mode) for 6 minutes. Then use quick pressure release. Meanwhile, place pinto beans in the food processor and pulse them for 1-2 times. Transfer the beans in the mixing bowl. Add bread crumbs, chili flakes, and dried basil. Then add cooked amaranth and rice flour. Mix up the mixture and make burgers. Brush the instant pot pan with avocado oil and place burgers in it. Put the pan in the instant pot and close the lid. Cook the burgers on Saute mode for 7 minutes.

Nutrition value/serving: calories 301, fat 2.6, fiber 10.2, carbs 54.8, protein 14.8

Turnip Patties
Prep time: 10 minutes | *Cooking time:* 9 minutes | *Servings:* 8

Ingredients:
- 1 ½ cup potatoes, peeled, chopped
- 1 cup turnip, chopped
- 2 tablespoons wheat flour
- ½ teaspoon salt
- 1 teaspoon white pepper
- 1 tablespoon sunflower oil
- 1 oz fresh dill, chopped
- 1 cup of water

Directions:
Put potatoes and turnip in the instant pot and add water. Close the lid and cook on Manual mode – High pressure for 5 minutes. Then make quick pressure release and strain the vegetables. Put them in the mixing bowl and mash. Add wheat flour, salt, white pepper, and dill. Mix it up and make patties. Brush instant pot bowl with sunflower oil and place patties inside. Close the lid and cook on Saute mode for 4 minutes. Flip the patties onto another side after 2 minutes of cooking if desired.

Nutrition value/serving: calories 56, fat 2, fiber 1.6, carbs 9.1, protein 1.6

Celery Patties
Prep time: 10 minutes | *Cooking time:* 11 minutes | *Servings:* 4

Ingredients:
- 2 potatoes, grated
- 6 oz celery root, peeled, grated
- 3 tablespoons wheat flour
- 1 tablespoon chives, chopped
- ¼ teaspoon minced garlic
- 1 teaspoon salt
- 1 teaspoon dried dill
- 1 teaspoon dried parsley
- ½ sweet red pepper, grinded
- 4 tablespoons bread crumbs
- Cooking spray

Directions:
In the big bowl mix up together grated potatoes and celery root. Add wheat flour, chives, minced garlic, salt, dried dill, parsley, and grinded sweet pepper. Stir the mass well with the help of a spoon. Then make medium size patties and coat them in bread crumbs. Spray the instant pot bowl with cooking spray and place patties. Close the lid and cook the meal on Saute mode for 6 minutes. Then flip patties onto another side and cook them for 5 minutes more or until they get light brown color.

Nutrition value/serving: calories 145, fat 0.7, fiber 4.1, carbs 31.4, protein 4.2

Farro Burger

Prep time: 20 minutes | *Cooking time:* 13 minutes | *Servings:* 4

Ingredients:
- 1 cup farro
- 2 cups vegetable broth
- 1 teaspoon salt
- ½ cup chickpea, cooked
- ¼ cup silken tofu, pureed
- ½ teaspoon ground coriander
- ½ teaspoon ground cumin
- ½ teaspoon ground nutmeg
- 1 teaspoon chili flakes
- 1 teaspoon coconut milk

Directions:
Combine together farro and water and transfer in the instant pot. Add salt and close the lid. Cook it on High for 10 minutes. Then allow natural pressure release for 10 minutes. Meanwhile, in the food processor combine together chickpea, silken tofu, ground coriander, cumin, nutmeg, chili flakes, and coconut milk. Blend the mixture for 20 seconds. Add cooked farro in the mixture and pulse it for 2-3 times, then make burgers with the help of the burger press and wrap them in the foil. After this, transfer the burgers in the instant pot and close the lid. Cook them on Manual mode (High pressure) for 3 minutes. Allow natural pressure release for 5 minutes. Remove the foil from the burgers.

Nutrition value/serving: calories 162, fat 2.9, fiber 5.2, carbs 24.5, protein 9.8

Yam Patties

Prep time: 10 minutes | *Cooking time:* 15 minutes | *Servings:* 4

Ingredients:
- 3 sweet yams, peeled
- 1 cup of water
- 1 tablespoon cornstarch
- 1 teaspoon turmeric
- 1 teaspoon salt
- 1 tablespoon coconut oil
- ¼ teaspoon garlic powder

Directions:
Pour water in the instant pot. Add yams and cook on Manual mode for 8 minutes (High pressure). Make a quick pressure release. Drain water and mash yams. Add cornstarch, turmeric, salt, and garlic powder. Mix up the mass and make patties. Preheat instant pot on Saute mode for 2 minutes, add coconut oil and melt it. Place patties and close the lid. Saute them for 5 minutes.

Nutrition value/serving: calories 40, fat 3.5, fiber 0.2, carbs2.5, protein 0.1

Barley Burger

Prep time: 10 minutes | Cooking time: 34 minutes | Servings: 8

Ingredients:
- 2 cups barley pearls
- 4 cups of water
- 1 teaspoon salt
- 1 cup sweet corn kernels, canned
- 1 tablespoon chives, chopped
- 2 tablespoons flax meal
- 4 tablespoons water
- Cooking spray

Directions:
Transfer barley pearls and water in the instant pot. Add salt and cook for 30 minutes on High. Then allow natural pressure release for 20 minutes. Combine together cooked barley pearls, corn kernels, chives, water, and flax meal. Make medium size burgers and spray them with cooking spray. Transfer burgers in the instant pot and cook on Manual for 4 minutes.

Nutrition value/serving: calories 200, fat 1.4, fiber 8.7, carbs 43.2, protein 5.9

Red Kidney Beans Burger

Prep time: 10 minutes | Cooking time: 10 minutes | Servings: 4

Ingredients:
- ½ cup Red kidney beans, cooked
- ¼ cup chickpea, cooked
- 1 tablespoon tahini paste
- ¼ cup cauliflower
- 3 tablespoons olive oil
- ½ cup panko bread crumbs
- 2 tablespoons almond milk

Directions:
In the food processor blend together chickpeas and kidney beans. When the mixture is smooth – add tahini paste and 2 tablespoons of olive oil. Pulse it for 5 seconds. Make burgers from the mixture and sprinkle with almond milk. Then coat burgers in bread crumbs Preheat instant pot on Saute mode for 3 minutes. Brush it with remaining olive oil and place burgers. Close the lid and cook on the same mode for 7 minutes.

Nutrition value/serving: calories 257, fat 15.9, fiber 5.2, carbs 23.8, protein 6.8

Bok Choy Patties
Prep time: 10 minutes | Cooking time: 10 minutes | Servings: 4

Ingredients:
- 1 sweet potato, grated
- 1 cup bok choy, grinded
- 1/3 cup polenta flour
- 1 teaspoon salt
- 1 tablespoon honey
- 1 tablespoon rice flour
- 1 cup water, for cooking

Directions:
Mix up together bok choy and sweet potato. Sprinkle the mixture with polenta flour and rice flour. Add honey and salt. Stir it carefully until smooth and not sticky. Add more rice flour if desired. Make balls from the mixture and press them gently to get patties shape. Pour water in instant pot and insert steamer rack. Wrap them in the foil and place on the instant pot rack. Cook the patties on Manual mode for 10 minutes (High pressure – Quick pressure release).

Nutrition value/serving: calories 65, fat 0.1, fiber 1.5, carbs 15.3, protein 1.3

Semolina-Cilantro Patties
Prep time: 10 minutes | Cooking time: 7 minutes | Servings: 4

Ingredients:
- ½ cup semolina
- 3 tablespoons hot water
- 1 tablespoon olive oil
- ¼ cup fresh cilantro, chopped
- 1 carrot, grated
- ¾ teaspoon grated ginger
- 3 oz firm tofu, scrambled
- 1 tablespoon Italian seasoning
- Cooking spray

Directions:
Place semolina in the bowl and add hot water and olive oil. Stir the mixture carefully until homogenous. After this, add chopped cilantro, grated carrot, ginger, tofu, and Italian seasoning. Mix up the mass and make patties. Spray instant pot bowl with cooking spray and place patties inside. Set Saute mode and cook patties with the open lid for 3 minutes. Then flip them onto another side and cook for 4 minutes more.

Nutrition value/serving: calories 108, fat 2.2, fiber 1.4, carbs 17.7, protein 4.6

Cranberry Patties

Prep time: 10 minutes | Cooking time: 7 minutes | Servings: 6

Ingredients:
- 1 ½ cup quinoa
- 3 cups of water
- ¼ cup dried cranberries, chopped
- 1/2 cup silken tofu, pureed
- 3 tablespoons wheat flour
- 2 tablespoons fresh dill, chopped
- ¾ teaspoon dried sage
- ½ cup chickpeas, cooked
- Cooking spray

Directions:
Combine together water and quinoa and place in the instant pot. Close the lid and cook on High for 1 minute. Allow natural pressure release for 5 minutes. Transfer the cooked quinoa in the big bowl. Blend chickpeas until smooth and add in the big bowl too. Then add fresh dill, pureed tofu, cranberries, wheat flour, and dried sage. Stir the mass with the spoon and form patties. Spray instant pot with cooking spray and place patties. Cook them on Saute mode for 3 minutes from each side.

Nutrition value/serving: calories 245, fat 4.1, fiber 6.3, carbs 41.7, protein 10.8

Sweet Pear Patties

Prep time: 10 minutes | Cooking time: 6 minutes | Servings: 3

Ingredients:
- 1 pear, grated
- ¾ cup almond milk
- ½ cup wheat flour
- 1 tablespoon white sugar
- ½ teaspoon ground cinnamon
- ¾ teaspoon ground cardamom
- 1 teaspoon almond butter

Directions:
Place all the ingredients except almond butter in the mixing bowl. With the help mix up the mass until homogenous. Preheat instant pot on Saute mode and add almond butter. Use 2 spoons to make patties from pear mixture. Transfer them in the hot almond butter. Cook sweet patties for 2.5 minutes from one side and then flip onto another side and cook for 2 minutes more.

Nutrition value/serving: calories 291, fat 17.6, fiber 4.2, carbs 31.9, protein 4.9

Mashed White Potato Patties
Prep time: 10 minutes | Cooking time: 8 minutes | Servings: 4

Ingredients:
- 3 white potatoes, mashed
- ¼ cup cauliflower, cooked
- ¼ cup flax meal
- 1 teaspoon salt
- 4 tablespoons bread crumbs
- 1 teaspoon dried rosemary
- 1 tablespoon olive oil

Directions:
Mash cauliflower and mix it up with potatoes, flax meal, salt, and dried rosemary. Make patties and coat them in bread crumb. Press the patties gently and place in the instant pot. Add olive oil and close the lid. Saute patties for 8 minutes. The cooked patties should have one golden brown side.

Nutrition value/serving: calories 199, fat 6.6, fiber 6.4, carbs 32.5, protein 5.2

Leek Patties
Prep time: 10 minutes | Cooking time: 10minutes | Servings: 2

Ingredients:
- 2 cups leek, chopped
- 1 teaspoon olive oil
- 1 tablespoon almond butter
- ¾ cup of water
- 1 tablespoon garam masala
- ¼ cup silken tofu, pureed
- 2 tablespoons rice flour
- 1 teaspoon salt

Directions:
Put leeks, almond butter, water, and salt in the instant pot. Close the lid and cook the mixture on High for 2 minutes. Then make quick pressure release. Transfer the mass in the bowl and mash gently with the help of a fork. Add garam masala, rice flour, tofu, and mix up well. Make patties and place them in instant pot. Add olive oil and cook them on Saute mode for 4 minutes from each side or until light brown.

Nutrition value/serving: calories 172, fat 7.8, fiber 2.7, carbs 22.5, protein 5.1

Asparagus Burger

Prep time: 10 minutes | Cooking time: 10 minutes | Servings: 4

Ingredients:
- 1-pound asparagus
- 1 cup of water
- 1 tablespoon salt
- ½ cup bread crumbs
- 1 teaspoon chili flakes
- 1 teaspoon minced garlic
- ¾ cup fresh parsley, chopped
- 1 teaspoon olive oil

Directions:

Put asparagus and water in the instant pot. Add salt and cook it on High for 3 minutes. Then use quick pressure release. Drain water from asparagus and transfer in the blender. Blend until smooth. Mix up together blended asparagus, bread crumbs, chili flakes, minced garlic, and parsley. When you get homogenous mass – make burgers. Preheat instant pot on Saute mode for 5 minutes. Add olive oil and place burgers. Cook burgers for 2 minutes from each side.

Nutrition value/serving: calories 91, fat 2.1, fiber 3.4, carbs 15.1, protein 4.7

Side Dishes

Glazed Bok Choy
Prep time: 15 minutes | Cooking time: 6 minutes | Servings: 4

Ingredients:
- 1-pound bok choy
- 1 tablespoon Maple syrup
- 1 tablespoon sesame oil
- 1 teaspoon ground cumin
- ½ teaspoon minced garlic
- 1 teaspoon ground ginger
- 1 tablespoon apple cider vinegar
- 1 tablespoon sesame seeds
- ½ cup of water

Directions:
Chop bok choy roughly and sprinkle with maple syrup, ground cumin, sesame oil, minced garlic, ground ginger, and apple cider vinegar. Mix up the vegetables and let them marinade for 10 minutes. Transfer the bok choy and all the liquid in the instant pot. Add water and cook on Manual mode (High pressure) for 4 minutes. Then make quick pressure release. Transfer the cooked bok choy in the serving bowls and sprinkle with sesame seeds.

Nutrition value/serving: calories 76, fat 4.9, fiber 1.5, carbs 7.1, protein 2.3

Pumpkin Puree
Prep time: 15 minutes | Cooking time: 15 minutes | Servings: 6

Ingredients:
- 2-pound pumpkin, peeled, chopped
- 1/3 cup almond milk
- 1 cup of water
- 1 teaspoon dried oregano

Directions:
Put chopped pumpkin in the instant pot. Add water and close the lid. Cook on Manual mode (High pressure) for 15 minutes. Use natural pressure release for 10 minutes. Strain pumpkin and transfer it in the food processor. Add almond milk and dried oregano. Blend the mixture until smooth. The pumpkin puree should be served only warm.

Nutrition value/serving: calories 83, fat 3.6, fiber 4.8, carbs 13.1, protein 2

Lemon Potatoes

Prep time: 7 *minutes* | *Cooking time:* 8 *minutes* | *Servings:* 4

Ingredients:
- 4 white potatoes
- 1 teaspoon lemon zest
- 1 teaspoon Pink salt
- 1 tablespoon fresh dill, chopped
- 1 teaspoon dried oregano
- 2 tablespoon lemon juice
- ¼ cup vegetable broth
- 1 tablespoon olive oil

Directions:
Wash potatoes carefully and chop roughly. Whisk together lemon juice, olive oil, dried oregano, and fresh dill. Pour olive oil mixture over the potatoes and sprinkle with salt. Shake well and transfer in the instant pot. Add vegetable broth and cook on Manual mode for 8 minutes. Allow natural pressure release.

Nutrition value/serving: calories 185, fat 3.9, fiber 5.4, carbs 34.5, protein 4.2

Quinoa with Basil and Lemongrass

Prep time: 15 *minutes* | *Cooking time:* 3 *minutes* | *Servings:* 3

Ingredients:
- 1 cup quinoa
- 1 cup vegetable broth
- 1 tablespoon lemongrass, chopped
- 1 teaspoon dried basil
- 1 tablespoon almond butter
- ¾ teaspoon ground nutmeg
- 1/3 teaspoon Pink salt

Directions:
Put quinoa in an instant pot. Add vegetable broth, ground nutmeg, and salt. Close the lid, seal it, and set Manual mode (high pressure). Cook quinoa for 3 minutes and allow natural pressure release for 10 minutes. In the cooked quinoa add almond butter, lemongrass and dried basil. Mix the side dish up. The side dish is cooked.

Nutrition value/serving: calories 259, fat 7.1, fiber 4.6, carbs 38.4, protein 10.8

Tender Yellow Couscous

Prep time: 15 *minutes* | *Cooking time:* 5 *minutes* | *Servings:* 4

Ingredients:
- 1 ½ cup yellow couscous
- 2 cups of water
- 1 tablespoon olive oil
- 1 teaspoon salt

Directions:
Preheat instant pot on Saute mode for 3 minutes. Pour olive oil inside it and add couscous. Stir it gently and saute for 2 minutes. Then add water and salt. Close the lid. Set manual mode (High pressure). Cook the side dish for 2 minutes. Release the pressure manually for 10 minutes.

Nutrition value/serving: calories 96, fat 3.6, fiber 0.8, carbs 13.5, protein 2.2

Mashed Potato

Prep time: 10 minutes | Cooking time: 10 minutes | Servings: 6

Ingredients:
- 6 potatoes, peeled, chopped
- 1 cup of water
- ¼ cup of coconut milk
- 1 tablespoon coconut yogurt
- 1 teaspoon salt
- 1 tablespoon chives, chopped

Directions:
Place potato and water in the instant pot. Add salt and close the lid. Cook the vegetables on Manual mode for 10 minutes. Then use quick pressure release. Open the lid, drain water from the potatoes and mash them. Add coconut yogurt, coconut milk, and chopped chives. Mix it up until soft and smooth.

Nutrition value/serving: calories 171, fat 2.6, fiber 5.3, carbs 34.2, protein 3.9

Vermicelli Bowl

Prep time: 10 minutes | Cooking time: 6 minutes | Servings: 2

Ingredients:
- 1 cup vermicelli, roasted
- ½ yellow onion, diced
- ½ jalapeno pepper, chopped
- 1 cup of water
- 1 teaspoon ground cumin
- ¼ teaspoon ground coriander
- 1 teaspoon dried rosemary
- 1 teaspoon ground ginger
- 2 red bell peppers, chopped
- 1 teaspoon olive oil

Directions:
Put diced onion, jalapeno pepper, ground cumin, coriander, rosemary, ginger, and bell peppers in the instant pot. Add olive oil, stir it and saute for 3 minutes. Then add vermicelli and water. Close the lid and set manual mode (High pressure) for 3 minutes. Make a quick pressure release. Shake the meal with the help of fork gently and transfer into the bowls.

Nutrition value/serving: calories 184, fat 3.6, fiber 3.8, carbs 34.3, protein 5.3

Broccoli Rice

Prep time: 10 minutes | Cooking time: 1 minutes | Servings: 4

Ingredients:
- 2 ½ cup broccoli florets
- 1 teaspoon salt
- 1 teaspoon grinded peppercorn
- ½ cup of water
- 1 teaspoon olive oil
- 1 teaspoon minced garlic

Directions:
Put broccoli florets in the food processor and blend until you get broccoli rice. Pour water in the instant pot. Then place broccoli rice in the instant pot pan. Add peppercorns, salt, olive oil, and minced garlic. Mix up the ingredients. Transfer the pan in the instant pot and close the lid. Set manual mode and cook on High for 1 minute. Make a quick pressure release. Chill the cauliflower rice for 2-5 minutes before serving.

Nutrition value/serving: calories 32, fat 1.4, fiber 1.6, carbs 4.4, protein 1.7

Sweet Potato Mash
***Prep time:** 10 minutes | **Cooking time:** 9 minutes | **Servings:** 6*

Ingredients:
- 2 cups sweet potatoes, peeled, chopped
- 1 teaspoon salt
- 1 teaspoon ground black pepper
- 1 cup vegetable broth
- 1 tablespoon fresh parsley, chopped

Directions:
Put potatoes, salt, and vegetable broth in the instant pot. Close the lid and set manual mode. Cook on High for 9 minutes. Then make quick pressure release, strain the sweet potatoes and mash until smooth. Add chopped parsley and ground black pepper in the mashed sweet potato. Mix up well.

Nutrition value/serving: calories 67, fat 0.3, fiber 2.2, carbs 14.4, protein 1.6

Red Cabbage with Apples
***Prep time:** 10 minutes | **Cooking time:** 7 minutes | **Servings:** 3*

Ingredients:
- 1-pound red cabbage
- 1 apple, chopped
- 1 teaspoon salt
- ¼ cup of coconut milk
- ¾ cup almond milk
- ½ teaspoon chili flakes

Directions:
Shred red cabbage and mix it up with salt. Transfer the mixture in the instant pot. Add coconut milk, almond milk, and chili flakes. Then add apple and set manual mode (High pressure). Cook the cabbage for 7 minutes. Then allow natural pressure release. Transfer the meal into the serving bowls and mix up well before serving.

Nutrition value/serving: calories 123, fat 5.1, fiber 6, carbs 20.2, protein 2.6

Garlic Spaghetti Squash
***Prep time:** 15 minutes | **Cooking time:** 10 minutes | **Servings:** 4*

Ingredients:
- 1 teaspoon minced garlic
- 1 teaspoon onion powder
- ½ teaspoon chili flakes
- 1 teaspoon apple cider vinegar
- 1-pound spaghetti squash, halved, seeds removed
- 1 tablespoon Italian seasoning
- 1 cup water, for cooking

Directions:
Pour water in the instant pot and insert steamer rack. Arrange spaghetti squash on the rack and close the lid. Cook it on High for 10 minutes. Then allow natural pressure release for 5 minutes. Check if the spaghetti squash is soft and shred the flesh with the help of a fork. Put the squash shred in the bowl. For serving the squash, add onion powder, minced garlic, chili flakes, apple cider vinegar, and Italian seasoning. Mix it up.

Nutrition value/serving: calories 49, fat 1.7, fiber 0, carbs 9, protein 0.8

Baked Potato

Prep time: 10 minutes | *Cooking time:* 11 minutes | *Servings:* 2

Ingredients:
- 2 potatoes
- 2 teaspoons vegan mayonnaise
- 1 teaspoon chives, chopped
- ½ cup of water

Directions:
Pour water in the instant pot and insert steamer rack. Put potatoes on the rack and close the lid. Set Manual mode (High pressure) and cook for 11 minutes. Then use quick pressure release. Transfer the potatoes on the plate and cut into halves. Sprinkle them with mayonnaise and chives.

Nutrition value/serving: calories 159, fat 1.4, fiber 5.1, carbs 33.8, protein 3.6

Vegan Applesauce

Prep time: 10 minutes | *Cooking time:* 10 minutes | *Servings:* 4

Ingredients:
- 5 apples
- 1/3 cup water
- 1 teaspoon ground cinnamon
- ¼ teaspoon vanilla extract

Directions:
Peel the apples and remove seeds. Put apples in the instant pot and sprinkle with ground cinnamon, vanilla extract, and water. Close the lid and cook on Manual mode (High pressure) for 10 minutes. After this, use quick pressure release. Transfer the mixture in the blender and blend until smooth. Place applesauce in the glass jar and let it rest in the fridge for 30 minutes before serving.

Nutrition value/serving: calories 147, fat 0.5, fiber 7.1, carbs 39, protein 0.8

Mexican Rice

Prep time: 10 minutes | *Cooking time:* 8 minutes | *Servings:* 4

Ingredients:
- 1 cup long grain rice
- 1 tablespoon tomato paste
- ¼ cup corn kernels, canned
- 1 teaspoon smoked paprika
- 1 teaspoon chili flakes
- 1 teaspoon salt
- 2 cups vegetable broth
- 1 carrot, chopped
- 2 tablespoons olive oil

Directions:
Pour olive oil in the instant pot and set Saute mode. Add rice and start to cook it. Add chili flakes, salt, and ¼ cup of vegetable broth. Stir it. Add tomato paste and stir until rice gets the red color. Then add corn kernels, smoked paprika, carrot, and all remaining vegetable broth. Set Manual mode (High pressure) and close the lid. Seal it. Cook rice for 4 minutes. Use quick pressure release.

Nutrition value/serving: calories 267, fat 8.2, fiber 1.6, carbs 41.8, protein 6.4

Polenta

Prep time: 5 minutes | *Cooking time:* 8 minutes | *Servings:* 5

Ingredients:
- 1 cup polenta
- 4 cups vegetable broth
- 2 tablespoons coconut milk
- ½ teaspoon ground black pepper
- 1 teaspoon salt

Directions:
Whisk together polenta and vegetable broth. Pour mixture in the instant pot. Add salt. Close the lid and cook it on Manual mode (High pressure) for 8 minutes. Use quick pressure release/ Transfer cooked polenta in the bowl and stir well. You need to get the creamy texture of the meal. Add ground black pepper and coconut milk. Stir it before serving.

Nutrition value/serving: calories 156, fat 2.8, fiber 1, carbs 25.5, protein 6.3

Pasta Marinara

Prep time: 5 minutes | *Cooking time:* 5 minutes | *Servings:* 4

Ingredients:
- 13 oz spaghetti
- 1 cup marinara sauce
- ½ cup of water
- 1 teaspoon dried basil

Directions:
Break spaghetti into half and put in the instant pot. Add marinara sauce and water. Close the lid. Seal it and cook on Manual mode (high pressure) for 5 minutes. Make a quick pressure release. Transfer cooked pasta in the bowl and sprinkle with dried basil.

Nutrition value/serving: calories 320, fat 3.8, fiber 1.6, carbs 59, protein 11.5

Butter Corn

Prep time: 5 minutes | *Cooking time:* 2 minutes | *Servings:* 4

Ingredients:
- 4 corn on the cob
- 4 teaspoon almond butter
- 1 teaspoon salt
- ½ teaspoon minced garlic
- ½ cup of water

Directions:
Pour water in the instant pot and insert trivet. Place corn on the cobs on the trivet and close the lid. Set manual mode (High pressure) and cook for 2 minutes. Use natural pressure release. Churn together almond butter, salt, and minced garlic. Spread the corn on the cobs with the churned mixture before serving.

Nutrition value/serving: calories 229, fat 9, fiber 3.5, carbs 34.7, protein 8.1

Artichoke Petals

Prep time: 5 minutes | Cooking time: 7 minutes | Servings: 4

Ingredients:
- 1-pound artichoke petals
- 1 teaspoon salt
- ½ cup of coconut milk

Directions:

Place artichoke petals, salt, and coconut milk in the instant pot. Close the lid and set Manual mode. Cook on High pressure for 7 minutes. Then allow natural pressure release for 5 minutes. Mix up the vegetables before serving.

Nutrition value/serving: calories 122, fat 7.3, fiber 6.8, carbs 13.6, protein 4.4

Beets

Prep time: 10 minutes | Cooking time: 17 minutes | Servings: 4

Ingredients:
- 2-pound beets, peeled
- 1 teaspoon ground black pepper
- 1 tablespoon olive oil
- 1 cup water, for cooking

Directions:

Cut the bets into the medium cubes. Pour water in the instant pot and insert trivet. Place beets on the trivet and close the lid. Cook the meal for 17 minutes on Manual mode (High pressure). Then use quick pressure. Transfer beets in the bowl and sprinkle with ground black pepper and olive oil before serving.

Nutrition value/serving: calories 131, fat 3.9, fiber 4.7, carbs 22.9, protein 3.9

Tender Sweet Peppers

Prep time: 10 minutes | Cooking time: 13 minutes | Servings: 4

Ingredients:
- 2 red sweet peppers
- 1 green bell pepper
- 1 yellow sweet pepper
- 1 garlic clove, peeled
- 1 tomato, chopped
- ¼ cup fresh dill, chopped
- 2 tablespoons sesame oil
- ½ cup of water

Directions:

Trim the peppers and cut into the strips. Preheat instant pot on Saute mode. Add olive oil, garlic clove, and chopped tomato. Saute the ingredients for 3 minutes. Mix up. Add pepper strips and add water. Close the lid and cook on Saute mode for 10 minutes. When the peppers are tender – they are cooked. Don't cook a long time to avoid overcooking.

Nutrition value/serving: calories 110, fat 7.3, fiber 2.2, carbs 11.5, protein 2

Spiced Okra

Prep time: *10 minutes* | ***Cooking time:*** *22 minutes* | ***Servings:*** *5*

Ingredients:
- 1-pound okra
- 1 teaspoon salt
- ½ teaspoon chili flakes
- ½ teaspoon cayenne pepper
- 1 teaspoon red chili pepper
- ½ cup of water
- 1 teaspoon almond butter

Directions:

Preheat instant pot on Saute mode for 2 minutes and place almond butter. Meanwhile, slice okra. Transfer it in the instant pot and sprinkle with chili flakes, salt, and red chili pepper. Add water and mix up gently. Close the lid and saute the vegetables for 20 minutes. Mix up the okra before serving.

Nutrition value/serving: calories 57, fat 2, fiber 3.3, carbs 7.6, protein 2.5

Sweet Baby Carrots

Prep time: *5 minutes* | ***Cooking time:*** *3 minutes* | ***Servings:*** *2*

Ingredients:
- 1 cup baby carrots
- 1 tablespoon honey
- 1 teaspoon ground cinnamon
- ¼ teaspoon pumpkin spices
- 1 teaspoon coconut oil
- ¼ cup of water

Directions:

Mix up together water, honey, ground cinnamon, and pumpkin spices. Whisk the liquid and pour it in the instant pot. Add baby carrots and coconut oil. Close the lid. Cook the side dish for 3 minutes on Manual mode (High pressure). Use the quick pressure release. Serve the cooked baby carrots with the sweet sauce from the instant pot.

Nutrition value/serving: calories 73, fat 2.3, fiber 2.2, carbs 13.7, protein 0.1

Soft Kale

Prep time: *10 minutes* | ***Cooking time:*** *3 minutes* | ***Servings:*** *2*

Ingredients:
- 1 cup kale
- ½ cup of water
- 1 teaspoon almond butter
- ½ teaspoon salt

Directions:

Chop the kale roughly and place in the instant pot. Add water. Close the lid and seal it. Set Manual mode (high pressure) and cook kale for 3 minutes. Then allow natural pressure release. Transfer the cooked kale in the bowls and sprinkle with salt and almond butter. Mix it up before serving.

Nutrition value/serving: calories 66, fat 4.5, fiber 1.3, carbs 5, protein 2.7

Cauliflower Rice

Prep time: 10 minutes | *Cooking time:* 12 minutes | *Servings:* 4

Ingredients:
- 1 ½-pound cauliflower head
- 1 cup of water
- 1 teaspoon salt
- 1 tablespoon fresh dill, chopped
- 2 tablespoons almond yogurt

Directions:

Pour water in the instant pot and insert steamer rack. Place cauliflower on the rack and close the lid. Seal it. Set manual mode (high pressure) and cook cauliflower for 12 minutes. Then make quick pressure release. Transfer cooked cauliflower in the big bowl. With the help of the potato masher mash it gently until you get cauliflower rice. Add dill, salt, and almond yogurt. Mix it up.

Nutrition value/serving: calories 50, fat 0.5, fiber 4.4, carbs 10.1, protein 3.7

Barley

Prep time: 20 minutes | *Cooking time:* 30 minutes | *Servings:* 3

Ingredients:
- 1 cup barley
- 2 cups of water
- 1 teaspoon salt
- 1 tablespoon olive oil
- 1 teaspoon turmeric
- ½ teaspoon smoked paprika

Directions:

Set saute mode and pour olive oil in the instant pot. Preheat it for 1-2 minutes and add barley. Stir it and cook for 3 minutes. After this, add salt, turmeric, smoked paprika, and water. Close the lid and switch on Manual mode (high pressure). Cook barley for 25 minutes. Allow natural pressure release for 15 minutes.

Nutrition value/serving: calories 261, fat 6.2, fiber 10.9, carbs 45.7, protein 7.8

Creamed Corn

Prep time: 8 minutes | *Cooking time:* 9 minutes | *Servings:* 3

Ingredients:
- 2 cups frozen corn
- 1 cup vegetable broth
- ½ teaspoon salt
- 1 teaspoon yeast
- 1 cup coconut cream
- ½ teaspoon turmeric
- ½ teaspoon chili flakes

Directions:

In the mixing bowl whisk together vegetable broth, salt, yeast, coconut cream, turmeric, and chili flakes. Place frozen corn in the instant pot bowl. Pour coconut cream mixture over the corn and close the lid. Set Manual mode (High pressure) and cook it for 9 minutes. Use quick pressure release.

Nutrition value/serving: calories 290, fat 20.8, fiber 4.9, carbs 24.8, protein 7.3

Mac'n Cheese

Prep time: 10 minutes | Cooking time: 7 minutes | Servings: 4

Ingredients:
- 2 cups macaroni
- 1 cup of water
- ½ cup cashew milk
- 1 teaspoon salt
- 5 oz vegan Parmesan, grated
- 1 teaspoon olive oil
- ½ teaspoon paprika

Directions:

Pour water in the instant pot. Add macaroni and salt. Close the lid. Set Manual mode (High pressure) and cook the mixture for 3 minutes. Then use quick pressure release. Drain the water from macaroni and return it back in the instant pot bowl. Add cashew milk, olive oil, paprika, and grated Parmesan. Mix up the meal. Close the lid and set Saute mode for 4 minutes. When the meal is cooked – all the cheese should melt. Mix it up carefully before serving.

Nutrition value/serving: calories 278, fat 2.1, fiber 1.4, carbs 38.9, protein 20

Green Beans with Nuts

Prep time: 8 minutes | Cooking time: 5 minutes | Servings: 4

Ingredients:
- 2 cups green beans
- 1 teaspoon salt
- 2 cups vegetable broth
- 1 tablespoon olive oil
- ½ teaspoon garlic powder
- ¼ cup walnuts, chopped

Directions:

Set Saute mode and toss green beans in the instant pot. Saute the vegetables for 2-3 minutes. Stir them from time to time. Then add vegetable broth and close the lid. Set Manual mode (High pressure) and cook the meal for 1 minute. Then use quick pressure release. Drain vegetable broth and sprinkle vegetables with garlic powder and walnuts. Shake well and close the lid. Saute the meal for 2-3 minutes more.

Nutrition value/serving: calories 116, fat 8.9, fiber 2.4, carbs 5.4, protein 5.4

Potato Salad

Prep time: 15 minutes | Cooking time: 6 minutes | Servings: 4

Ingredients:
- 3 red potatoes, peeled, chopped
- 1 cup green peas, frozen
- 1 tablespoon vegan mayonnaise
- 1 teaspoon mustard
- ½ teaspoon paprika
- 3 tablespoons fresh dill, chopped
- 2 tablespoons fresh parsley, chopped
- 1 teaspoon salt
- 1 cup water, for cooking

Directions:
Pour water in instant pot and insert steamer rack. Place potatoes in the instant pot pan and transfer it in the instant pot. Close the lid and cook the vegetables on Manual (High pressure) for 6 minutes. After this, allow natural pressure release for 5 minutes. Transfer the cooked potatoes in the salad bowl. Then return back the pan in the instant pot and add frozen green peas. Close the lid and cook them on Manual (High pressure) for 1 minute. Use quick pressure release. Transfer the green peas in the salad bowl. Add fresh dill and parsley. In the separate small bowl whisk together paprika, mustard, salt, and vegan mayonnaise. Pour the sauce over the salad mixture and mix up well.

Nutrition value/serving: calories 161, fat 1.6, fiber 5.2, carbs 32.7, protein 5.8

Cilantro Brussels Sprouts

Prep time: 5 minutes | Cooking time: 4 minutes | Servings: 2

Ingredients:
- 1 cup Brussels sprouts
- 1 garlic clove, peeled
- ½ cup of water
- 1 tablespoon dried cilantro
- ½ teaspoon salt
- 1 tablespoon olive oil

Directions:
Pour water and add Brussels sprouts in the instant pot. Close the lid and cook vegetables on High pressure for 2 minutes. Then use quick pressure release and drain water. Chop garlic and add in Brussels sprouts. Then add dried cilantro, salt, and olive oil. Mix up the vegetables and saute on Saute mode for 2 minutes.

Nutrition value/serving: calories 81, fat 7.2, fiber 1.7, carbs 4.5, protein 1.6

Mushroom Risotto

Prep time: 10 minutes | *Cooking time:* 12 minutes | *Servings:* 4

Ingredients:

- 1 cup mushrooms, chopped
- 1 tablespoon olive oil
- 1 white onion, diced
- ½ cup green peas, frozen
- ½ teaspoon dried thyme
- 1 teaspoon salt
- 1 ½ cups of rice
- 1 teaspoon garlic powder
- 2 ½ cups vegetable broth
- 1 teaspoon dried parsley
- 1 oz vegan Parmesan, grated

Directions:

Preheat instant pot on Saute mode. Add olive oil, mushrooms, and diced onion. Saute vegetables for 5 minutes. Stir time to time. Then add green peas, dried thyme, salt, garlic powder, and dried parsley. Mix up well and add rice. Then add vegetable broth and mix up. Close the lid and cook risotto on Manual mode (High pressure) and cook it for 7 minutes. Then use quick pressure release. Open the lid and add grated vegan Parmesan. Mix up well.

Nutrition value/serving: calories 361, fat 5, fiber 2.7, carbs 63.9, protein 12.8

Ratatouille

Prep time: 10 minutes | *Cooking time:* 15 minutes | *Servings:* 6

Ingredients:

- 1 cup tomatoes, chopped
- 3 sweet peppers, chopped
- 1 red onion, diced
- 2 garlic cloves, peeled
- 1 zucchini, chopped
- ½ eggplant, chopped
- 2 tablespoons sesame oil
- 1 tablespoon fresh parsley, chopped
- 1 teaspoon tomato paste
- 1 teaspoon dried cilantro
- ¼ teaspoon dried oregano
- 1 tablespoon Italian seasoning
- 1 jalapeno, pepper, chopped
- 2 cups vegetable broth

Directions:

Set instant pot on Saute mode for 8 minutes and pour sesame oil. Add sweet peppers, tomatoes, and onions. Stir the mixture. Then add zucchini, garlic clove, eggplant, and jalapeno pepper. Mix up the vegetables and keep cooking. Add parsley, dried oregano, Italian seasoning, and tomato paste. When the time of sauteing is over – add vegetable broth and close the lid. Cook the meal on Manual mode (High pressure) for 2 minutes. Allow natural pressure release for 5 minutes.

Nutrition value/serving: calories 110, fat 6.1, fiber 3.4, carbs 12, protein 3.6

Pineapple Rice

Prep time: 5 minutes | Cooking time: 8 minutes | Servings: 4

Ingredients:
- 1 ½ cup of rice
- 2 cups of water
- 1 cup pineapple juice
- 1 can pineapples, chopped
- 1 teaspoon coconut cream

Directions:
Pour water and pineapple juice in the instant pot. Add rice and chopped pineapple, and close the lid. Set Manual mode (high pressure) for 8 minutes. Then use quick pressure release. Transfer the cooked pineapple rice in the bowl and add coconut cream. Stir it.

Nutrition value/serving: calories 310, fat 0.9, fiber 1.6, carbs 69, protein 5.4

Mongolian Stir Fry

Prep time: 5 minutes | Cooking time: 4 minutes | Servings: 4

Ingredients:
- 1 tablespoon minced ginger
- 1 teaspoon minced garlic
- 1 tablespoon avocado oil
- 4 tablespoons soy sauce
- 1 teaspoon chili flakes
- 1 teaspoon cornstarch
- 1 tablespoon brown sugar
- 8 tablespoon water
- ½ teaspoon cayenne pepper
- 1-pound seitan, chopped

Directions:
In the mixing bowl whisk together minced ginger, minced garlic, avocado oil, soy sauce, chili flakes, cornstarch, brown sugar, cayenne pepper, and water. Preheat instant pot bowl on Saute mode until hot. Transfer ginger mixture in the instant pot and cook it for 1 minute. Then add chopped seitan and stir well. Close the lid and set Manual mode (high pressure) for 1 minute. Use quick pressure release. Mix up the side dish well before serving.

Nutrition value/serving: calories 59, fat 0.9, fiber 0.8, carbs 5.6, protein 6.6

Mushroom "Bacon"

Prep time: 5 minutes | Cooking time: 2 minutes | Servings: 5

Ingredients:
- 6 oz shiitake mushrooms
- 1 teaspoon salt
- ¼ teaspoon cayenne pepper
- 1 tablespoon olive oil

Directions:
Slice the mushrooms onto bacon shape strips and sprinkle every strip with olive oil, cayenne pepper, and salt. Then place mushroom "bacon" in the instant pot and close the lid. Set Manual mode (high pressure) and cook mushrooms for 2 minutes. Then use quick pressure release. The time of cooking depends on mushroom strips size.

Nutrition value/serving: calories 43, fat 2.9, fiber 0.7, carbs 4.7, protein 0.5

Crushed Baby Potatoes
Prep time: 10 minutes | Cooking time: 10 minutes | Servings: 2

Ingredients:
- 1 ½ cup baby potatoes
- 1 teaspoon salt
- 4 tablespoons olive oil
- 1 tablespoon dried rosemary
- 1 teaspoon dried oregano

Directions:
Wash baby potatoes carefully and crush with the help of the knife. Then sprinkle the crushed potatoes with salt, olive oil, dried rosemary, and oregano. Shake well until homogenous. Transfer potatoes in the instant pot and close the lid. Cook the meal on Manual mode (high pressure) for 4 minutes. Then use natural pressure release for 5 minutes. Don't mix up potatoes anymore.

Nutrition value/serving: calories 325, fat 28.4, fiber 3.7, carbs 19.2, protein 2.1

Bang Bang Broccoli
Prep time: 10 minutes | Cooking time: 4 minutes | Servings: 2

Ingredients:
- 2 tablespoons vegan mayo
- 1 teaspoon chili paste
- 1 tablespoon Maple syrup
- 1 cup broccoli
- ¼ cup almond milk
- 1 teaspoon cornstarch
- 2 tablespoons wheat flour
- 1 teaspoon olive oil
- 1/3 cup panko bread crumbs
- 1 tablespoon lemon juice
- ½ cup water for cooking

Directions:
For the sauce: whisk together vegan mayo and chili paste. For the broccoli batter: in the separated bowl whisk together almond milk, wheat flour, olive oil, cornstarch, and lemon juice. Cut broccoli into the florets and dip into the batter. Then coat every broccoli floret in the panko bread crumbs. Pour water in the instant pot bowl and insert rack. Place coated broccoli on the rack and close the lid. Cook the vegetables on Manual mode (High pressure) for 4 minutes. Use quick pressure release. Transfer the cooked broccoli in the bowl and sprinkle with sauce.

Nutrition value/serving: calories 280, fat 14.7, fiber 2.9, carbs 33.7, protein 5.4

Tikka Masala with Cauliflower

Prep time: 10 minutes | Cooking time: 10 minutes | Servings: 4

Ingredients:
- 1 teaspoon garam masala
- ½ teaspoon salt
- 1 cup cauliflower, chopped
- 1/3 cup coconut yogurt
- 1 teaspoon ground cumin
- ½ teaspoon ground coriander
- 1 onion, diced
- ½ teaspoon garlic, diced
- ¼ teaspoon minced ginger
- 1 cup tomatoes, canned

Directions:

Set instant pot on Saute mode. Add olive oil, diced onion, garlic, and minced ginger. Then sprinkle the mixture with ground cumin, coriander, salt, and garam masala. Mix up well. Add canned tomatoes and mix up well. Saute the mixture for 5 minutes. After this, add chopped cauliflower and stir well. Close the lid and seal it. Cook the meal on Manual mode (High pressure) for 3 minutes. Then use quick pressure release and open the lid. Add coconut yogurt and mix up well. Serve the meal hot

Nutrition value/serving: calories 67, fat 4.1, fiber 1.8, carbs 7.2, protein 1.7

Vegetable En Papillote

Prep time: 10 minutes | Cooking time: 3 minutes | Servings: 4

Ingredients:
- 1 cup baby carrot
- ½ cup green beans
- 1 teaspoon dried rosemary
- 1 teaspoon salt
- 1 tablespoon avocado oil
- 1 garlic clove, diced
- 1 teaspoon fresh oregano
- 1 tablespoon lemon juice
- 1 teaspoon turmeric

Directions:

In the mixing bowl mix up together baby carrot and green beans. Sprinkle the vegetables with dried rosemary, salt, avocado oil, garlic, oregano, lemon juice, and turmeric. Shake the ingredients well. Then Wrap the vegetables in the baking paper and transfer in the instant pot. Close the lid and seal it. Cook the vegetables on Manual mode (High pressure) for 3 minutes. Then allow natural pressure release for 5 minutes and remove vegetables from the baking paper.

Nutrition value/serving: calories 30, fat 0.7, fiber 2.3, carbs 5.8, protein 0.7

Brown Rice

Prep time: 15 minutes | *Cooking time:* 18 minutes | *Servings:* 4

Ingredients:
- 1 ½ cup brown rice
- 3 cups of water
- 1 tablespoon olive oil
- 1 teaspoon salt

Directions:
Set Saute mode and preheat instant pot. Add olive oil and brown rice and stir it well. Cook the rice for 3 minutes. Add water and salt. Close and seal the lid. Set Manual mode (high pressure) and cook the meal for 15 minutes. Allow natural pressure release for 10 minutes more. Mix up the rice before serving.

Nutrition value/serving: calories 57, fat 3.9, fiber 0, carbs 5.3, protein 0.4

Fragrant Bulgur

Prep time: 5 minutes | *Cooking time:* 19 minutes | *Servings:* 3

Ingredients:
- 1 cup bulgur
- 1 teaspoon tomato paste
- 2 cup of water
- 1 teaspoon olive oil
- 1 teaspoon salt

Directions:
Preheat instant pot on Saute mode and add olive oil. Place bulgur in the oil and stir well. Saute it for 4 minutes. Then add tomato paste and salt. Stir well. Add water and mix up bulgur until you get a homogenous liquid mixture. Close the lid and set Manual mode (low pressure). Cook bulgur for 15 minutes. The bulgur will be cooked when it soaks all the liquid.

Nutrition value/serving: calories 174, fat 2.2, fiber 8.6, carbs 35.8, protein 5.8

Baked Apples

Prep time: 5 minutes | *Cooking time:* 9 minutes | *Servings:* 6

Ingredients:
- 4 red apples, chopped
- 1 teaspoon ground cinnamon
- 1 tablespoon brown sugar
- 1 teaspoon maple syrup
- ¼ cup cashew milk

Directions:
Place apples in the instant pot and sprinkle with ground cinnamon, brown sugar, and maple syrup. Close the lid and set Saute mode. Cook the apples for 5 minutes. Then add cashew milk and mix up the side dish well. Cook it for 4 minutes more.

Nutrition value/serving: calories 88, fat 0.4, fiber 3.8, carbs 23.1, protein 0.4

Scalloped Potatoes

Prep time: 15 minutes | *Cooking time:* 4 minutes | *Servings:* 4

Ingredients:
- 4 potatoes, peeled, sliced
- 1 cup almond milk
- 1 teaspoon nutritional yeast
- 1 teaspoon dried rosemary
- ½ teaspoon salt
- 1 teaspoon garlic powder
- 1 teaspoon cashew butter
- 1 teaspoon ground nutmeg

Directions:

Mix up together nutritional yeast, dried rosemary, salt, garlic powder, and ground nutmeg. Whisk together almond milk and spice mixture. Grease the instant pot bowl with cashew butter. Place the sliced potatoes inside instant pot bowl by layers. Then pour almond milk mixture over the potatoes and close the lid. Cook scalloped potatoes on Manual mode (High pressure) for 4 minutes. Then allow natural pressure release for 10 minutes. Sprinkle the cooked meal with your favorite vegan cheese if desired.

Nutrition value/serving: calories 302, fat 15.5, fiber 7, carbs 38.5, protein 5.7

Glazed White Onions

Prep time: 5 minutes | *Cooking time:* 20 minutes | *Servings:* 4

Ingredients:
- 3 white onions, peeled, sliced
- 1 tablespoon sugar
- ½ teaspoon ground black pepper
- 3 tablespoons coconut oil
- ½ teaspoon baking soda

Directions:

Set Saute mode and preheat instant pot until hot. Toss coconut oil and melt it. When the coconut oil is liquid, add sugar, baking soda, and ground black pepper. Stir the mixture gently. Add sliced onions and mix the ingredients up. Close the lid and saute onions for 15 minutes. When the side dish is cooked it will have a light brown color and tender texture.

Nutrition value/serving: calories 133, fat 10.3, fiber 1.8, carbs 10.9, protein 0.9

Spicy Garlic

Prep time: 10 minutes | *Cooking time:* 10 minutes | *Servings:* 4

Ingredients:
- 4 garlic bulbs, trimmed
- 2 teaspoons olive oil
- ½ teaspoon salt
- ¼ teaspoon chili flakes
- ½ cup water, for cooking

Directions:

Pour water in the instant pot and insert rack. Place garlic bulbs on the rack and sprinkle with olive oil, salt, and chili flakes. Close the lid and set Poultry mode. Cook garlic for 10 minutes. Then allow natural pressure release for 5 minutes more. Serve the garlic when it reaches room temperature.

Nutrition value/serving: calories 35, fat 2.3, fiber 0, carbs 3, protein 0

Pasta and Green Peas Side Dish

Prep time: 5 minutes | Cooking time: 10 minutes | Servings: 2

Ingredients:
- ½ cup pasta
- 1 cup of water
- 1/3 cup green peas, frozen
- 1 teaspoon salt
- ¼ teaspoon minced garlic
- 1 teaspoon tomato paste

Directions:

Mx up together water, tomato paste, minced garlic, and salt. Pout liquid in the instant pot. Add green peas and pasta. Mix up gently. Close the lid and set Manual mode (High pressure). Cook the side dish for 10 minutes. Then use quick pressure release. Drain ½ part of the liquid and transfer the meal into the serving bowl.s

Nutrition value/serving: calories 207, fat 1.6, fiber 1.4, carbs 39.1, protein 8.7

Almond Milk Millet

Prep time: 5 minutes | Cooking time: 10 minutes | Servings: 3

Ingredients:
- ½ teaspoon salt
- 1 cup millet
- 1 cup almond milk

Directions:

Pour almond milk in the instant pot bowl. Add millet and salt. Close and seal the lid and set Manual mode (High pressure). Cook the side dish for 10 minutes. Allow natural pressure release.

Nutrition value/serving: calories 436, fat 21.9, fiber 7.4, carbs 53, protein 9.2

Stir Fried Kale

Prep time: 5 minutes | Cooking time: 5 minutes | Servings: 4

Ingredients:
- 2 cup kale, chopped
- ½ teaspoon nutritional yeast
- 1 teaspoon coconut oil
- ½ teaspoon ground black pepper
- 2 tablespoon bread crumbs
- 4 tablespoons water

Directions:

Preheat instant pot on Saute mode until hot. Toss coconut oil and melt it. Add chopped kale and sprinkle it with ground black pepper and nutritional yeast. Add water and saute kale for 2 minutes. Then mix up kale well and sprinkle with bread crumbs. Close the lid and cook on Manual mode (high pressure) for 1 minute. Allow quick pressure release. Shake the kale well before serving.

Nutrition value/serving: calories 42, fat 1.3, fiber 0.8, carbs 6.3, protein 1.7

Zoodles

Prep time: 10 minutes | *Cooking time:* 25 minutes | *Servings:* 4

Ingredients:
- 2 zucchini
- ½ teaspoon salt
- ¾ cup vegetable broth
- ¼ teaspoon ground black pepper

Directions:
Wash and trim zucchini well. With the help of the spiralizer make the zucchini zoodles. Sprinkle them with ground black pepper and salt. Transfer zoodles in the instant pot bowl and add vegetable broth. Close and seal the lid. Set Manual moe (high pressure) and cook meal for 1 minute. Use natural pressure release.

Nutrition value/serving: calories 23, fat 0.4, fiber 1.1, carbs 3.5, protein 2.1

Buckwheat

Prep time: 10 minutes | *Cooking time:* 15 minutes | *Servings:* 4

Ingredients:
- 2 cups buckwheat
- 2.5 cup of water
- 1 tablespoon sunflower oil
- 1 teaspoon salt
- 1 tablespoon almond butter

Directions:
Pour sunflower oil in the instant pot. Add almond butter and saute the ingredients for 3 minutes on Saute mode. Then add buckwheat and stir it carefully. Saute the mixture for 3 minutes. Add water and stir well. Close and seal the lid. Set manual mode (high pressure) and cook buckwheat for 4 minutes. Then use quick pressure release. Mix up the buckwheat carefully before serving.

Nutrition value/serving: calories 347, fat 8.6, fiber 8.9, carbs 61.5, protein 12.1

Grains and Pasta

Japgokbap

Prep time: 8 minutes | Cooking time: 20 minutes | Servings: 6

Ingredients:
- ¼ cup white rice
- 1/3 cup red beans
- ¼ cup sorghum
- 1/3 cup millet
- ¼ cup chickpea
- 3 cups of water
- ¼ teaspoon of sea salt

Directions:
Put white rice, red beans, sorghum, millet, chickpea, and sea salt in the instant pot bowl. Mix up the ingredients with the help of the wooden spatula. Add water, close and seal the lid. Set Manual mode (high pressure) and cook the meal for 20 minutes. Then use quick pressure release. Mix up the meal gently before serving.

Nutrition value/serving: calories 175, fat 1.1, fiber 4, carbs 35.9, protein 5.7

Proso Millet

Prep time: 5 minutes | Cooking time: 15 minutes | Servings: 2

Ingredients:
- 1 cup proso millet
- 2 cups vegetable broth
- 1 teaspoon salt
- ¼ teaspoon chili flakes
- 1 teaspoon coconut oil

Directions:
Preheat instant pot on Saute mode and toss coconut oil. Melt it and add salt, chili flakes, and proso millet. Stir it gently and cook for 3 minutes. Then add vegetable broth, close, and seal the lid. Set Manual moe (high pressure) and cook meal for 10 minutes. Use the quick pressure release to prevent mushy texture of the proso millet.

Nutrition value/serving: calories 436, fat 7.9, fiber 8.5, carbs 73.8, protein 15.9

Sweet Rice

Prep time: 5 minutes | Cooking time: 13 minutes | Servings: 3

Ingredients:
- 1 cup white rice
- 2 tablespoons mango puree
- 1 cup of water
- 1 cup of coconut milk
- 1 tablespoon sugar
- ½ teaspoon ground cinnamon
- 1 teaspoon cashew butter

Directions:
Place white rice in the instant pot bowl. Add water, coconut milk, and sugar. Close and seal the lid and set Rice mode for 13 minutes. Use queek pressure release. Then open the lid and add cashew butter and ground cinnamon. Mix it up well and transfer into the serving bowls.

Nutrition value/serving: calories 440, fat 20.4, fiber 2.9, carbs 59.6, protein 6.6

Basmati Rague

Prep time: 10 minutes | Cooking time: 26minutes | Servings: 4

Ingredients:
- 1 cup basmati rice
- 2 cup of water
- 1 sweet pepper, chopped
- 1 red onion, diced
- 1 teaspoon salt
- 1 teaspoon tomato paste
- 1 teaspoon turmeric

Directions:
Mix up together turmeric, tomato paste, salt, and water. Stir until liquid is homogenous. Pour it in the instant pot bowl and add basmati rice. Then close the lid, set Manual mode (high pressure) and cook rice for 3 minutes. Use quick pressure release and open the lid. Add sweet pepper and onion and mix up well. Close and seal the lid and cook on Manual (high pressure) for 3 minutes more. Use the quick pressure release. Mix up ragout before serving.

Nutrition value/serving: calories 192, fat 0.5, fiber 1.8, carbs 42.4, protein 4

Arborio Rice

Prep time: 10 minutes | Cooking time: 6 minutes | Servings: 5

Ingredients:
- 2 cups Arborio rice
- 4 cups of water
- 1 teaspoon salt
- 1 teaspoon coconut oil
- ½ onion, diced
- 4 oz vegan Parmesan, grated

Directions:
Preheat instant pot on Saute mode well and toss coconut oil. Melt it. Add diced onion and saute it for 3 minutes. Then add Arborio rice and salt. Mix it up and toast mixture until light brown. Add water and close the lid. Set Rice mode (high pressure) and cook a meal for 6 minutes. Then use quick pressure release and open the lid. Transfer the rice into the serving bowls and sprinkle with grated Parmesan.

Nutrition value/serving: calories 355, fat 1.3, fiber 2.3, carbs 66.1, protein 14.4

Vanilla Rice Pudding

Prep time: 10 minutes | Cooking time: 14 minutes | Servings: 4

Ingredients:
- 1 cup of rice
- 1 teaspoon cornstarch
- 2 teaspoon vanilla extract
- 1 cup almond milk
- ½ cup of water
- 1 cup of coconut milk
- 4 tablespoons maple syrup
- ¼ teaspoon ground nutmeg
- ½ teaspoon ground cardamom
- 4 teaspoon raisins

Directions:
Whisk together cornstarch, water, vanilla extract, almond milk, coconut milk, ground nutmeg, and ground cardamom. Place rice in the instant pot bowl, add liquid mixture, and mix it up. Close and seal the lid and set Rice mode. Set timer for 4 minutes (High pressure). Then allow natural pressure release for 10 minutes. Open the lid and mix up pudding. Transfer it into the bowls and sprinkle with raisins and maple syrup.

Nutrition value/serving: calories 393, fat 15.4, fiber 2.1, carbs 59.2, protein 5.1

Oatmeal with Tender Onions

Prep time: 15 minutes | Cooking time: 5 minutes | Servings: 5

Ingredients:
- 2 cups cut oats
- 1 red onion, sliced
- 1 tablespoon coconut oil
- ½ teaspoon salt
- 2 cups of water
- ½ teaspoon white pepper

Directions:
Preheat instant pot on Saute mode and toss coconut oil inside. Melt it and add onions, salt, and white pepper. Mix it up and saute for 2 minutes. Then add cut oats and water. Close and seal the lid and set Manual mode (high pressure). Cook oatmeal for 3 minutes. Then allow natural pressure release for 15 minutes more. Mix up the cooked meal well before serving.

Nutrition value/serving: calories 99, fat 4.2, fiber 2.1, carbs 13.4, protein 2.6

Cayenne Pepper Corn

Prep time: 5 minutes | *Cooking time:* 4 minutes | *Servings:* 4

Ingredients:
- 2 cups corn, frozen
- 1 teaspoon cayenne pepper
- 1 teaspoon fresh parsley, chopped
- ½ cup vegetable broth
- 1 teaspoon olive oil
- ½ teaspoon salt

Directions:

Place corn and vegetable broth in the instant pot bowl. Sprinkle the ingredients with parsley, cayenne pepper, salt, and olive oil. Stir the mixture gently with the help of the spatula, close and seal the lid. Cook the corn on Manual mode (high pressure) for 4 minutes. Then use quick pressure release.

Nutrition value/serving: calories 82, fat 2.3, fiber 2.2, carbs 14.9, protein 3.2

PopCorn

Prep time: 2 minutes | *Cooking time:* 10 minutes | *Servings:* 2

Ingredients:
- ½ cup of corn
- 1 teaspoon olive oil
- 1 teaspoon salt

Directions:

Set Saute mode and pour olive oil in the instant pot. Preheat it and add corn. Sprinkle corn with salt and stir carefully. Close the lid and cook popcorn on Saute mode for 7-10 minutes or until it is cooked.

Nutrition value/serving: calories 53, fat 2.8, fiber 1.1, carbs 7.3, protein 1.3

Teff in Tomato Paste

Prep time: 10 minutes | *Cooking time:* 6 minutes | *Servings:* 3

Ingredients:
- 1 cup teff
- 2 cups vegetable broth
- 1 teaspoon salt
- 1 teaspoon tomato paste
- 1 teaspoon coconut oil

Directions:

Toss coconut oil in the instant pot bowl. Set Saute mode and preheat coconut oil until it is melted. Add tomato paste and salt. Stir gently. After this, add teff and stir well. Saute it for 3 minutes. Add vegetable broth, close and seal the lid. Cook the meal on Manual mode (High pressure) for 3 minutes. Then use quick pressure release. Mix up the meal before serving.

Nutrition value/serving: calories 255, fat 3.2, fiber 8.1, carbs 45, protein 11.3

Amaranth Banana Porridge

Prep time: 10 minutes | Cooking time: 6 minutes | Servings: 4

Ingredients:
- 1 ½ cup amaranth
- 1 cup almond milk
- 2 cups of water
- 2 bananas, peeled, sliced
- ¼ cup brown sugar
- 1 teaspoon vanilla extract
- 1 teaspoon almond butter

Directions:
Place amaranth, almond milk, and water in the instant pot. Add sugar and almond butter, close and seal the lid. Cook amaranth for 6 minutes on Manual mode (High pressure). Then use quick pressure release. Open the lid and add vanilla extract. Mix up well. Transfer the porridge into the serving bowls and garnish with sliced bananas.

Nutrition value/serving: calories 526, fat 21.5, fiber 10.1, carbs 75, protein 13.4

Basic Amaranth Recipe

Prep time: 5 minutes | Cooking time: 6 minutes | Servings: 2

Ingredients:
- ½ cup amaranth
- 1 cup of water
- ½ teaspoon salt

Directions:
Put all the ingredients in the instant pot bowl. Close and seal the lid. Set Manual mode (High pressure). Cook amaranth for 6 minutes. Then use quick pressure release.

Nutrition value/serving: calories 182, fat 3.2, fiber 4.5, carbs 32.3, protein 7

Multi-Grain Porridge

Prep time: 5 minutes | Cooking time: 30minutes | Servings: 4

Ingredients:
- ¼ cup red beans, soaked
- 1/3 cup black beans, soaked
- 1/3 cup brown rice
- 1 teaspoon salt
- ¼ cup barley
- 4 cups of water

Directions:
Place red and black beans in the instant pot. Add brown rice, salt, barley, and water. Close the lid and set Chili mode for 30 minutes. When the meal is cooked, mix it up carefully.

Nutrition value/serving: calories 192, fat 1, fiber 6.7, carbs 37.6, protein 8.7

Green Buckwheat

Prep time: 5 minutes | Cooking time: 9 minutes | Servings: 4

Ingredients:
- 2 cups green buckwheat
- 1 tablespoon almond butter
- ½ teaspoon turmeric
- 1 teaspoon paprika
- 2 cup vegetable broth
- 1 teaspoon salt

Directions:
Place almond butter in the instant pot and preheat it on Saute mode. Then add green buckwheat and sprinkle it with turmeric, paprika, and salt. Stir gently. Saute the buckwheat for 5 minutes. Add vegetable broth, close and seal the lid. Set Rice mode (High pressure). Cook buckwheat for 4 minutes. Use the quick pressure release.

Nutrition value/serving: calories 122, fat 3.6, fiber 2.8, carbs 17, protein 5.8

Balsamic Rice Noodles

Prep time: 10 minutes | Cooking time: 2 minutes | Servings: 4

Ingredients:
- 10 oz of rice noodles
- 1 tablespoon balsamic vinegar
- 1 teaspoon olive oil
- 1 tablespoon tamari sauce
- ½ teaspoon minced garlic
- 1 teaspoon minced ginger
- 1 ½ cup water
- ½ teaspoon sriracha

Directions:
Whisk together balsamic vinegar, olive oil, tamari sauce, minced garlic, ginger, and sriracha. Place rice noodles in the instant pot. Mix up together balsamic vinegar mixture and water and transfer the liquid in the instant pot. Close and seal the lid. Set Manual mode (High pressure) and cook a meal for 2 minutes. Transfer the cooked rice noodles in the serving bowls with ½ part of the liquid.

Nutrition value/serving: calories 94, fat 1.3, fiber 0.8, carbs 18.7, protein 1.2

Rosemary Creamed Polenta
Prep time: 8 minutes | Cooking time: 15 minutes | Servings: 5

Ingredients:
- 2 cups polenta
- 1 cup coconut cream
- 3 cups of water
- 1 teaspoon dried rosemary
- 1 teaspoon Pink salt
- 1 teaspoon minced garlic
- 1 tablespoon coconut oil

Directions:
Place coconut oil in the instant pot and melt it on Saute mode. Add Pink salt, minced garlic, and dried rosemary. Saute the mixture for 3 minutes. Then add coconut cream and bring the mixture to boil. Then add water and polenta. Stir it well. Close and seal the lid. Set manual mode (high pressure).Cook polenta for 8 minutes. Use quick pressure release. Stir the cooked polenta well before serving.

Nutrition value/serving: calories 357, fat 14.8, fiber 2.8, carbs 51.7, protein 5.8

Pasta Puttanesca
Prep time: 10 minutes | Cooking time: 15 minutes | Servings: 2

Ingredients:
- 1 cup penne pasta
- 2 cups vegan pasta sauce
- 1 cup of water
- 1/3 teaspoon chili flakes
- ½ teaspoon salt
- ½ teaspoon minced garlic
- 1 teaspoon capers

Directions:
Preheat instant pot on Saute mode and place minced garlic inside. Add salt, chili flakes, and pasta sauce. Then add water and caper. Mix up the mixture and cook it on saute mode for 10 minutes. After this, add penne pasta and stir gently. Close and seal the lid. Cook pasta on Manual mode (High pressure) for 5 minutes. Then use quick pressure release. Open the lid and mix up the pasta carefully.

Nutrition value/serving: calories 606, fat 25.6, fiber 3.5, carbs 77.9, protein 16.5

Pasta Fagioli

Prep time: 10 minutes | Cooking time: 14 minutes | Servings: 5

Ingredients:
- 1 cup red kidney beans, canned
- 1 teaspoon minced garlic
- 1 carrot, chopped
- 1 white onion, chopped
- 2 oz celery, chopped
- 1 cup tomatoes, canned
- 2 cups vegetable broth
- 1 ½ cup shell pasta
- 1 teaspoon salt
- 1 teaspoon dried oregano
- 1 teaspoon dried dill
- 1 bay leaf
- ½ teaspoon chili flakes
- 1 tablespoon coconut oil

Directions:
Toss coconut oil in the instant pot and melt it. Add chili flakes, bay leaf, dried dill, oregano, salt, canned tomatoes, celery, onion, and carrot. Mix up the ingredients and saute for 10 minutes. Then add red kidney beans, minced garlic, shell pasta, and vegetable broth. Close and seal the lid. Set Manual mode (high pressure) for 4 minutes. Then use quick pressure release. Mix up the pasta well before serving.

Nutrition value/serving: calories 397, fat 4.8, fiber 9.1, carbs 69.4, protein 18.1

Mushroom Tetrazzini

Prep time: 10 minutes | Cooking time: 15 minutes | Servings: 4

Ingredients:
- 1 cup mushroom, chopped
- 1 tablespoon olive oil
- ½ white onion, diced
- 1 teaspoon dried basil
- 1 tablespoon dried parsley
- 1 teaspoon wheat flour
- 1 cup spaghetti noodles
- ½ cup coconut cream
- 1 tablespoon bread crumbs
- 1 cup of water

Directions:
Pour olive oil in the instant pot. Set Saute mode and add chopped mushrooms and onion. Saute the vegetables until light brown. Then add dried basil, dried parsley, and stir well. Transfer the mushroom mixture in the bowl. Place wheat flour, coconut cream, and water in the instant pot bowl. Stir it carefully until smooth. Add spaghetti noodles and close the lid. Seal the lid and set Manual mode (high pressure) for 5 minutes. Then use quick pressure release. Mix up together cooked spaghetti and mushroom mixture. Sprinkle the meal with bread crumbs before serving.

Nutrition value/serving: calories 318, fat 11.8, fiber 3.3, carbs 47.3, protein 8.7

Arrabiatta Pasta

Prep time: 5 minutes | Cooking time: 16 minutes | Servings: 3

Ingredients:
- 1 tablespoon Italian seasoning
- 1 teaspoon minced garlic
- 1 tomato, chopped
- 3 oz yellow onion, diced
- 1 cup pasta
- 1 cup of water
- 1 cup pasta sauce
- 1 teaspoon sesame oil

Directions:
Pour sesame oil in the instant pot. Set Saute mode on instant pot. Add minced garlic, chopped tomato, yellow onion, and saute ingredients for 7 minutes. Add pasta sauce and water. Then add pasta and close the lid. Seal the lid and set Manual mode (high pressure) and timer for 7 minutes. Then use quick pressure release. Chill the cooked pasta for 2-3 minutes.

Nutrition value/serving: calories 362, fat 7.2, fiber 3.1, carbs 62.4, protein 11.7

Bolognese

Prep time: 10 minutes | Cooking time: 15 minutes | Servings: 4

Ingredients:
- 6 oz firm tofu
- ½ white onion, diced
- 1 celery stalk, chopped
- 4 oz mushrooms, chopped
- 1 teaspoon olive oil
- ½ teaspoon chili flakes
- ¼ teaspoon garlic powder
- 1 tablespoon Italian seasoning
- 3 tablespoon marinara sauce
- 10 oz penne pasta
- 1 cup tomatoes, canned
- 2 cups of water

Directions:
Crumble tofu and place it in the instant pot. Sprinkle it with chili flakes, garlic powder, Italian seasoning, and 1 teaspoon of olive oil. Cook tofu on saute mode for 5 minutes. Transfer the cooked crumbled tofu in the separated bowl. Place mushrooms, celery stalk, and onion in the instant pot. Add remaining olive oil. Stir it and saute for 2-3 minutes. Then add cooked crumbled tofu, canned tomatoes, water, penne pasta, and marinara sauce. Close and seal the lid. Set Manual mode (High pressure) and cook the meal for 6 minutes. Then use quick pressure release. Mix up bolognese gently with the help of the wooden spatula.

Nutrition value/serving: calories 296, fat 7.3, fiber 1.9, carbs 45.7, protein 13.2

Italian Style Pasta

Prep time: 5 minutes | *Cooking time:* 5 minutes | *Servings:* 4

Ingredients:
- 9 oz penne pasta
- 1 cup marinara sauce
- ¼ cup of coconut yogurt
- 1 teaspoon ground black pepper
- 1 teaspoon paprika
- 1 cup of water
- 6 oz vegan Parmesan, shredded
- 1 tablespoon dried oregano

Directions:
Place marinara sauce in the instant pot bowl. Add penne pasta. Then pour coconut yogurt and water. Sprinkle the mixture with ground black pepper, paprika, and dried oregano. Close and seal the lid. Set Manual mode (high pressure) and cook pasta for 5 minutes. Use quick pressure release. Transfer the cooked pasta in the serving bowls and sprinkle generously with shredded Parmesan.

Nutrition value/serving: calories 393, fat 4.2, fiber 2.5, carbs 55.4, 26.8

Tomato Spaghetti

Prep time: 10 minutes | *Cooking time:* 10 minutes | *Servings:* 4

Ingredients:
- 10 oz spaghetti
- 2 tomatoes, chopped
- 1 tablespoon tomato paste
- 1 teaspoon chili flakes
- 1 teaspoon paprika
- ½ teaspoon salt
- 1 teaspoon dried basil
- ½ teaspoon dried oregano
- 2 cups vegetable stock
- 1 teaspoon dried cilantro
- 1 teaspoon wheat flour

Directions:
On the instant pot set Saute mode and place chopped tomatoes inside. Sprinkle the vegetables with chili flakes, tomato paste, paprika, salt, dried basil, dried oregano, and cilantro. Saute the mixture for 3 minutes. Add vegetable stock and wheat flour. Mix up the liquid until the flour is smooth and cook for 2 minutes more. Then add spaghetti, close and seal the lid. Cook the meal on Manual mode (high pressure) for 5 minutes. Use the quick pressure release and open the lid. Chill the cooked meal for 5 minutes before serving.

Nutrition value/serving: calories 229, fat 2, fiber 1.7, carbs 43.8, protein 9.3

Tofu Spaghetti

Prep time: 15 minutes | Cooking time: 10 minutes | Servings: 2

Ingredients:
- 6 oz firm tofu, chopped
- 1 teaspoon sesame oil
- 1 tablespoon soy sauce
- 1 tablespoon lemon juice
- 1 teaspoon sriracha
- 8 oz spaghetti
- 1 ½ cup vegetable stock
- 1 tablespoon coconut cream
- 1 teaspoon salt

Directions:
Whisk together sesame oil, soy sauce, lemon juice, and sriracha, Then coat the tofu cubes in the soy mixture and let it marinate for 5 minutes. Meanwhile, preheat instant pot on Saute mode. Place chopped tofu in the preheated instant pot and saute for 2 minutes from each side. Transfer the tofu in the bowl. Place spaghetti, salt, and vegetable stock in the instant pot. Add coconut cream and close the lid. Seal the lid and cook on High pressure for 6 minutes. Then use quick pressure release. Mix up together cooked spaghetti with tofu and transfer in the serving bowls.

Nutrition value/serving: calories 440, fat 11.8, fiber 1, carbs 66.7, protein 20.5

Pumpkin Mac and Cheese

Prep time: 10 minutes | Cooking time: 5 minutes | Servings: 3

Ingredients:
- 1 cup elbow macaroni
- 1 teaspoon salt
- 2 cups of water
- 3 tablespoons pumpkin puree
- 4 oz vegan Cheddar cheese, grated
- 1 tablespoon chives, chopped

Directions:
Place elbow macaroni and water in the instant pot bowl. Add salt, close and seal the lid. Set manual mode and cook macaroni for 5 minutes. Use quick pressure release. Then open the lid, add pumpkin puree and grated cheese. яMix the macaroni carefully.

Nutrition value/serving: calories 216, fat 7.2, fiber 2.7, carbs 28.9, protein 4.5

Basil Pasta

Prep time: 5 minutes | Cooking time: 6 minutes | Servings: 4

Ingredients:
- 10 oz spaghetti
- 3 cups vegetable stock
- 1 tablespoon coconut cream
- 1 teaspoon salt
- 1 tablespoon dried basil
- 4 oz Vegan Parmesan, grated

Directions:
Pour vegetable stock in the instant pot bowl. Add spaghetti and salt. Close and seal the lid. Set Manual mode (High pressure) and cook spaghetti for 6 minutes. Then use quick pressure release and open the lid. Drain water from spaghetti. Mix up spaghetti with dried dill, Parmesan, and coconut cream. Mix it up carefully.

Nutrition value/serving: calories 307, fat 4, fiber 0.1, carbs 46.3, protein 19.7

Buckwheat Pasta with Mushroom Sauce

Prep time: 10 minutes | Cooking time: 20 minutes | Servings: 3

Ingredients:
- 8 oz buckwheat pasta
- 2 cups of water
- 1 teaspoon salt
- 1 teaspoon almond butter
- 1 cup mushrooms, chopped
- 1 teaspoon olive oil
- 1/3 cup almond milk
- 1 teaspoon ground black pepper
- ½ onion, diced

Directions:
Preheat instant pot on the Saute mode. Add olive oil, chopped mushrooms, and diced onion. Saute the ingredients for 7-10 minutes or until light brown. Add almond milk and stir it. Cook for 1 minute more. Transfer mushroom sauce in the bowl. Place buckwheat pasta, water, and almond butter in the instant pot. Close and seal the lid. Set manual mode and cook pasta for 10 minutes (High pressure). Then use quick pressure release. Mix up together mushroom sauce and pasta before serving.

Nutrition value/serving: calories 373, fat 12.4, fiber 5.9, carbs 54.5, protein 13.3

Classic Wheat Berries

Prep time: 5 minutes | Cooking time: 32 minutes | Servings: 4

Ingredients:
- 1 ½ cup wheat berries
- 4 ½ cup vegetable broth
- 1 teaspoon salt
- 1 teaspoon coconut oil

Directions:
Place wheat berries, vegetable broth, salt, and coconut oil in the instant pot bowl. Close and seal the lid. Set the Manual mode (High pressure) and cook wheat berries for 32 minutes. When the time is over, use the quick pressure release and open the lid. Mix up wheat berries gently before serving.

Nutrition value/serving: calories 133, fat 3.2, fiber 0.5, carbs 18.3, protein 8.5

Freekeh Tacos

Prep time: 15 minutes | Cooking time: 15 minutes | Servings: 4

Ingredients:
- ½ red onion, diced
- 1 tablespoon almond butter
- 1 cayenne pepper, chopped
- 1 green bell pepper, chopped
- ¼ teaspoon minced garlic
- ½ cup of salsa
- ½ teaspoon ground coriander
- 1 teaspoon paprika
- ½ cup red kidney beans, canned
- ½ cup freekeh
- 2 cups of water
- 1 teaspoon Taco seasoning
- 8 taco shells

Directions:
Place almond butter in the instant pot and set Saute mode. Melt almond butter. Add cayenne pepper, bell pepper, minced garlic, and ground coriander. Then add paprika, kidney beans, and Taco seasoning. Mix up the mixture. Saute it for 7 minutes. After this, add salsa, water, and freekeh. Stir it gently. Close and seal the lid. Set Manual mode (High pressure) and cook the mixture for 8 minutes. Then allow natural pressure release for 10 minutes. Open the lid. Fill taco shells with the instant pot mixture and transfer tacos on the serving plate.

Nutrition value/serving: calories 345, fat 11.7, fiber 7.9, carbs 50.6, protein 11.1

Quinoa and Freekeh Mix

Prep time: 8 minutes | Cooking time: 8 minutes | Servings: 2

Ingredients:
- 1/3 cup freekeh
- ½ cup quinoa
- ½ cup of corn
- ¼ cup green peas
- 3 cups of water
- 1 teaspoon salt
- 1 teaspoon almond butter

Directions:
Place freekeh, water, and almond butter in the instant pot. Close and seal the lid. Set Manual mode (High pressure) and cook the mixture for 6 minutes. Then use quick pressure release. Open the lid and add quinoa, corn, green peas, and mix up the mixture gently. Close and seal the lid. Cook the meal for 2 minutes more on High pressure. Then use quick pressure release. Open the lid, mix up the meal and let it chill till the room temperature.

Nutrition value/serving: calories 275, fat 7.8, fiber 6.4, carbs 43, protein 11.3

Sorgotto

Prep time: 10 minutes | Cooking time: 30 minutes | Servings: 4

Ingredients:
- 1 cup sorghum grain, soaked
- 4 cups of water
- ¼ teaspoon rosemary
- 5 oz vegan Parmesan, grated
- 1 teaspoon coconut oil
- ½ white onion, diced
- ¼ cup white wine
- ½ teaspoon salt
- ½ teaspoon ground black pepper

Directions:
Toss coconut oil in the instant pot and preheat it on Saute mode. Add diced onion, salt, ground black pepper, and rosemary Saute onion until it is light brown. Then add water and wine. Saute the mixture for 5 minutes. Add sorghum grains and close the lid. Seal the lid and set Manual mode (High pressure) for 20 minutes. Use quick pressure release when the meal is cooked. Open the lid and mix up the meal with the grated cheese before serving. Wait till Parmesan starts to melt.

Nutrition value/serving: calories 317, fat 2.2, fiber 8.4, carbs 48.2, protein 19.7

Tuscan Sorghum

Prep time: 10 minutes | Cooking time: 35 minutes | Servings: 5

Ingredients:
- 1/3 cup sorghum
- 1 tomato, chopped
- ½ teaspoon salt
- 1/3 cup chard stems, chopped
- 1 onion, diced
- 4 oz celery stalk, chopped
- 1 tablespoon olive oil
- ½ zucchini, chopped
- 4 cups vegetable broth
- 1 teaspoon turmeric
- ½ teaspoon ground coriander
- 1 teaspoon dried cilantro
- 1/3 cup beans, canned

Directions:
Set Saute mode and pour olive oil inside instant pot. Add chopped chard stem, diced onion, celery stalk, and zucchini. Mix up the vegetables and saute them for 5 minutes. Stir from time to time. Then add chopped tomato, salt, vegetable broth, turmeric, ground coriander, cilantro, and beans. Add sorghum. Close and seal the lid. Set Pressure cooker mode and cook meal for 30 minutes. Use quick pressure release and open the lid. Transfer the meal into the bowls.

Nutrition value/serving: calories 141, fat 4.1, fiber 1.6, carbs 22, 4.8

Rye Berries

Prep time: 30 minutes | Cooking time: 29 minutes | Servings: 8

Ingredients:
- 2 cups rye berries
- 8 cups of water
- 1 teaspoon salt
- 1 tablespoon olive oil

Directions:
Pour olive oil in the instant pot and preheat it on Saute mode. Add rye berries and saute it for 4 minutes. Stir it from time to time. Then add water and salt. Mix it up and close the lid. Seal the lid and set Manual mode (High pressure). Cook the meal for 25 minutes. Allow natural pressure release for 20 minutes and then open the lid. Transfer the cooked meal in the serving bowls.

Nutrition value/serving: calories 165, fat 2.7, fiber 6, carbs 33, protein 6

Soba Noodles with Curry Tofu

Prep time: 15 minutes | Cooking time: 15 minutes | Servings: 2

Ingredients:
- 7 oz soba noodles
- 6 oz firm tofu, chopped
- 1 teaspoon curry paste
- 4 tablespoons soy sauce
- 1 teaspoon apple cider vinegar
- 1 teaspoon coconut oil
- 2 cups vegetable broth

Directions:
Mix up together curry paste, soy sauce, and apple cider vinegar. Whisk it. Then stir together curry paste mixture and chopped tofu. Leave it for 10 minutes to marinate. Meanwhile, preheat instant pot on Saute mode. Place tofu and all remaining sauce in the instant pot and saute for 2-3 minutes. Stir it from time to time. Transfer cooked tofu in the bowl. Clean the instant pot and put the soba noodles inside. Add coconut oil and vegetable broth. Close and seal the lid. Set Manual mode (High pressure) and cook a meal for 10 minutes. Use quick pressure release. Drain the liquid from noodles if desired. Mix up together soba noodles and tofu.

Nutrition value/serving: calories 485, fat 9.4, fiber 1, carbs 79.6, protein 28.2

Mac with Artichokes
Prep time: 10 minutes | Cooking time: 4 minutes | Servings: 4

Ingredients:
- 3 cups vegetable broth
- 1 ½ cup macaroni
- ½ cup artichoke hearts, canned, chopped
- 5 oz vegan Parmesan, grated
- ½ cup spinach, chopped
- ½ teaspoon ground black pepper
- ½ teaspoon chili flakes

Directions:
In the instant pot combine together vegetable broth, macaroni, and ground black pepper. Close and seal the lid. Set manual mode (High pressure) and cook macaroni for 4 minutes. Use quick pressure release and open the lid. Add grated cheese, chili flakes, artichokes, and spinach. Mix up the meal till the cheese is melted. The meal is cooked.

Nutrition value/serving: calories 263, fat 1.6, fiber 2, carbs 33.4, protein 22.9

Pesto Pasta
Prep time: 10 minutes | Cooking time: 4 minutes | Servings: 5

Ingredients:
- 2 cups fresh basil
- 1 teaspoon minced garlic
- 4 oz pine nuts
- 6 oz vegan Parmesan, grated
- 1/3 cup olive oil
- ½ teaspoon kosher salt
- 12 oz pasta
- 3 cups vegetable broth

Directions:
Pour vegetable broth in the instant pot bowl. Add pasta and close the lid. Seal it and cook on High pressure for 4 minutes. Use quick pressure release. Meanwhile, in the food processor blend together grated cheese, pine nuts, minced garlic, basil, kosher salt, and olive oil. When the mixture is smooth – pesto sauce is cooked. Transfer cooked pasta in the serving bowls, add pesto sauce and mix it up carefully before serving.

Nutrition value/serving: calories 594, fat 31.4, fiber 1, carbs 48.1, protein 27.9

Curry Rice

Prep time: 15 minutes | *Cooking time:* 4 minutes | *Servings:* 4

Ingredients:
- 1 ½ cup jasmine rice
- 1 tablespoon curry paste
- ½ cup fresh cilantro, chopped
- 1 tablespoon coconut oil
- ¼ cup almond milk
- 3 cups of water
- 1 teaspoon salt
- 1 tablespoon pine nuts

Directions:
Mix up together almond milk, salt, and curry paste. Place jasmine rice in the instant pot bowl. Add almond milk mixture. Then add coconut oil, water, and pine nuts. Mix the mixture up until homogenous. Close and seal the lid. Set High-pressure mode and cook rice for 4 minutes. Then allow natural pressure release for 10 minutes. Season cooked curry rice with cilantro.

Nutrition value/serving: calories 344, fat 10.7, fiber 3.5, carbs 56.2, protein 5.4

Taco Pasta

Prep time: 10 minutes | *Cooking time:* 5 minutes | *Servings:* 5

Ingredients:
- 15 oz pasta
- 4 cups of water
- 1 teaspoon salt
- 1 tablespoon almond butter
- 1 tablespoon Taco seasoning
- ¼ cup of coconut yogurt

Directions:
Pour water in the instant pot bowl. Add pasta and salt. Close and seal the lid. Set High-pressure mode and cook pasta for 3 minutes. Use quick pressure release. Then open the lid, add almond butter, Taco seasoning, yogurt, and mix up the pasta well. Close the lid and saute it for 1 minute more. Stir the cooked meal before serving.

Nutrition value/serving: calories 271, fat 3.8, fiber 0.3, carbs 48.5, protein 10.4

Caprese Pasta

Prep time: 10 minutes | Cooking time: 10 minutes | Servings: 4

Ingredients:
- 9 oz pasta
- 3 cups vegetable broth
- 1 cup fresh basil
- ½ cup tomatoes, chopped
- 1 teaspoon salt
- ½ teaspoon ground black pepper
- 1 onion, diced
- 1 tablespoon olive oil
- 4 oz firm tofu, chopped
- 4 oz vegan Parmesan, grated

Directions:
Set Saute mode and pour olive oil. Add ½ cup of fresh basil and onion. Saute the ingredients for 5 minutes. Stir from time to time. Then add salt, chopped tomatoes, ground black pepper, and pasta. Mix up the mixture carefully. Add remaining basil. Close the lid. Set Pressure mode and cook for 5 minutes. Then use quick pressure release. Open the lid and add tofu and cheese and Parmesan. Mix up the pasta well before serving.

Nutrition value/serving: calories 366, fat 7.3, fiber 1.3, carbs 45.6, protein 25.5

Pizza Pasta

Prep time: 10 minutes | Cooking time: 6 minutes | Servings: 4

Ingredients:
- 1 cup pizza sauce
- 1 cup macaroni
- 2 cups spaghetti sauce
- 1 teaspoon salt
- 6 oz vegan Cheddar cheese, grated
- 5 oz firm tofu, crumbled
- 1 teaspoon Italian seasoning
- 4 corn tortillas, chopped

Directions:
Pour pizza sauce in the instant pot. Add the layer of macaroni and sprinkle it with salt. After this, add Italian seasoning and spaghetti sauce. Close the lid and cook meal for 5 minutes on Manual mode (high pressure). Use quick pressure release and open the lid. Mix up the mixture, add grated Cheddar cheese and crumbled tofu. Mix up well. Then add chopped tortillas and close the lid. Cook it on High for 1 minute more. Use quick pressure release. Mix up the cooked meal gently.

Nutrition value/serving: calories 359, fat 15.7, fiber 6.5, carbs 50.1, protein 10

Pasta Alfredo

Prep time: 10 minutes | Cooking time: 10minutes | Servings: 4

Ingredients:
- 12 oz spaghetti
- 3 cups vegetable broth
- 1 teaspoon salt
- 1 teaspoon minced garlic
- 1 cup cauliflower, chopped
- 1 cup of water
- ½ cup cashew, chopped
- 1 teaspoon coconut oil

Directions:
Place coconut oil and minced garlic in the instant pot. Add salt, cashew, and cauliflower. Then add water and close the lid. Cook it on High pressure for 4 minutes. Use the quick pressure release, open the lid and transfer the mixture in the blender. Blend it until smooth. After this, add vegetable broth and spaghetti in the instant pot. Close and seal the lid. Cook it on High pressure for 5 minutes (quick pressure release). Drain the vegetable broth and transfer spaghetti in the bowls. Pour the cauliflower Alfredo sauce over the spaghetti and serve it warm.

Nutrition value/serving: calories 389, fat 12.1, fiber 1.2, carbs 54.4, protein 16.4

Penne Rigate

Prep time: 10 minutes | Cooking time: 20 minutes | Servings: 2

Ingredients:
- 8 oz penne pasta
- 1 teaspoon tomato paste
- 1 teaspoon salt
- 3 cups vegetable broth
- 1 onion, diced
- ½ zucchini, chopped
- 1 tablespoon olive oil
- ¼ cup mushrooms, chopped
- ¼ teaspoon minced garlic
- 1 teaspoon dried oregano

Directions:
Pour olive oil in the instant pot. Add salt, diced onion, zucchini, and mushrooms. Then add dried oregano and minced garlic. Stir it carefully and saute for 15 minutes. After this, add tomato paste, vegetable broth, and penne pasta. Mix it up and close the lid. Seal the lid and set Manual mode (high pressure). Cook pasta for 4 minutes. Use the quick pressure release. Open the lid and mix up the meal carefully before serving.

Nutrition value/serving: calories 481, fat 1.9, fiber 2.3, carbs 71.6, protein 21.8

Dill Orzo

Prep time: 10 minutes | Cooking time: 10minutes | Servings: 3

Ingredients:
- 1 cup orzo
- 1 ½ cup water
- 1 teaspoon salt
- 1 teaspoon dried dill
- 1 teaspoon coconut oil
- 1 tomato, chopped

Directions:
Toss coconut oil in the instant pot and melt it on Saute mode. Add orzo, salt, dried dill, and chopped tomato. Mix it up and saute for 5 minutes. After this, add water and close the lid. Seal it. Set Manual mode (High pressure) and cook orzo for 5 minutes. Use quick pressure release. Open the lid and mix up the cooked orzo carefully.

Nutrition value/serving: calories 230, fat 2.6, fiber 2.3, carbs 43.4, protein 7.3

Tomato Farfalle with Arugula

Prep time: 10 minutes | Cooking time: 4 minutes | Servings: 3

Ingredients:
- 1 cup farfalle
- ½ cup arugula
- ¼ teaspoon garlic, diced
- ½ cup cherry tomatoes, halved
- 4 oz vegan Parmesan, grated
- 1/3 cup walnuts, chopped
- 4 tablespoon olive oil
- 3 cups of water

Directions:
Pour water in the instant pot bowl and add farfalle. Close and seal the lid. Cook farfalle on Manual mode (High pressure) for 4 minutes. Then use quick pressure release. Drain water from the farfalle. After this, in the food processor blend together garlic, arugula, vegan cheese, walnuts, and olive oil. When the mixture is smooth, transfer it over the farfalle. Mix up well. Transfer the cooked meal on the plates and garnish with cherry tomato halves.

Nutrition value/serving: calories 636, fat 28.3, fiber 4, carbs 66.6, protein 28.5

Buckwheat Groats

Prep time: 10 minutes | Cooking time: 15 minutes | Servings: 2

Ingredients:
- 1 cup buckwheat groats
- 1 teaspoon dried dill
- 1 carrot, grated
- 1 tablespoon olive oil
- 1 teaspoon salt
- 2 cups of water

Directions:
Pour olive oil in the instant pot and add grated carrot. Saute it for 10 minutes. Stir it from time to time. Then add buckwheat groats, dried dill, and salt. Add water, close and seal the lid. Set Manual mode (High pressure) and cook buckwheat for 4 minutes. Use quick pressure release and open the lid. Mix up the buckwheat groats and transfer into the serving bowls.

Nutrition value/serving: calories 275, fat 8.9, fiber 6.8, carbs 45.6, protein 7.9

Creamy Spelt Berries

Prep time: 5 minutes | Cooking time: 25 minutes | Servings: 4

Ingredients:
- 1 cup spelt berries, unsoaked
- 1 teaspoon coconut oil
- 1 teaspoon salt
- 1 ½ cup vegetable broth

Directions:
Put spelt berries, coconut oil, salt, and vegetable broth in the instant pot bowl. Close the lid and set Manual mode (high pressure). Seal the lid and cook meal for 25 minutes. Then use quick pressure release. Open the lid and stir it gently before serving.

Nutrition value/serving: calories 182, fat 2.4, fiber 5.5, carbs 33.1, protein 5.2

Bulgur Salad

Prep time: 10 minutes | Cooking time: 10 minutes | Servings: 3

Ingredients:
- 1/3 cup bulgur
- 1 cup of water
- 1 teaspoon salt
- 1 teaspoon tomato paste
- 1 onion, diced
- 1 bell pepper, chopped
- ½ cup tomatoes
- ½ cup arugula, chopped
- 1 teaspoon olive oil

Directions:
Pour olive oil in the instant pot. Add bell pepper and diced onion. Mix up the vegetables and saute for 3-4 minutes. After this, add bulgur, tomato paste, salt, and water. Mix it up carefully. Close the lid and cook the meal on High for 4 minutes. Then use quick pressure release. Meanwhile, in the salad bowl, mix up together chopped tomatoes and arugula. When the bulgur is cooked, open the lid and chill it till the room temperature. Add chilled bulgur in the salad bowl and mix up well.

Nutrition value/serving: calories 102, fat 2, fiber 4.7, carbs 19.9, protein 3.1

Vegan Quinoa Pilaf

Prep time: 10 minutes | *Cooking time:* 1 minutes | *Servings:* 6

Ingredients:
- 3 cups quinoa
- 3 cups vegetable broth
- 1 teaspoon salt
- 1 teaspoon dried dill
- 1 teaspoon dried cilantro
- 1 garlic clove, peeled
- 1 teaspoon turmeric
- 1 teaspoon onion powder
- 1 tablespoon almond butter
- ¼ cup fresh parsley, chopped

Directions:
Mix up together salt, dried dill, cilantro, turmeric, and onion powder. In the instant pot combine together dill mixture with quinoa. Add garlic clove, almond butter, and vegetable broth. Close and seal the lid. Set Manual mode for 1 minute (High pressure) and cook quinoa. When the time is over, use quick pressure release. Open the lid, transfer the cooked quinoa in the bowls and sprinkle with fresh parsley.

Nutrition value/serving: calories 353, fat 7.4, fiber 6.4, carbs 56.5, protein 15.2

Rice Garden Salad

Prep time: 10 minutes | *Cooking time:* 6 minutes | *Servings:* 4

Ingredients:
- 1 cup of rice
- 2 cups of water
- 1 teaspoon salt
- ½ cup spinach, chopped
- 1 cucumber, chopped
- ½ cup tomatoes, chopped
- 1 tablespoon olive oil
- 1 teaspoon chili flakes
- ½ cup green peas, canned
- 1 tablespoon fresh dill, chopped

Directions:
Cook rice: place it in the instant pot, add salt and water. Close and seal the lid. Set manual mode (high pressure) for 6 minutes. When the time is over, use quick pressure release. Meanwhile, in the salad bowl mix up together chopped spinach, cucumber, tomatoes, chili flakes, olive oil, dill, and green peas. When the rice is cooked, chill it till room temperature and transfer in the salad bowl. Mix up the salad carefully and serve it warm.

Nutrition value/serving: calories 232, fat 4.1, fiber 2.4, carbs 43.8, protein 5.3

Lemon Pasta

*Prep time: 15 minutes | **Cooking time:** 15 minutes | **Servings:** 4*

Ingredients:
- 1 cup almond milk
- ½ lemon
- 12 oz spaghetti
- 3 cups of water
- 1 teaspoon wheat flour
- 1 teaspoon salt
- 1 teaspoon ground black pepper
- 1 teaspoon almond butter
- 1 tablespoon cashew, chopped
- 1 teaspoon fresh basil

Directions:
Cook spaghetti: place it in the instant pot bowl, add water and salt. Close and seal the lid and cook on Manual (high pressure) for 4 minutes. Then use quick pressure release Drain the water and transfer spaghetti in the big bowl. After this, pour almond milk in the instant pot bowl. Add wheat flour, ground black pepper, and juice from ½ lemon. Stir it gently and cook on Saute mode for 10 minutes. Stir it constantly. When the liquid starts to be thick, add cooked spaghetti and mix up well. Switch off the instant pot and close the lid. Let the pasta rest for 2-3 minutes or until it is serving time. Garnish spaghetti with chopped cashew.

Nutrition value/serving: calories 426, fat 19.6, fiber 2.1, carbs 52.9, protein 12.4

Beans and Lentils

Baked Beans
Prep time: 10 minutes | Cooking time: 55 minutes | Servings: 4

Ingredients:
- 1 cup white beans
- 5 cups of water
- 2 tablespoons tomato paste
- 1 teaspoon salt
- 1 teaspoon dried dill
- 1 teaspoon sugar
- ½ cup barbecue sauce
- ½ cup vegetable broth
- 1 carrot, chopped
- ½ teaspoon ground black pepper

Directions:
Place white bean and water in the instant pot. Close and seal the lid and cook on High for 30 minutes. Then use quick pressure release. Drain water from beans. In the instant pot, add tomato paste, salt, dried dill, barbecue sauce, vegetable broth, chopped carrot, and ground black pepper. Mix up the beans mixture until homogenous. Close the lid and set Saute mode. Cook beans for 25 minutes more.

Nutrition value/serving: calories 238, fat 0.8, fiber 8.7, carbs 46.2, protein 13

Mexican Pinto Beans
Prep time: 10 minutes | Cooking time: 50 minutes | Servings: 5

Ingredients:
- 2 cups pinto beans
- 6 cups of water
- 1 teaspoon salt
- 1 teaspoon ground black pepper
- ½ cup fresh cilantro, chopped
- 1 jalapeno pepper, chopped
- 1 teaspoon onion powder
- 1 teaspoon garlic powder
- 1 tablespoon almond butter
- 3 tablespoon coconut yogurt
- 1 tablespoon tomato paste

Directions:
Put all the ingredients in the instant pot bowl. Mix up the mixture well until it gets the red color. Then close and seal the lid. Set Manual mode (High pressure). Cook pinto beans for 50 minutes. After this, use quick pressure release. Mix up the cooked beans carefully before serving.

Nutrition value/serving: calories 300, fat 3, fiber 12.7, carbs 51.3, protein 17.8

Vegan Black Beans

Prep time: 10 minutes | Cooking time: 45 minutes | Servings: 4

Ingredients:
- 1 ½ cup black beans
- 3 cups of water
- 1 teaspoon salt
- ¼ teaspoon peppercorn
- 1 tablespoon chives, chopped
- 1 tablespoon coconut oil
- 1 teaspoon chili flakes

Directions:
Place black beans, salt, peppercorn, and water in the instant pot. Close and seal the lid. Set Manual mode and cook beans on High for 30 minutes. Then make quick pressure release and open the lid. Add chopped chives, chili flakes, coconut oil, and mix up well. Close the lid and saute black beans for 15 minutes more on Saute mode. The cooked beans should be served warm.

Nutrition value/serving: calories 278, fat 4.4, fiber 11.1, carbs 45.5, protein 15.8

Lentil Radish Salad

Prep time: 10 minutes | Cooking time: 10 minutes | Servings: 2

Ingredients:
- 1 cup radish
- 1 cup lettuce, chopped
- ½ cup lentils
- ½ cup vegetable broth
- 1 teaspoon garam masala
- 1 teaspoon coconut yogurt
- 1 teaspoon olive oil
- ½ teaspoon minced garlic

Directions:
Place lentils and vegetable broth in the instant pot. Add garam masala and close the lid. Set Manual mode and cook lentils for 10 minutes. Then make quick pressure release. Meanwhile, slice radish and place in the salad bowl. Add chopped lettuce. In the separated small bowl whisk together coconut yogurt, olive oil, and minced garlic. Add lentils in radish mixture and stir gently. Pour the salad with garlic mixture and stir only before serving.

Nutrition value/serving: calories 214, fat 3.3, fiber 15.8, carbs 32.2, protein 14.2

Lebanese Lemon and Beans Salad

Prep time: 5 *minutes* | *Cooking time:* 6 *minutes* | *Servings:* 4

Ingredients:
- 2 cups green beans
- 1 teaspoon chili pepper
- ½ lemon, sliced
- 1 cup tomatoes, chopped
- 1 white onion, chopped
- 2 tablespoons tomato sauce
- ½ teaspoon salt
- 1 teaspoon ground coriander
- ½ teaspoon cayenne pepper
- ½ cup of coconut milk

Directions:
Chop the green beans roughly and place them in the instant pot. Add chili pepper, chopped tomatoes, onion, tomato sauce, salt, ground coriander, cayenne pepper, and coconut milk. Mix up all the ingredients very carefully and top with the sliced lemon. Close the lid and set Manual mode (High pressure). Cook salad for 6 minutes. Then use quick pressure release. Open the lid and discard sliced lemon. Transfer the cooked salad into the serving bowls.

Nutrition value/serving: calories 110, fat 7.4, fiber 4.1, carbs 11.3, protein 2.6

Lentil Tacos

Prep time: 10 *minutes* | *Cooking time:* 10 *minutes* | *Servings:* 6

Ingredients:
- 1 cup lentils
- 1 teaspoon salt
- 1 cup vegetable broth
- 2 cups salsa
- 1 teaspoon garlic powder
- ½ teaspoon onion powder
- 6 tablespoons coconut yogurt
- 6 corn tortillas

Directions:
Place lentil, salt, salsa, and vegetable broth in the instant pot bowl. Add garlic powder and onion powder. Close the lid. Cook the lentils on Manual for 10 minutes. Then make quick pressure release. When the lentils are cooked, open the lid and chill them at least till the room temperature. Fill corn tortillas with the lentils mixture and sprinkle with coconut yogurt.

Nutrition value/serving: calories 200, fat 1.4, fiber 12.9, carbs 37.2, protein 11.3

Red Kidney Beans Burrito

Prep time: 10 minutes | *Cooking time:* 15 minutes | *Servings:* 2

Ingredients:
- ½ avocado, sliced
- 1 bell pepper, sliced
- ½ onion, peeled
- 1 tablespoon olive oil
- 1 teaspoon tomato paste
- ½ teaspoon chili flakes
- ½ cup red kidney beans, canned
- ½ teaspoon ground cumin
- ½ teaspoon ground coriander
- ½ cup fresh cilantro, chopped
- 2 burritos

Directions:

Preheat instant pot on Saute mode for 3 minutes. Pour olive oil and add sliced bell pepper. Start to saute vegetable, stir it from time to time. Meanwhile cut the onion into the petals and add in the instant pot too. Add chili flakes, ground cumin, coriander, and tomato paste. Stir it and add red kidney beans. Mix it up. Close the lid and saute the mixture for 10 minutes. Then switch off the instant pot and open the lid. Fill the burritos with the bean mixture, add cilantro, avocado, and roll.

Nutrition value/serving: calories 352, fat 17.6, fiber 11.9, carbs 40.3, protein 12.4

Lentil Meatballs

Prep time: 10 minutes | *Cooking time:* 20 minutes | *Servings:* 4

Ingredients:
- 1 ½ cup lentils
- 3 cups of water
- 1 teaspoon salt
- 1 tablespoon olive oil
- 1 teaspoon turmeric
- 1 teaspoon dried oregano
- 1 teaspoon dried dill
- 1 carrot, grated
- 2 tablespoons oatmeal flour
- 1 onion, diced

Directions:

Pour water in the instant pot. Add lentils and salt and close the lid. Cook it on Manual mode for 7 minutes. Then use quick pressure release. Meanwhile, mix up together grated carrot and diced onion. Transfer the cooked lentils in the mixing bowl. Pour olive oil in the instant pot and add carrot mixture. Close the lid and saute it for 10 minutes. Open the lid and stir it from time to time. When the carrot mixture is cooked, transfer it in the lentils. Add turmeric, dried oregano, and dill. Then add oatmeal flour and mix up until smooth and homogenous. Make the medium size meatballs from the lentil mixture and transfer in the instant pot. Set Saute mode, close the lid and cook the meal for 3 minutes.

Nutrition value/serving: calories 313, fat 4.5, fiber 23.5, carbs 49.4, protein 19.5

Black Beans Chili

***Prep time:** 10 minutes | **Cooking time:** 15 minutes | **Servings:** 4*

Ingredients:
- 1 cup black beans, canned
- 1 cup vegetable broth
- 1 cup tomato sauce
- 1 cup fresh cilantro, chopped
- 1 teaspoon chili flakes
- 1 teaspoon ground coriander
- 1 teaspoon dried rosemary
- 1 chipotle pepper, chopped
- 2 sweet green pepper, chopped
- 1 garlic clove, diced
- 3 tomatoes, chopped
- 1 red onion, roughly chopped
- 1 tablespoon almond butter
- 1 teaspoon garlic powder

Directions:

Melt the almond butter in the instant pot on Saute mode. Add diced garlic onion, garlic powder, green pepper, chipotle, rosemary, coriander, chili flakes, vegetable broth, and stir well. Saute the ingredients for 10 minutes. After this, add black beans and tomato sauce. Mix up the chili very carefully. Add tomatoes, close and seal the lid. Set Manual mode and cook chili for 3 minutes, use quick pressure release. Open the lid and mix up chili well. Transfer the cooked meal in the serving bowls and sprinkle with chopped cilantro.

Nutrition value/serving: calories 264, fat 3.8, fiber 11.9, carbs 45.6, protein 15.5

Burrito Bowl

***Prep time:** 10 minutes | **Cooking time:** 7 minutes | **Servings:** 2*

Ingredients:
- 1 cup of water
- 1 cup quinoa
- 1 teaspoon salt
- 1 teaspoon ground cumin
- ½ cup red beans, cooked
- 1 bell pepper, chopped
- ½ avocado, sliced
- ¼ cup of coconut milk

Directions:

Transfer quinoa and water in the instant pot. Add salt, bell pepper, and close the lid. Seal and set Manual mode. Cook the ingredients for 7 minutes. Then use quick pressure release. Transfer the cooked quinoa mixture in the bowl. Add red beans and ground cumin. Mix up well. Add avocado slices and sprinkle the meal with the coconut milk.

Nutrition value/serving: calories 662, fat 23, fiber 17.9, carbs 93.7, protein 24.8

Cowboy Caviar

Prep time: 10 minutes | Cooking time: 6 minutes | Servings: 4

Ingredients:
- ½ black-eyed peas
- 1 cup of water
- 4 tomatoes, chopped
- 1 tablespoon apple cider vinegar
- 1 tablespoon lemon juice
- 1 jalapeno pepper, chopped
- ½ cup fresh parsley, chopped
- 2 tablespoons olive oil
- ½ teaspoon salt

Directions:
In the instant pot combine together black-eyed peas and water. Close the lid. Set manual mode and cook on Pressure for 6 minutes. Then make quick pressure release. In the mixing bowl mix up together chopped tomatoes, jalapeno pepper, parsley, and apple cider vinegar. When the black-eyed peas are chilled, add them in the tomato mixture . Add olive oil, salt, and lemon juice. Mix up the caviar carefully before serving.

Nutrition value/serving: calories 99, fat 7.5, fiber 2.4, carbs 7.6, protein 2.1

Chipotle Chili with Hot Sauce

Prep time: 10 minutes | Cooking time: 15 minutes | Servings: 4

Ingredients:
- 1 tablespoon almond butter
- ½ cup mushrooms, chopped
- 1 teaspoon chipotle powder
- 1 cup black beans, canned
- ¼ cup hot sauce
- 1 cup tomato sauce
- ½ cup of water
- 2 garlic cloves, diced
- 1 tomato, chopped
- 1 red bell pepper, chopped

Directions:
Melt almond butter in the instant pot on Saute mode. Add mushrooms, diced garlic, tomato, and bell pepper. Saute the vegetables for 10 minutes. Then sprinkle the mixture with chipotle powder. Add hot sauce, tomato sauce, water, and black beans. Mix up carefully. Close the lid. Set Manual mode and cook chili for 5 minutes more. Then make quick pressure release. Chill the cooked chili for 5-10 minutes before serving.

Nutrition value/serving: calories 223, fat 3.3, fiber 9.4, carbs 38.2, protein 13

Vaquero Beans Chili with Tempeh

Prep time: 15 minutes | *Cooking time:* 35 minutes | *Servings:* 4

Ingredients:
- 7 oz tempeh, chopped
- 1 tablespoon olive oil
- 1 teaspoon salt
- ¼ cup onion, diced
- 2 cups vaquero beans, canned
- ½ cup of water
- ½ cup tomato juice
- 1 teaspoon paprika
- 1 teaspoon turmeric
- 1 teaspoon ground black pepper
- ½ cup tomatoes, canned

Directions:
Saute onion with olive oil in the instant pot for 5 minutes. Then add chopped tempeh, salt, vaquero beans, water, tomato juice, paprika, turmeric, and ground black pepper. Add canned tomatoes and mix up mixture gently. Close the lid. Cook chili on Saute mode for 30 minutes. When the time is over, open the lid and chill chili for 10 minutes.

Nutrition value/serving: calories 160, fat 9.2, fiber 2.9, carbs 12.4, protein 10.9

Creamy Kidney Beans

Prep time: 10 minutes | *Cooking time:* 25 minutes | *Servings:* 4

Ingredients:
- 2 cups kidney beans
- 2 cups of water
- 2 cups almond milk
- 1 tablespoon coconut oil
- 1 teaspoon salt
- 1 tablespoon tomato paste
- 1 garlic clove, peeled
- 1 tablespoon Taco seasoning

Directions:
Place kidney beans, water, almond milk, coconut oil, salt, tomato paste, garlic clove, and Taco seasoning in the instant pot. Mix up the ingredients until homogenous. Close and seal the lid. Set manual mode and cook meal for 25 minutes. Then use quick pressure release. Mix up the kidneys gently before serving.

Nutrition value/serving: calories 620, fat 33, fiber 16.8, carbs 64.1, protein 23.7

Spicy Tacos with Beans

Prep time: 10 minutes | Cooking time: 15minutes | Servings: 2

Ingredients:
- 4 oz red cabbage, shredded
- 1 tablespoon tomato paste
- ¼ onion, diced
- 1 teaspoon olive oil
- 1 jalapeno pepper, chopped
- 1/3 cup black beans, canned
- ½ cup of water
- ½ teaspoon salt
- 1 tablespoon vegan mayonnaise
- 2 taco shells

Directions:
Mix up together tomato paste, salt, water, black beans, jalapeno pepper, and diced onion in the instant pot. Add olive oil and close the lid. Saute the ingredients for 15 minutes on Saute mode. Then chill bean mixture till the room temperature. Fill the tacos shells with bean mixture and red cabbage. Sprinkle the tacos with mayonnaise before serving.

Nutrition value/serving: calories 276, fat 9.1, fiber 8.1, carbs 40.3, protein 9.8

Edamame Dip

Prep time: 10 minutes | Cooking time: 6 minutes | Servings: 4

Ingredients:
- 1 cup edamame beans
- 1 cup of water
- 1 tablespoon miso paste
- 4 tablespoons vegetable broth
- ½ teaspoon minced garlic
- ¼ teaspoon minced ginger
- 1 teaspoon onion powder
- 1/3 cup fresh dill, chopped
- ½ cup of coconut milk

Directions:
In the instant pot, combine together edamame beans and water. Close and seal the lid. Set manual mode and cook beans for 6 minutes. Then use quick pressure release. Transfer all the remaining ingredients in the food processor. Drain water from the cooked beans and chill them. Add edamame beans into the food processor too. Blend the mixture until smooth and soft. Transfer the cooked dip in the bowl.

Nutrition value/serving: calories 114, fat 8.4, fiber 2.3, carbs 7.5, protein 4.1

Zoodles with Lentils

Prep time: 10 minutes | Cooking time: 8 minutes | Servings: 4

Ingredients:
- 1 cup lentils
- 1 cup of water
- 1 zucchini
- 1 teaspoon chili flakes
- 1 tablespoon cashew milk

Directions:

Place lentils and water in the instant pot bowl. Close the lid and cook on Manual for 5 minutes. Then use quick pressure release. After this, spiralize the zucchini with the help of the spiralizer. Sprinkle zoodles with chili flakes and transfer in the lentils. Add cashew milk and mix up it well. Close the lid and saute the meal for 3 minutes on Saute mode.

Nutrition value/serving: calories 178, fat 0.6, fiber 15.2, carbs 30.5, protein 13

Buffalo Chickpea

Prep time: 5 minutes | Cooking time: 5 minutes | Servings: 4

Ingredients:
- 2 cups chickpea, cooked
- 3 tablespoons Buffalo hot sauce
- 1 tablespoon olive oil
- 1 teaspoon dried dill

Directions:

Place chickpeas and Buffalo hot sauce in the instant pot. Add olive oil and dried dill. Mix up the ingredients and close the lid. Set Saute mode and cook meal for 5 minutes. Stir it from time to time.

Nutrition value/serving: calories 417, fat 9.6, fiber 17.4, carbs 66, protein 19.4

Mung Beans Croquettes

Prep time: 10 minutes | Cooking time: 10 minutes | Servings: 6

Ingredients:
- 1 cup mung beans, soaked
- 1 green bell pepper, chopped
- ½ chipotle pepper, chopped
- ½ teaspoon minced garlic
- 1 tablespoon sesame oil

Directions:

Place mung beans in the food processor and blend well. Add bell pepper, chipotle, and minced garlic. Blend the mixture until smooth. Then transfer it in the mixing bowl. Wet your hands and make the small croquettes. Set saute mode and preheat instant pot. Add sesame oil and croquettes. Cook them for 2 minutes from each side or until light brown.

Nutrition value/serving: calories 148, fat 2.7, fiber 6, carbs 23.5, protein 8.5

Pinto Beans Quinoa Salad

Prep time: 10 minutes | Cooking time: 2 minutes | Servings: 2

Ingredients:
- ½ cup quinoa
- 1 cup of water
- ½ cup pinto beans, canned
- 1 cup fresh cilantro, chopped
- 1 sweet red pepper, chopped
- 1 tablespoon olive oil
- 1 teaspoon salt

Directions:
In the instant pot combine together quinoa and water. Close and seal the lid. Cook it on Manula mode for 2 minutes. Use quick pressure release. Then open the lid and chill quinoa till the room temperature. Transfer it in the salad bowl. Add fresh cilantro, pinto beans, salt, and olive oil. Mix up the salad carefully.

Nutrition value/serving: calories 405, fat 10.4, fiber 11.5, carbs 62.2, protein 17.1

Beanballs

Prep time: 20 minutes | Cooking time: 25 minutes | Servings: 2

Ingredients:
- 1 cup red kidney beans, soaked
- 4 cups of water
- 1 teaspoon salt
- 1 teaspoon onion powder
- 1 teaspoon garlic powder
- 1 teaspoon paprika
- ½ teaspoon chili flakes

Directions:
In the instant pot put red kidney beans and water. Close and seal the lid. Cook beans on Manual mode (high pressure) for 25 minutes. Then allow natural pressure release for 15 minutes. Drain water and transfer beans in the food processor. Add onion powder, garlic powder, paprika, chili flakes, and salt. Blend the mixture until it has puree texture. Then make the bean balls. Store them in the fridge before serving.

Nutrition value/serving: calories 322, fat 1.1, fiber 14.6, carbs 59, protein 21.3

Lentil Stew with Spinach
Prep time: 10 minutes | *Cooking time:* 10 minutes | *Servings:* 2

Ingredients:
- 1 cup green lentils
- 1 cup of water
- 1 cup tomatoes, canned
- 1 teaspoon ground black pepper
- 2 cups spinach, chopped
- 1 teaspoon paprika
- 1 teaspoon turmeric
- 1 teaspoon olive oil
- 1 carrot, chopped

Directions:
Place lentils, water, tomatoes, ground black pepper, paprika, turmeric, and carrot in the instant pot. Add olive oil and close the lid. Seal it and set High-pressure mode. Cook the ingredients for 6 minutes. After this, use quick pressure release. Then open the lid. Add chopped spinach and mix up it well. Close the lid and set Saute mode. Cook stew for 4 minutes more.

Nutrition value/serving: calories 404, fat 3.9, fiber 32.7, carbs 67.3, protein 27

Bean Loaf
Prep time: 10 minutes | *Cooking time:* 4 minutes | *Servings:* 4

Ingredients:
- 1 cup red beans, canned
- 1 tablespoon oatmeal
- 1 tablespoon wheat flour
- 1 teaspoon salt
- 1 teaspoon tahini paste
- 1 potato, peeled, boiled
- 1 tablespoon tomato sauce
- 1 teaspoon olive oil

Directions:
Mash red beans and potato until you get soft puree mixture. Add oatmeal, wheat flour, salt, tahini paste, and tomato sauce. Mix up the mixture until smooth. Then take instant pot loaf pan and line it with parchment. Place mixture into the loaf pan and make the shape of the loaf. Brush it with the olive oil. Pour water in the instant pot and insert rack. Place loaf pan on the rack and close the lid. Then seal it and set High-pressure mode. Cook the bean loaf for 4 minutes. Then use quick pressure release. Chill the bean loaf well and them a slice.

Nutrition value/serving: calories 218, fat 2.5, fiber 8.3, carbs 38.4, protein 11.9

Bean Enchiladas

Prep time: 15 minutes | *Cooking time:* 15 minutes | *Servings:* 6

Ingredients:
- 6 corn tortillas
- ½ cup corn kernels
- 3 tablespoon Enchilada sauce
- 2 sweet potatoes, chopped
- 1 yellow onion, chopped
- 1 cup kidney beans, cooked
- 2 red sweet peppers, chopped
- 1 teaspoon paprika
- 1 teaspoon ground cumin
- ½ teaspoon ground black pepper
- 1 teaspoon salt
- 7 oz vegan Parmesan, grated
- 1 tablespoon olive oil
- 1 jalapeno, sliced

Directions:

Preheat instant pot on Saute mode, when it shows "hot" add olive oil. Then add sweet peppers and yellow onion. Cook the vegetables for 5 minutes. After this, add corn sweet potato, Enchilada sauce, corn kernels, paprika, ground cumin, ground black pepper, salt, and sliced jalapeno. Mix the ingredients up. Close and seal the lid. Set Manual mode and cook the meal for 6 minutes. When the time is over, make quick pressure release. Chop the corn tortillas. Open the lid and place tortillas over the mixture. Then make the cheese layer. Close the lid and cook meal for 3 minutes more on Saute mode. Switch off the instant pot and let the cooked meal rest for 10 minutes before serving.

Nutrition value/serving: calories 319, fat 3.9, fiber 8.5, carbs 46, protein 23.3

Rice and Beans Bowl

Prep time: 10 minutes | *Cooking time:* 30 minutes | *Servings:* 4

Ingredients:
- 1 cup black beans, soaked
- 1 cup of rice
- 1 teaspoon salt
- 4 cups of water
- 1 cup of salsa
- 1cup fresh parsley, chopped
- 1 tablespoon almond butter

Directions:

Place black beans, rice, water, salsa, salt, and almond butter in the instant pot. Close and seal the lid. Set Manual mode (high pressure) and cook a meal for 30 minutes. Then use quick pressure release. After this, open the lid and mix up the meal well. Add parsley and mix it up one more time. Transfer the cooked meal into the serving bowls.

Nutrition value/serving: calories 382, fat 3.5, fiber 9.9, carbs 73, protein 16.1

Frijoles Negros

Prep time: 10minutes | Cooking time: 60minutes | Servings: 4

Ingredients:
- 1 cup black beans
- 1 tablespoon BBQ seasoning
- 1 teaspoon salt
- 1 teaspoon garlic powder
- 1 teaspoon onion powder
- 3 cups vegetable broth
- 1 teaspoon dried cilantro

Directions:
Place black beans in the instant pot. Sprinkle them with BBQ seasoning, salt, garlic powder, onion powder, and dried cilantro. Add vegetable broth and stir gently. Close and seal the lid. Set Manual mode and cook meal for 40 minutes. When the time is over, allow natural pressure release for 20 minutes more.

Nutrition value/serving: calories 201, fat 1.7, fiber 7.5, carbs 32.2, protein 14.3

Bean Casserole

Prep time: 10 minutes | Cooking time: 50 minutes | Servings: 6

Ingredients:
- 2 golden potatoes, peeled, sliced
- 6 oz vegan Parmesan, grated
- ½ cup mushrooms, sliced
- 1 cup green beans, roughly chopped
- 4 tablespoons bread crumbs
- 1 yellow onion, sliced
- 1 teaspoon coconut oil
- ½ cup of coconut yogurt
- 1 teaspoon salt
- 1 teaspoon ground black pepper
- 1 teaspoon paprika

Directions:
Mix up together paprika, ground black pepper, and salt. Then grease instant pot pan with coconut oil. Place the layer of sliced potato inside and sprinkle it with the small amount of paprika mixture. Then add a layer of mushrooms and sliced onion. Sprinkle the layers with the remaining paprika mixture and add green beans. Sprinkle the green beans with bread crumbs. Pour coconut yogurt over the mixture. Cover the casserole with the foil and secure the edges. Transfer it in the instant pot. Close the lid. Set Saute mode and cook meal for 50 minutes.

Nutrition value/serving: calories 179, fat 1.5, fiber 2.3, carbs 23.9, protein 14.5

Spaghetti Squash Bean Bowl

Prep time: 15 minutes | *Cooking time:* 8 minutes | *Servings:* 4

Ingredients:
- 1 cup red kidney beans, canned
- 1-pound spaghetti squash, seeded, cut into halves
- ¼ cup fresh parsley, chopped
- 1 teaspoon minced garlic
- 1 tablespoon tomato sauce
- ½ teaspoon white pepper
- 3 oz vegan Cheddar, grated
- 1 cup water, for cooking

Directions:
Pour water in the instant pot and insert steamer rack. Put spaghetti squash on the rack, close and seal the lid. Set Manual mode and cook it for 8 minutes. When the time is over, use quick pressure release. Remove the squash from the instant pot and shred spaghetti squash flesh. Do it carefully to get spaghetti squash cups from the squash skin. Mix up together shredded squash with kidney beans, fresh parsley, minced garlic, tomato sauce, white pepper, and fill the spaghetti squash bowls. Sprinkle the meal with grated Cheddar cheese.

Nutrition value/serving: calories 262, fat 7.2, fiber 8, carbs 42.1, protein 12.1

Red Beans Cauliflower Rice

Prep time: 15 minutes | *Cooking time:* 60minutes | *Servings:* 2

Ingredients:
- ½ cup cauliflower, shredded
- ½ teaspoon turmeric
- ½ teaspoon salt
- 1 cup black beans, soaked
- 3 cups of water
- 1 teaspoon ground black pepper
- ½ cup of coconut milk
- 1 teaspoon Italian seasoning
- ½ cup water, for cooking

Directions:
Place black beans and 3 cups of water in the instant pot. Close and seal the lid. Cook it for 40 minutes on Manual mode. Then allow natural pressure release for 20 minutes Transfer the beans in the bowl and clean the instant pot. After this, pour ½ cup of water in the instant pot and insert rack. Take a pan and place shredded cauliflower inside. Add salt, turmeric, ground black pepper, and mix it up. Insert the pan on the rack and close the lid. Set Manual mode or High pressure and cook cauliflower for 1 minute. Then use quick pressure release. Transfer the cauliflower over the beans and mix up. Whisk together Italian seasoning and coconut milk. Pour liquid over the cauliflower-beans mixture.

Nutrition value/serving: calories 487, fat 16.5, fiber 17.1, carbs 66.4, protein 23

Stuffed Sweet Potato with Beans

Prep time: 10 minutes | Cooking time: 10 minutes | Servings: 4

Ingredients:
- 2 sweet potatoes
- 1 tablespoon chives, chopped
- 1 cup red kidney beans, canned
- 1 tablespoon lemon juice
- 1 teaspoon salt
- 1 teaspoon cayenne pepper
- 1 tablespoon fresh parsley
- 1 cup water, for cooking

Directions:
Pour water in the instant pot and insert steamer rack. Cut sweet potatoes into halves and place on the steamer rack. Close the lid and cook on Manual for 7 minutes. Then allow natural pressure release for 3 minutes. Meanwhile, mix up together chives, red kidney beans, lemon juice, salt, cayenne pepper, and parsley. Shred the flesh of cooked sweet potatoes and mix it up with the beans mixture. Fill the sweet potato skins with this mixture and transfer on the serving plates.

Nutrition value/serving: calories 159, fat 0.6, fiber 7.2, carbs 28.8, protein 10.5

Curry White Beans

Prep time: 5 minutes | Cooking time: 2 hours | Servings: 6

Ingredients:
- 1 cup of brown rice
- 2 cups white beans
- 1 tablespoon curry paste
- 1 teaspoon ground cumin
- 1 teaspoon salt
- 7 cups of water
- 1 tablespoon dried dill
- 1 teaspoon tomato paste
- 1 garlic clove, peeled

Directions:
Place all the ingredients in the instant pot and mix them up until you get a homogenous liquid mixture. Then close the lid. Set Saute mode and cook the meal for 2 hours. When the time is over, open the instant pot lid and mix it up.

Nutrition value/serving: calories 360, fat 3, fiber 11.5, carbs 66.2, protein 18.5

Kidney Beans Koftas with Mushrooms

Prep time: 15 minutes | *Cooking time:* 10 minutes | *Servings:* 4

Ingredients:
- 1 cup red kidney beans, canned
- ½ cup mushrooms
- 1 tablespoon tomato paste
- ½ cup of water
- 1 teaspoon salt
- ½ onion, diced
- 1 teaspoon ground black pepper
- 1 teaspoon dried dill
- 1 tablespoon wheat flour
- 1 tablespoon bread crumbs
- 1 teaspoon chili flakes

Directions:
Put red kidney beans and mushrooms in the food processor. Blend the mixture until smooth and transfer in the mixing bowl. Add diced onion, dried dill, wheat flour, bread crumbs, and chili flakes. Mix it up until smooth. After this, pour water in the instant pot. Add tomato paste, salt, and ground black pepper. Stir it until homogenous. Start to preheat the liquid on Saute mode for 5 minutes. Meanwhile, make medium size bowls (koftas) from the bean mixture. Put them in the preheated tomato mixture and close instant pot lid. Set Manual mode and cook the meal for 4 minutes. Then allow quick pressure release. Chill the cooked koftas for 10 minutes before serving.

Nutrition value/serving: calories 182, fat 0.7, fiber 7.8, carbs 33.7, protein 11.5

Stuffed Peppers with Kidney Beans

Prep time: 15 minutes | *Cooking time:* 4 minutes | *Servings:* 2

Ingredients:
- 2 big sweet peppers
- 1 cup kale, chopped
- ¼ cup red kidney beans, canned
- 3 oz vegan Parmesan, grated
- 1 tablespoon coconut cream
- ½ teaspoon cayenne pepper

Directions:
Chop kale into the tiny pieces. Mash red kidney beans. In the mixing bowl mix up together kale, mashed beans, coconut cream, and cayenne pepper. Cut the sweet peppers into halves and remove seeds. Then fill peppers with beans mixture and sprinkle with grated cheese. Wrap the stuffed peppers in the foil and place in the instant pot. Close and seal the lid. Cook the meal on Manual for 4 minutes. Then use quick pressure release.

Nutrition value/serving: calories 281, fat 2.4, fiber 5.9, carbs 35.9, protein 25

Chickpea Shakshuka

Prep time: 10 minutes | *Cooking time:* 15 minutes | *Servings:* 2

Ingredients:
- ½ cup tomato puree
- 1 shallot, diced
- 1 bell pepper, chopped
- ½ cup chickpeas, cooked
- ¼ teaspoon ground cinnamon
- 1 tablespoon coconut oil
- 1 teaspoon tomato puree
- 1 tablespoon chives, chopped
- 1 tablespoon fresh dill, chopped
- 2 oz mushrooms, sliced
- ¼ cup of water

Directions:
Set instant pot on Saute mode. Add coconut oil and melt it. Then add diced shallot and mushrooms. Mix the ingredients up and saute for 5 minutes. Then add chopped pepper, tomato puree, and tomato paste. ix it up. Add chickpeas, water, dill, chives, and ground cinnamon. Mix the meal up and close the lid. Saute it for 10 minutes. When the time is over, mix up the cooked shakshuka one more time.

Nutrition value/serving: calories 296, fat 10.3, fiber 11.4, carbs 42.8, protein 12.6

Buddha Bowl

Prep time: 10 minutes | *Cooking time:* 10 minutes | *Servings:* 4

Ingredients:
- 2 yams, chopped
- 2 tablespoons almond butter
- 1 cup chickpeas, cooked
- 1 teaspoon harissa
- ½ cup of water
- 1 cup spinach, chopped
- 1 tablespoon lemon juice
- 1 teaspoon garlic powder

Directions:
Place almond butter in the instant pot and melt it on Saute mode. Then add chopped yams, sprinkle them with harissa and close the lid. Saute the vegetables for 7 minutes. After this, open the lid, stir the yams gently, add chickpeas, spinach, and water. Sprinkle the ingredients with harissa, lemon juice, and garlic powder. Mix it up. Close and seal the lid. Set Manual mode (high pressure) and cook a meal for 3 minutes. Then use quick pressure release. Open the lid and transfer the meal into the bowls.

Nutrition value/serving: calories 266, fat 7.9, fiber 10.7, carbs 39.1, protein 12.4

Chickpea Curry

Prep time: 10 minutes | *Cooking time:* 60 minutes | *Servings:* 4

Ingredients:
- 1 ½ cup chickpeas, soaked
- 1 cup tomatoes, chopped
- 1 tablespoon curry powder
- ½ cup fresh cilantro, chopped
- 5 cups of water
- 1 teaspoon salt
- 1 teaspoon ground coriander
- ½ teaspoon ground cumin
- ½ teaspoon ground nutmeg
- ½ teaspoon minced garlic
- 1 white onion, diced
- ½ cup of coconut milk

Directions:
Place all the ingredients in the instant pot and mix up carefully until homogenous and gets a light yellow color. Then close and seal the lid. Set Manual (pressure cook) mode and cook the meal for 40 minutes. When the time is over, allow natural pressure release for 20 minutes. Then open the lid and mix up cooked curry well. Transfer it into the serving bowls.

Nutrition value/serving: calories 370, fat 12.2, fiber 15.5, carbs 52.8, protein 16.2

Chickpea Salad

Prep time: 20 minutes | *Cooking time:* 25 minutes | *Servings:* 5

Ingredients:
- 1 cup chickpea
- 1 red onion, sliced
- ½ cup fresh parsley, chopped
- 1 tablespoon olive oil
- 1 teaspoon salt
- 3 cups vegetable broth
- 1 teaspoon garam masala

Directions:
Place chickpeas and vegetable broth in the instant pot. Add garam masala. Close and seal the lid. Set High-pressure mode and cook chickpeas for 25 minutes. After this, allow naturally pressure release for 10 minutes. In the salad bowl combine together cooked chickpeas, chopped parsley, sliced onion, salt, and olive oil. Mix up the salad carefully before serving.

Nutrition value/serving: calories 184, fat 5.3, fiber 7.8, carbs 27.3, protein 8.2

Buffalo Chickpea

Prep time: 20 minutes | Cooking time: 45 minutes | Servings: 4

Ingredients:
- ¼ cup Buffalo sauce
- ½ cup tomato puree
- 1 cup chickpeas, soaked
- 3 cups of water
- ½ teaspoon chili powder

Directions:
In the instant pot combine together Buffalo sauce, tomato puree, and water. Add chili powder and stir it carefully with the help of the spoon until you get homogenous liquid. Then add chickpeas and close the lid. Set High-pressure cook mode, close and seal the lid. Cook chickpeas for 45 minutes. Allow natural pressure release for 15 minutes. Open the lid and mix up the meal.

Nutrition value/serving: calories 196, fat 3.2, fiber 9.5, carbs 33.5, protein 10.2

Edamame Toast

Prep time: 15 minutes | Cooking time: 10 minutes | Servings: 4

Ingredients:
- 4 bread slices, toasted
- 1 avocado, peeled
- ½ cup edamame beans
- 2 cups of water
- 1 teaspoon salt
- 1 teaspoon chili flakes
- 1 teaspoon ground black pepper
- 1 tablespoon cashew milk

Directions:
Pour water in the instant pot. Add edamame beans and salt. Close the lid and set Manual mode. Cook the beans for 10 minutes. Then allow natural pressure release for 10 minutes more. Meanwhile, in the food processor blend together avocado, chili flakes, ground black pepper, and cashew milk. When the mixture is smooth, transfer it into the bowl. Chill the cooked edamame beans till the room temperature and blend in the food processor until smooth. Mix up together edamame beans and avocado mixture. You will get the paste. Spread the bread toasts with the paste.

Nutrition value/serving: calories 164, fat 12, fiber 5.1, carbs 10.2, protein 5.2

Lentils Shepherd's Pie

Prep time: 25 minutes | Cooking time: 10 minutes | Servings: 2

Ingredients:
- 1 cup lentils
- 2 cups of water
- 1 teaspoon salt
- 1 teaspoon chili flakes
- 1 teaspoon ground black pepper
- 1 teaspoon dried dill
- 1 teaspoon dried oregano
- 2 carrots, chopped
- 1 onion, diced
- ½ cup almond milk
- 1 teaspoon cayenne pepper
- 1-pound cauliflower

Directions:
Place lentils, carrots, and onion in the instant pot. Add water, almond milk, and stir the mixture. Insert steamer rack and put cauliflower on it. Close and seal the lid. Set Manual mode and cook ingredients for 7 minutes. Then allow natural pressure release for 10 minutes. Open the lid and transfer the cauliflower in the food processor. Add salt and blend it until smooth. Add chili flakes, ground black pepper, dried dill and oregano, cayenne pepper in the lentils mixture and mix it up. Transfer it in the serving bowls. Place smooth cauliflower puree over lentils.

Nutrition value/serving: calories 197, fat 5.3, fiber 13.3, carbs 28.7, protein 10.7

Lentil Bolognese

Prep time: 57 minutes | Cooking time: 7 minutes | Servings: 2

Ingredients:
- ½ cup green lentils
- 1 cup of water
- 1 oz celery stalk, chopped
- 1 tablespoon fresh parsley, chopped
- 1 tablespoon fresh dill, chopped
- 1 teaspoon salt
- ½ cup tomato puree
- 1 teaspoon paprika
- 1 tablespoon fresh basil, chopped
- 1 bell pepper, chopped

Directions:
Place all the ingredients in the instant pot and mix up gently. Close and seal the lid. Set Manual (High pressure) mode. Cook the meal for 7 minutes. Then make quick pressure release and open the lid. Mix up lentil bolognese carefully before serving.

Nutrition value/serving: calories 222, fat 1.1, fiber 17.5, carbs 41, protein 14.7

Lentil Loaf

Prep time: 10 minutes | Cooking time: 20 minutes | Servings: 6

Ingredients:
- 2 cups lentils
- 6 cups of water
- 1 teaspoon salt
- 1 teaspoon ground black pepper
- 1 onion, diced
- ½ cup mushrooms, chopped
- 1 tablespoon olive oil
- 2 tablespoons tomato paste
- 2 tablespoons wheat flour
- 1 tablespoon flax meal
- 1 tablespoon dried oregano
- 1 tablespoon dried cilantro
- 1 tablespoon coconut oil

Directions:

Cook lentils: Place lentils, water, and salt in the instant pot. Set manual mode and cook the mixture for 7 minutes. Then make quick pressure release. After this, open the lid and transfer lentils in the mixing bowl. Clean the instant pot and pour olive oil inside. Add diced onion and mushrooms. Cook the vegetables on Saute mode for 10 minutes or until tender. Stir them from time to time. Then transfer the cooked vegetables in the lentils. Add wheat flour, flax meal, dried oregano, cilantro, and mix it up until smooth. Grease the instant pot bowl with coconut oil and place lentil mixture inside. Flatten it well and spread with tomato paste. Close and seal the lid. Cook the lentil loaf on Manual mode for 3 minutes. Use quick pressure release. Chill the cooked meal for 1-2 hours before slicing.

Nutrition value/serving: calories 296, fat 5.9, fiber 21, carbs 44.4, protein 17.8

Lentil Chili

Prep time: 15 minutes | Cooking time: 6 minutes | Servings: 4

Ingredients:
- ½ cup tomatoes, canned
- 1 jalapeno pepper, chopped
- 1 onion, chopped
- 1 cup green lentils
- 2 cups of water
- 1 teaspoon chili flakes
- 1 teaspoon salt
- 1 teaspoon paprika
- 1 teaspoon oregano
- ½ teaspoon minced garlic
- 4 oz vegan Cheddar, grated

Directions:

Put the canned tomatoes, jalapeno pepper, onion, green lentils, and water in the instant pot. Add chili flakes, salt, paprika, oregano, and minced garlic. Close and seal the lid. Cook chili for 6 minutes on Manual mode (high pressure). Then allow natural pressure release for 5 minutes and open the lid. Stir the cooked lentil chili well and transfer in the serving bowls. Sprinkle the grated cheese over the chili before serving.

Nutrition value/serving: calories 279, fat 8.7, fiber 17, carbs 40.2, protein 14.1

Sloppy Lentils

Prep time: 10 minutes | Cooking time: 7 minutes | Servings: 4

Ingredients:
- 1 cup lentils
- 1 white onion, sliced
- 2 carrots, diced
- 2 cups of water
- 1 teaspoon salt
- 1 teaspoon paprika
- 1 teaspoon ground black pepper
- ¼ teaspoon ground nutmeg
- ½ teaspoon minced garlic
- 1 tablespoon mustard
- 1 tablespoon tomato sauce
- 3 tablespoons ketchup
- 4 burger buns

Directions:
Place lentils, water, carrot, salt, paprika, ground black pepper, ground nutmeg, minced garlic, mustard, tomato sauce, and ketchup in the instant pot. Stir it gently. Close the lid and cook on High-pressure mode for 7 minutes. Then make quick pressure release. Open the lid and stir the mixture well. Fill the burger buns with the lentils mixture and sliced onion and serve.

Nutrition value/serving: calories 222, fat 1.5, fiber 18.9, carbs 78.3, protein 21.2

Masala Lentils

Prep time: 15 minutes | Cooking time: 5 minutes | Servings: 2

Ingredients:
- 1 teaspoon ginger powder
- 1 teaspoon turmeric
- 1 tablespoon garam masala
- 1 cup almond milk
- ½ cup lentils
- 1 teaspoon minced garlic
- 1 tablespoon fresh parsley, chopped
- 1 teaspoon salt

Directions:
Put lentils and all spices in the instant pot. Add minced garlic and almond milk and close the lid. Set Manual mode and cook the meal for 5 minutes. Then allow natural pressure release for 10 minutes. Mix up the cooked lentils well and transfer into the bowls. Garnish the meal with fresh parsley.

Nutrition value/serving: calories 455, fat 29.3, fiber 17.7, carbs 37.4, protein 15.5

Lentil Ragout

Prep time: 15 minutes | Cooking time: 15 minutes | Servings: 4

Ingredients:
- 1 tomato, roughly chopped
- 2 oz celery, chopped
- 1 carrot, chopped
- 1 cup lentils
- 1 ½ cup vegetable broth
- 1 teaspoon salt
- 1 teaspoon oregano
- 1 teaspoon chili flakes
- 2 teaspoons olive oil
- 1 teaspoon tomato paste

Directions:
Pour olive oil in the instant pot and set Saute mode. Add chopped celery, carrot, and mix up the ingredients. Saute them for 5 minutes, Then add tomato and lentils. Stir and cook for 3 minutes more. After this, sprinkle the mixture with salt, oregano, and chili flakes Add tomato paste and vegetable broth. Stir it until homogenous. Close and seal the lid. Set Manual or High-pressure mode and cook ragout for 5 minutes. Then allow natural pressure release for 10 minutes. Open the lid and transfer cooked ragout into the bowls. Do not stir it anymore.

Nutrition value/serving: calories 209, fat 2.9, fiber 16, carbs 33, protein 12.9

Lentil Mash

Prep time: 10 minutes | Cooking time: 8 minutes | Servings: 4

Ingredients:
- 2 cup lentils
- 3 cups of water
- ½ cup tomato sauce
- ½ cup kale, chopped

Directions:
Place all the ingredients in the instant pot. Close and seal the lid. Set High-pressure mode and cook the mass for 8 minutes. After this, use quick pressure release and open the lid. Use the hand blender to blend the mixture until you get mash. Transfer the mash into the serving bowls. It is recommended to eat the meal until it is warm.

Nutrition value/serving: calories 350, fat 1.1, fiber 29.9, carbs 60.2, protein 25.4

Red Lentil Dal

Prep time: 15 minutes | Cooking time: 10 minutes | Servings: 3

Ingredients:
- 1 cup red lentils
- 2 cups of water
- 1 tablespoon coconut oil
- ½ teaspoon cumin
- 1 tablespoon garlic, diced
- ½ chipotle pepper, chopped
- 1 tomato, chopped
- 1 teaspoon ground coriander
- ¾ teaspoon ground nutmeg
- 1 teaspoon salt
- ½ teaspoon chili powder

Directions:
Preheat instant pot on Saute mode and add coconut oil. Melt it. Add tomato, chipotle pepper, and diced garlic. Stir it and saute for 3 minutes. After this, add cumin, ground coriander, nutmeg, salt, and chili powder. Mit it up and cook for 2 minutes more. Then add red lentils and water. Close and seal the lid. Cook lentil dal for 5 minutes on Manual mode. Then allow natural pressure release for 10 minutes. Open the lid and stir the meal. Season it with salt or any other spices if needed.

Nutrition value/serving: calories 281, fat 5.6, fiber 20.2, carbs 41.6, protein 17.2

Lentil Tomato Salad

Prep time: 10 minutes | Cooking time: 7 minutes | Servings: 5

Ingredients:
- 2 cups baby spinach
- 1 cup lentils
- 2 cups of water
- 1 teaspoon salt
- 1 teaspoon ground black pepper
- 3 tomatoes, chopped
- 1, sliced
- 2 tablespoons olive oil
- 1 tablespoon lemon juice

Directions:
Cook lentils: mix up lentils, water, and salt. Transfer the mixture in the instant pot. Close and seal the lid and cook on Manual for 7 minutes. Then use quick pressure release. Meanwhile, make all the remaining preparations: combine together baby spinach with tomatoes, and red onion in the salad bowl. Sprinkle with lemon juice, olive oil, and ground black pepper. Don't stir the salad. Chill the cooked lentils till the room temperature and add in the salad bowl. Mix up the cooked meal carefully and serve it warm.

Nutrition value/serving: calories 210, fat 6.3, fiber 13.5, carbs 28.8, protein 11.2

Cabbage Rolls with Lentils

Prep time: 15 minutes | *Cooking time:* 21 minutes | *Servings:* 4

Ingredients:
- 9 oz cabbage, petals
- ½ cup lentils
- 1 onion, diced
- 1 carrot, diced
- 1 cup of water
- 1 teaspoon salt
- 1 teaspoon ground black pepper
- ½ cup tomato juice
- ¼ cup almond milk
- ½ teaspoon cayenne pepper

Directions:

Put lentils and water in the instant pot. Add diced onion and carrot. Close and seal the lid. Cook the ingredients for 6 minutes on High-pressure mode. Then open the lid and transfer lentil mixture in the bowl. Add salt, ground black pepper, and mix it up. Fill the cabbage petals with the mixture and roll them. Place the cabbage rolls in the instant pot. Add tomato juice and almond milk. Sprinkle the meal with cayenne pepper and close the lid. Cook it on Saute mode for 15 minutes. Chill the meal for 10-15 minutes before serving.

Nutrition value/serving: calories 160, fat 4, fiber 10.5, carbs 24.8, protein 8.1

Soup and Stews

Wild Rice Soup
Prep time: 10 minutes | Cooking time: 45 minutes | Servings: 4

Ingredients:
- 2 cups vegetable stock
- 1 carrot, chopped
- 4 oz celery, chopped
- ½ onion, chopped
- ¼ cup coconut cream
- ½ cup wild rice
- 1 teaspoon salt
- ½ teaspoon chili flakes
- 1 teaspoon ground black pepper
- 1 tablespoon fresh parsley

Directions:
Place all the ingredients in the instant pot. Mix them up carefully and close the lid. Set Saute mode and cook soup for 45 minutes. When the time is over, open the instant pot lid and mix up soup well.

Nutrition value/serving: calories 129, fat 4.9, fiber 2.9, carbs 20.8, protein 3.9

Pumpkin Cream Soup
Prep time: 10 minutes | Cooking time: 20 minutes | Servings: 5

Ingredients:
- 2 cups coconut cream
- 2 cups of water
- 3 cups pumpkin, chopped
- 1 teaspoon salt
- 1 teaspoon paprika
- ¼ teaspoon ground cardamom
- ½ teaspoon turmeric
- 1 potato, peeled
- 1 tablespoon wheat flour

Directions:
Whisk together water with wheat flour until smooth and pour mixture in the instant pot. Add coconut cream, chopped pumpkin, salt, paprika, ground cardamom, and turmeric. Grate potato and add it in the instant pot too. Close and seal the instant pot lid. Set Manual mode (High pressure) and cook soup for 20 minutes. Then use quick pressure release. Open the lid and with the help of the hand mixer blend the soup until smooth. Ladle the cooked soup into the serving bowls.

Nutrition value/serving: calories 305, fat 23.4, fiber 7.4, carbs 24.8, protein 4.8

Classic Vegetable Soup

Prep time: 15 minutes | *Cooking time:* 17 minutes | *Servings:* 4

Ingredients:
- 2 cups of water
- 1 carrot, chopped
- 1 yellow onion, diced
- ½ teaspoon minced garlic
- 1 teaspoon ground black pepper
- 2 tablespoons avocado oil
- 1 teaspoon salt
- 2 potatoes, chopped
- 1 cup tomatoes, chopped
- ½ cup fresh dill, chopped

Directions:
Preheat instant pot on Saute mode and add avocado oil. Then add onion and carrot. Saute the vegetables for 5 minutes. Stir them from time to time. Then sprinkle the ingredients with minced garlic, ground black pepper, salt, and chopped tomatoes. Saute vegetables for 5 minutes more. Add dill, potato, and water, Mix it up. Close and seal the lid. Set Manual mode and cook soup for 7 minutes. Then allow natural pressure release for 8 minutes.

Nutrition value/serving: calories 125, fat 1.4, fiber 5.3, carbs 26.8, protein 4

Cauliflower Soup

Prep time: 10 minutes | *Cooking time:* 15 minutes | *Servings:* 4

Ingredients:
- 1-pound cauliflower head
- ¼ cup coconut cream
- 2 cups of water
- 2 tablespoon lemon juice
- 1 tablespoon olive oil
- 1 onion, diced
- 1 teaspoon salt
- ½ teaspoon ground black pepper
- ½ cup water, for cooking

Directions:
Pour ½ cup of water in the instant pot and insert steamer rack. Place cauliflower on the rack and close the lid. Cook it on Manual mode for 5 minutes. Then use quick pressure release. Remove the cauliflower head from the instant pot. Remove water. Pour olive oil into the instant pot. Add diced onion and saute it for 4 minutes. Sprinkle the onion with salt and ground black pepper. Chop cooked cauliflower and add into the instant pot. Then add water and coconut cream. Close and seal the lid. Set Manual mode and cook the meal for 4 minutes. Use quick pressure release. Open the lid and blend the mixture until smooth. Ladle the soup in the bowls and sprinkle with lemon juice.

Nutrition value/serving: calories 106, fat 7.3, fiber 3.9, carbs 9.7, protein 3

Noodle Soup
Prep time: 10 minutes | Cooking time: 7 minutes | Servings: 4

Ingredients:
- ¼ teaspoon fresh ginger, grated
- 1 teaspoon salt
- ½ teaspoon ground black pepper
- 4 cups of water
- 5 oz noodles, cooked
- 4 oz celery stalk, chopped
- 1 teaspoon garlic powder
- 1 cup baby carrots
- 1 teaspoon sesame oil

Directions:
Preheat instant pot on Saute mode and pour sesame oil. Add chopped celery stalk and saute it for 2-3 minutes. Meanwhile, cut baby carrots into the halves. Add them in the instant pot too Sprinkle the ingredients with salt, ground black pepper, and garlic powder. Then add water and grated ginger. Close and seal the lid. Set Manual mode (High pressure) and cook soup for 4 minutes. Then use quick pressure release. Add cooked noodles, mix up soup well and ladle into the bowls.

Nutrition value/serving: calories 82, fat 1.9, fiber 2, carbs 14, protein 2.5

Potato Chowder with Corn
Prep time: 10 minutes | Cooking time: 10 minutes | Servings: 2

Ingredients:
- ¼ cup mushrooms, chopped
- ½ onion, diced
- 1 cup coconut cream
- 1 cup of water
- ½ cup corn kernels
- 1 teaspoon salt
- 1 teaspoon paprika
- ½ teaspoon chili flakes
- 1 cup potato, chopped
- 1 teaspoon olive oil

Directions:
In the instant pot mix up together diced onion and mushrooms. Add olive oil and saute vegetables for 3-4 minutes or until golden brown. Then transfer vegetables in the bowl. Add water and coconut cream in the instant pot. Then add potato and corn kernels. Sprinkle the mixture with salt, paprika, and chili flakes. Set Manual mode (High pressure), close and seal the lid. Cook chowder for 5 minutes. Then allow natural pressure release for 5 minutes. Ladle the cooked chowder in the bowls and sprinkle with cooked onion and mushrooms.

Nutrition value/serving: calories 374, fat 31.6, fiber 5.6, carbs 23.9, protein 5.5

Leek Soup

Prep time: 10 minutes | Cooking time: 35 minutes | Servings: 4

Ingredients:
- 3 cups leek, chopped
- 2 tablespoons coconut oil
- 1 teaspoon minced garlic
- 1 cup potatoes, chopped
- 1 tablespoon corn flour
- ½ cup coconut cream
- 3 cups of water
- ½ cup celery root, chopped
- 1 teaspoon salt
- 1 teaspoon chili flakes
- ½ teaspoon ground ginger
- ½ teaspoon white pepper
- 4 teaspoons chives, chopped

Directions:

Place leek with coconut oil in the instant pot. Add minced garlic, and saute the mixture for 5 minutes. Stir it from time to time. When the vegetables are soft, sprinkle them with corn flour. Add chopped celery root, potatoes, coconut cream, water, chili flakes, ground ginger, and white pepper. Mix it up and close the lid. Set Saute mode and cook soup for 30 minutes. Then blend the soup until you get a creamy mixture. Garnish the cooked soup with chopped chives.

Nutrition value/serving: calories 212, fat 14.4, fiber 3.4, carbs 20.8, protein 2.9

French Onion Soup

Prep time: 10 minutes | Cooking time: 25 minutes | Servings: 2

Ingredients:
- 3 cups onion, diced
- 2 tablespoons coconut oil
- ¼ cup of water
- 2 cups vegetable broth
- 1 teaspoon salt
- 1 teaspoon ground black pepper
- 1 teaspoon minced garlic
- ½ teaspoon ground nutmeg
- 3 oz vegan Parmesan, grated

Directions:

Place diced onions and coconut oil in the instant pot. Set saute mode and start to cook them. Sprinkle the vegetables with salt, ground black pepper, minced garlic, and ground nutmeg. Stir well. When the onions start to become tender, add water and mix up the mixture well. Close and seal the lid. Set Manual mode (High pressure) and cook onions for 12 minutes. Then use quick pressure release. Add vegetable broth and stir the soup well. Close the lid and cook on Saute mode for 10 minutes more. Mix up the soup carefully and ladle into the serving bowls. Top the cooked onion soup with vegan Parmesan.

Nutrition value/serving: calories 332, fat 14, fiber 4.6, carbs 27.7, protein 19.5

Potato Cream Soup

Prep time: 5 minutes | *Cooking time:* 15 minutes | *Servings:* 4

Ingredients:
- 1 cup of coconut milk
- 2 cups of water
- 2 cups potatoes, chopped
- 1 onion, sliced
- 1 teaspoon turmeric
- 1 teaspoon salt
- 1 tablespoon avocado oil
- 1 teaspoon chili flakes
- ½ cup fresh cilantro, chopped

Directions:
Pour avocado oil in the instant pot and preheat it on Saute mode. When the oil is hot, add sliced onion and chopped potatoes. Sprinkle the vegetables with turmeric, salt, and chili flakes. Mix up the ingredients and saute for 5 minutes. Then add coconut milk and water. Close and seal the lid. Cook soup on Manual mode for 10 minutes. Then use quick pressure release. Open the lid and blend soup with the help of the hand blender. When the liquid is smooth, transfer it into the serving bowls. Sprinkle the soup with cilantro before serving.

Nutrition value/serving: calories 208, fat 14.9, fiber 4.1, carbs 18.3, protein 3.1

Quinoa Tomato Soup

Prep time: 5 minutes | *Cooking time:* 15minutes | *Servings:* 3

Ingredients:
- 1 carrot, diced
- ½ onion, diced
- 1 cup quinoa
- 1 cup tomato puree
- 1 tablespoon fresh dill
- ½ bell pepper, chopped
- 1 cup of water
- 1 teaspoon salt
- 1 teaspoon cayenne pepper
- 1/3 cup green peas
- 1 teaspoon almond butter

Directions:
Toss butter in the instant pot and melt it on Saute mode. Add carrot, onion, and bell pepper. Saute the ingredients for 10 minutes. Mix p them from time to time. After this, add quinoa, green peas, cayenne pepper, salt, fresh dill, and water. Add tomato puree, mix up the soup and close the lid. Set Manual (high pressure) mode and cook soup for 3 minutes. Then use quick pressure release. Mix up the cooked soup well before serving.

Nutrition value/serving: calories 313, fat 6.9, fiber 8.4, carbs 53.3, protein 12.2

Lentil Soup

Prep time: 15 minutes | Cooking time: 15 minutes | Servings: 2

Ingredients:
- 1 cup red lentils
- 1 potato, chopped into tiny pieces
- ½ onion, diced
- 5 cups of water
- 1 teaspoon salt
- 1 teaspoon ground black pepper
- 1 tablespoon coconut oil
- 1 teaspoon chili flakes
- 1 tablespoon tomato paste

Directions:
Melt coconut oil on Saute mode. Then add onion and chopped potato. Saute the vegetables for 7 minutes. After this, sprinkle vegetables with salt, ground black pepper, chili flakes, and tomato paste. Mix the mixture up until it gets the red color. Add lentils. Add water and mix up again. Close and seal the lid. Set Manual mode and cook soup for 8 minutes. Then allow natural pressure release for 10 minutes.

Nutrition value/serving: calories 483, fat 8, fiber 32.4, carbs 77.3, protein 27.3

Butternut Squash Ginger Soup

Prep time: 10 minutes | Cooking time: 10 minutes | Servings: 5

Ingredients:
- 3 cups of coconut milk
- 2 cups butternut squash, chopped
- 1 tablespoon fresh ginger, peeled, chopped
- 1 teaspoon turmeric
- 1 teaspoon salt
- 1 teaspoon paprika
- 1 garlic clove, diced
- 1 tablespoon olive oil
- ½ teaspoon ground nutmeg
- 1 cup of water
- 1 teaspoon ground ginger

Directions:
In the instant pot place together coconut milk. Butternut squash, fresh ginger, turmeric, salt, paprika, diced garlic, olive oil, ground nutmeg, water, and ground ginger. Close and seal the lid and set Manual mode for 10 minutes. Cook the soup. When the time is over, use quick pressure release. Open the lid and blend the soup with the help of the immersion blender. When the mixture is smooth, the soup is cooked.

Nutrition value/serving: calories 388, fat 37.4, fiber 4.7, carbs 15.8, protein 4.1

Minestrone

Prep time: 15 minutes | Cooking time: 15minutes | Servings: 4

Ingredients:
- 2 tablespoons almond butter
- 1 red onion, diced
- 1 tablespoon minced garlic
- 1 teaspoon tomato paste
- 5 oz carrot, chopped
- 4 oz celery, chopped
- 1 zucchini, chopped
- 1 cup tomatoes, chopped
- 1 teaspoon salt
- 1 teaspoon thyme
- 1 teaspoon ground black pepper
- ½ teaspoon ground nutmeg
- 1 cup red kidney beans, canned, drained
- 1 bay leaf
- ½ cup spinach
- ¼ cup elbow pasta
- 4 cups of water

Directions:
Melt almond butter in the instant pot on Saute mode. Add diced onion, minced garlic, tomato paste, chopped carrot, and celery. Then add zucchini and tomatoes. Sprinkle the mixture with salt, thyme, ground black pepper, and nutmeg. Mix up the mixture well. Add water, elbow pasta, and bay leaf. Close and seal the lid. Set High-pressure mode and cook soup for 5 minutes. Then allow natural pressure release for 10 minutes. Meanwhile, chop the spinach. Open the instant pot lid and add chopped spinach. Cook minestrone on Saute mode for 10 minutes more.

Nutrition value/serving: calories 273, fat 5.5, fiber 11.4, carbs 44.5, protein 14.7

Carrot Soup

Prep time: 10 minutes | Cooking time: 10 minutes | Servings: 4

Ingredients:
- ½ lemon
- 3 cups vegetable broth
- 2 cups carrot, chopped
- 1 oz ginger, peeled, chopped
- ½ onion, chopped
- 1 teaspoon thyme
- 1 teaspoon salt
- ¼ cup coconut cream
- 1 tablespoon coconut oil

Directions:
Place coconut oil, chopped ginger, and onion in the instant pot. Set saute mode and cook ingredients for 3-5 minutes. Stir them from time to time. After this, add carrot. Sprinkle the vegetables with thyme and salt, mix them up. Add vegetable broth and close the lid. Set High-pressure mode (manual mode) and cook soup for 6 minutes. Then use quick pressure release. Open the lid and smooth the mixture with the help of the immersion blender. Add coconut cream and mix the soup up.

Nutrition value/serving: calories 148, fat 8.5, fiber 3.2, carbs 14.1, protein 5.3

Kale and Sweet Potato Soup

Prep time: 10 minutes | *Cooking time:* 15 minutes | *Servings:* 2

Ingredients:
- 1 sweet potato, chopped
- 2 cups kale
- ½ cup almond milk
- 2 cups vegetable broth
- 1 teaspoon ground coriander
- 1 teaspoon olive oil
- ¼ teaspoon minced garlic
- ½ teaspoon Italian seasoning

Directions:
Chop the kale. Then pour olive oil in the instant pot. Add chopped sweet potato and saute it on Saute mode for 10 minutes. Mix it up every 2 minutes. Then sprinkle sweet potatoes with ground coriander, minced garlic, and Italian seasoning. Add chopped kale, almond milk, and vegetable broth. Close and seal the lid. Set Manual mode (high pressure) and cook soup for 4 minutes. When the time is over, allow the natural pressure release. Chill the soup till the room temperature before serving.

Nutrition value/serving: calories 254, fat 17.1, fiber 4.7, carbs 23.9, protein 4.5

Beta Carotene Booster Soup

Prep time: 10 minutes | *Cooking time:* 20 minutes | *Servings:* 4

Ingredients:
- 1 teaspoon sesame seeds
- 2 tablespoons lime juice
- 1 teaspoon turmeric
- 2 carrots, chopped
- ½ cup red lentils
- 2 tomatoes, chopped
- 1 teaspoon salt
- 1 teaspoon ground coriander
- ½ teaspoon chili powder
- 1 red bell pepper, chopped
- 2 cups of water
- 1 garlic clove, diced
- 2 tablespoons coconut cream

Directions:
In the instant pot combine together turmeric, chopped carrot, red lentils, chopped tomatoes, salt, ground coriander, chili powder, bell pepper, diced garlic clove, and water. Close and seal the lid. Set manual mode (high pressure) for 5 minutes. Then allow natural pressure release for 15 minutes more. Blend the cooked mixture until you get smooth liquid mass. Ladle the soup in the serving bowls and top it with sesame seeds.

Nutrition value/serving: calories 144, fat 2.7, fiber 9.7, carbs 23.5, protein 7.7

Beet Soup

Prep time: 15 minutes | Cooking time: 15 minutes | Servings: 8

Ingredients:
- 1 carrot, grated
- 1 bell pepper, chopped
- ½ cup beet, chopped
- 1 tablespoon tomato paste
- 4 potatoes, chopped
- 1 cup white cabbage, shredded
- 1 teaspoon salt
- ¼ cup coconut cream
- 1 onion, diced
- 1 tablespoon coconut oil
- 1/3 cup fresh parsley, chopped
- ¼ chili pepper, chopped
- 7 cups of water

Directions:

Toss coconut oil in the instant pot. Set Saute mode and preheat it for 3 minutes. Then add grated carrot and onion. Cook the ingredients for 3-4 minutes. Stir them from time to time. After this, add beet and cook the vegetables for 5 minutes more. Then add tomato paste, bell pepper, potato, shredded cabbage, salt, coconut cream, parsley, and chili pepper. Add water, close and seal the lid. Set manual mode (High pressure) and cook soup for 7 minutes. Then allow natural pressure release for 10 minutes.

Nutrition value/serving: calories 128, fat 3.7, fiber 4, carbs 22.4, protein 2.8

Anti-Inflammatory Soup

Prep time: 10 minutes | Cooking time: 10 minutes | Servings: 2

Ingredients:
- 1 teaspoon grated ginger
- 1 teaspoon turmeric
- 1 teaspoon minced garlic
- 2 potatoes, chopped
- ½ carrot, grated
- 1 onion, grated
- 1 teaspoon salt
- 1 teaspoon chili flakes
- ½ teaspoon ground black pepper
- 1 oz celery stalk, chopped
- 1 cup of water
- ½ cup of coconut milk

Directions:

Place coconut milk in the instant pot and preheat it on Saute mode for 3 minutes. Add grated ginger, turmeric, minced garlic, salt, chili flakes, and ground black pepper. Saute the liquid until you get light spice smell. Then add chopped potato, grated carrot, onion, and celery stalk. Add water, close and seal the lid. Set manual mode (high pressure) and cook soup for 5 minutes. Allow natural pressure release for 5 minutes. Open the lid and blend the mixture with the help of the hand blender. Ladle the smooth soup into the serving bowls.

Nutrition value/serving: calories 326, fat 14.8, fiber 8.7, carbs 46, protein 6.1

Creamy Tomato Soup
Prep time: 15 minutes | Cooking time: 7 minutes | Servings: 4

Ingredients:
- 1 cup tomato juice
- ½ cup tomato puree
- ½ cup fresh cilantro, chopped
- 1 green bell pepper, chopped
- 1 garlic clove, diced
- 1 tablespoon olive oil
- ½ cup lentils
- 1 cup of water
- 1 teaspoon salt
- 1 teaspoon white pepper
- 1 teaspoon ground coriander

Directions:
Pour olive oil in the instant pot. Add garlic clove, salt, white pepper, and ground coriander. Saute the garlic for 2 minutes. Stir it from time to time. Then add lentils, tomato puree, bell pepper, and fresh cilantro. Mix up well and saute for 1 minute. Add water, tomato juice, and close the lid. Cook tomato soup on Manual mode (high pressure) for 4 minutes. Then allow natural pressure release for 5 minutes more. Open the lid and using immersion blender blend the soup well. Add salt and pepper if needed.

Nutrition value/serving: calories 149, fat 4, fiber 8.8, carbs 22.7, protein 7.6

Taco Soup
Prep time: 10minutes | Cooking time: 10minutes | Servings: 6

Ingredients:
- 1 cup corn kernels
- 1 cup red kidney beans, canned
- ¼ cup onion, chopped
- 1 teaspoon garlic, diced
- 1 oz fresh cilantro, chopped
- 1 jalapeno, chopped
- 1 teaspoon oregano
- 1 tablespoon Taco seasoning
- 5 cups of water
- 1 teaspoon sesame oil

Directions:
Saute chopped onion, diced garlic, and jalapeno pepper with sesame oil in the instant pot on Saute mode. When the onion is light brown, add red kidney beans, oregano, taco seasoning, water, cilantro, and corn kernels. Close and seal the lid. Cook soup on Manual mode (high pressure) for 5 minutes. Then allow natural pressure release for 5 minutes more. Open the lid and mix up the soup carefully before serving.

Nutrition value/serving: calories 142, fat 1.5, fiber 5.8, carbs 25.7, protein 8

Chickpea Soup

Prep time: 5 minutes | *Cooking time:* 25 minutes | *Servings:* 3

Ingredients:
- 1 cup chickpeas, canned
- 1 teaspoon garam masala
- ½ cup coconut cream
- 2 cups of water
- 1 teaspoon onion powder
- 1 teaspoon garlic powder
- 1 tomato, diced
- 1 carrot, chopped
- ¼ cup green beans, chopped

Directions:
Place all the ingredients in the instant pot and mix them up. Close the lid and set Saute mode. Cook soup for 25 minutes. When the soup is cooked, all the ingredients should be tender. Add salt and pepper if needed and transfer soup into the serving bowls.

Nutrition value/serving: calories 355, fat 13.6, fiber 13.7, carbs 47.4, protein 14.6

Cabbage Detox Soup

Prep time: 25 minutes | *Cooking time:* 10 minutes | *Servings:* 2

Ingredients:
- ½ cup white cabbage, shredded
- ¼ cup cherry tomatoes
- ½ red onion, diced
- ½ carrot, diced
- 1 tablespoon apple cider vinegar
- 2 cups of water
- 1 teaspoon salt
- 1/3 teaspoon sage
- 1 tablespoon fresh parsley, chopped

Directions:
Place the cabbage in the big bowl and sprinkle with salt. Mix it up and let cabbage rest for 5-10 minutes or until it starts to give juice. Then place cabbage in the instant pot. Add red onion, carrot, apple cider vinegar, water, sage, and cherry tomatoes. Mix up the soup mixture with the help of the spoon. Close and seal the lid. Set High-pressure mode and cook soup for 10 minutes. After this, allow natural pressure release for 10 minutes more. Sprinkle the cooked soup with fresh chopped parsley.

Nutrition value/serving: calories 28, fat 0.1, fiber 1.8, carbs 6.2, protein 0.9

Spinach and Lentils Soup

Prep time: 5 *minutes* | *Cooking time:* 11 *minutes* | *Servings:* 4

Ingredients:
- 1 cup green lentils
- 2 cups spinach, chopped
- 6 cups of water
- 1 teaspoon salt
- 1 teaspoon red pepper
- 1 bell pepper, chopped
- ¼ teaspoon cayenne pepper
- 1 tablespoon coconut oil

Directions:
Place coconut oil and green lentils in the instant pot. Cook the ingredients on Saute mode for 4 minutes. Stir the lentils constantly. After this, add water, red pepper, chopped bell pepper, cayenne pepper, and spinach. Close and seal the lid. Cook soup on Manual mode (high pressure) for 7 minutes. Then use quick pressure release and open the lid. Mix up the soup carefully before serving.

Nutrition value/serving: calories 222, fat 4.2, fiber 15.8, carbs 33.9, protein 13.4

Tuscan Soup

Prep time: 10 *minutes* | *Cooking time:* 10 *minutes* | *Servings:* 4

Ingredients:
- 1 cup curly kale
- 1 cup cannellini beans, canned
- 1 carrot, chopped
- 1 cup tomatoes, canned
- 3 cups vegetable stock
- 1 teaspoon salt
- ½ teaspoon dried rosemary
- ½ teaspoon dried coriander
- 1 teaspoon garlic powder
- 1 teaspoon ground black pepper
- 1 tablespoon avocado oil

Directions:
In the instant pot combine together avocado oil and chopped carrot. Cook the carrot for 6 minutes on Saute mode. After this, add canned tomatoes, salt, dried rosemary, coriander, garlic powder, and ground black pepper. Mix up the mixture. Chop the curly kale roughly. Add cannellini beans, kale, and vegetable stock in the instant pot. Mix the soup up and close the lid. Cook the meal on High-pressure mode for 4 minutes. Then allow natural pressure release for 5 minutes.

Nutrition value/serving: calories 208, fat 2.9, fiber 14.6, carbs 37.9, protein 13.8

Broccoli Soup

Prep time: 10 minutes | Cooking time: 8 minutes | Servings: 4

Ingredients:
- ¼ cup almond flakes
- 1 cup broccoli, chopped
- 1 cup spinach, chopped
- 1 oz celery stalk, chopped
- 2 tablespoons coconut oil
- 1 teaspoon cilantro
- 1 teaspoon ground ginger
- 3 cups of water
- 1 teaspoon salt
- 1 avocado, peeled
- 1 potato, chopped

Directions:

Place potato, salt, water, ground ginger, cilantro, coconut oil, celery stalk, spinach, and broccoli in the instant pot. Close and seal the lid. Cook the mixture on Manual mode (high pressure) for 8 minutes. Then allow natural pressure release. Chop the avocado. Add it in the cooked broccoli mixture. Use the immersion blender to blend the soup well. Ladle the cooked soup into the serving bowls and sprinkle with almond flakes.

Nutrition value/serving: calories 245, fat 20.1, fiber 5.9, carbs 14.7, protein 4.1

Tortilla Soup

Prep time: 10 minutes | Cooking time: 20 minutes | Servings: 4

Ingredients:
- ½ cup tomatoes, chopped
- ½ cup corn kernels
- ½ cup red kidney beans, canned
- 1 teaspoon ground black pepper
- 1 teaspoon chili flakes
- 1 teaspoon salt
- 1 teaspoon dried cilantro
- 1 teaspoon dried oregano
- 2 cups of water
- ½ cup of coconut milk
- ½ jalapeno pepper, chopped
- 1 tablespoon tomato paste
- ½ teaspoon dried thyme
- ½ teaspoon dried cumin
- 4 corn tortillas
- ½ cup fresh cilantro, chopped

Directions:

In the instant pot combine together chopped tomatoes, corn kernels, red kidney beans, ground black pepper, chili flakes, salt, dried cilantro, oregano, water, coconut milk, jalapeno pepper, tomato paste, thyme, and cumin. Close and seal the lid. Set Manual mode (high pressure) and cook soup for 11 minutes; allow natural pressure release for 9 minutes. Meanwhile, cut corn tortillas into the strips. Ladle the cooked soup into the bowls. Top the soup with corn tortillas and chopped cilantro.

Nutrition value/serving: calories 228, fat 8.5, fiber 7.1, carbs 32.7, protein 8.5

Mushroom Cream Soup
Prep time: 15 minutes | Cooking time: 60 minutes | Servings: 6

Ingredients:
- 2 cups mushrooms, chopped
- 1 onion, peeled, diced
- ½ cup coconut cream
- 1 teaspoon salt
- 1 teaspoon ground black pepper
- 1 tablespoon olive oil
- 2 potatoes, chopped
- 4 cups of water

Directions:
Place mushrooms, onion, and olive oil in the instant pot. Saute the vegetables for 10 minutes or until they are half cooked. Then add coconut cream, salt, ground black pepper, and potatoes. Add water and close the lid. Set Saute mode and cook soup for 50 minutes. When the time is over and all the ingredients are tender, blend the soup with the help of the hand blender until it is smooth. Let the cooked soup rest for 10 minutes before serving.

Nutrition value/serving: calories 128, fat 7.3, fiber 2.9, carbs 15, protein 2.6

Penne Pasta Soup
Prep time: 15 minutes | Cooking time: 7 minutes | Servings: 2

Ingredients:
- 1 red bell pepper, chopped
- 2 cups of water
- 5 oz penne pasta
- 1 teaspoon salt
- ¼ cup fresh dill
- 1 potato, chopped
- 1 teaspoon olive oil
- ½ teaspoon paprika

Directions:
Cook bell pepper with olive for 3 minutes on Saute mode. Add penne pasta, potato, paprika, and salt. Then add water, close and seal the lid. Cook soup on Manual mode (high pressure) for 7 minutes. When the time is over, use the quick pressure release. Chop the dill and add it in the soup. Mix it up and let it rest for 10-15 minutes.

Nutrition value/serving: calories 325, fat 4.5, fiber 3.7, carbs 61.8, protein 11.6

Winter Stew
Prep time: 10 minutes | Cooking time: 20 minutes | Servings: 6

Ingredients:
- ½ cup red lentils
- 1 cup mushrooms, chopped
- 1 yellow onion, chopped
- 2 sweet potatoes, chopped
- 1 carrot, chopped
- ½ cup red kidney beans, canned
- 1 tablespoon tomato paste
- 2 cups of water
- ½ cup almond milk
- 1 teaspoon salt
- ½ teaspoon peppercorns
- 1 teaspoon olive oil

Directions:
Cook mushrooms with onion and olive oil on Saute mode for 10 minutes. Then add red lentils, sweet potatoes, carrot, red kidney beans, tomato paste, almond milk, water, salt, and peppercorns. Mix up the ingredients gently. Close and seal the lid. Set High-pressure mode and cook the stew for 10 minutes. Then allow natural pressure release. Mix up the cooked stew carefully.

Nutrition value/serving: calories 177, fat 5.9, fiber 8.6, carbs 23.8, protein 8.8

Vegan "Beef" Stew
Prep time: 10 minutes | Cooking time: 45 minutes | Servings: 2

Ingredients:
- ½ yellow onion, chopped roughly
- 1 oz celery stalk, chopped
- ¼ cup carrot, chopped
- 1 garlic clove, diced
- 1 tablespoon tomato sauce
- ¼ cup green peas
- 1 tomato, chopped
- 1 cup vegetable stock
- 1 teaspoon salt
- 1 teaspoon thyme
- 2 Yukon potatoes

Directions:
Chop Yukon potatoes roughly and transfer them in the instant pot. Add celery stalk, yellow onion, carrot, garlic, tomato sauce, green peas, tomato, salt, thyme, and mix up. Then add vegetable stock and close the lid. Set Saute mode and cook the stew for 45 minutes. When the time is over, check if all the ingredients are cooked and mix up the stew gently.

Nutrition value/serving: calories 100, fat 1.2, fiber 4.5, carbs 22.4, protein 3

Egyptian Stew

Prep time: 10 minutes | *Cooking time:* 12 minutes | *Servings:* 2

Ingredients:

- 1 tablespoon tomato paste
- 1 tablespoon olive oil
- 1 tablespoon red pepper
- 1 teaspoon paprika
- 4 potatoes, peeled, chopped
- 2 cups lentils
- 6 cups of water
- 1 teaspoon salt
- 1 cup fresh dill, chopped
- 3 tablespoons lemon juice

Directions:

Place tomato paste, paprika, potatoes, lentils, water, and salt in the instant pot. Close and seal the lid. After this, set Manual mode and cook the stew for 12 minutes. Then use quick pressure release. Open the lid and add lemon juice. Mix it up. Transfer the stew in the serving bowls. Then mix up together red pepper and olive oil. Pour the mixture over the stew. Garnish the meal with fresh dill.

Nutrition value/serving: calories 451, fat 4.4, fiber 29.5, carbs 81.1, protein 25.1

Moroccan Stew

Prep time: 10 minutes | *Cooking time:* 18 minutes | *Servings:* 4

Ingredients:

- 1 cup butternut squash, chopped
- ½ cup chickpeas, canned
- 1 teaspoon turmeric
- 1 teaspoon sage
- 1 teaspoon ground coriander
- 1 teaspoon thyme
- 1 teaspoon harissa
- 1 teaspoon ground ginger
- ¼ teaspoon saffron
- 1 lemon slice
- 1 teaspoon salt
- 1 teaspoon tomato paste
- 2 cups of water

Directions:

In the instant pot, combine together water, tomato paste, salt, saffron, ground ginger, harissa, thyme, ground coriander, sage, turmeric, and canned chickpeas. Add butternut squash and mix the ingredients. Add lemon slice and close the lid. Set Manual mode (high pressure) and cook the stew for 8 minutes. Then allow natural pressure release for 10 minutes more. Open the lid and chill the stew till the room temperature.

Nutrition value/serving: calories 117, fat 1.9, fiber 5.5, carbs 21.1, protein 5.5

Peas and Carrot Stew

Prep time: 5 minutes | *Cooking time:* 20 minutes | *Servings:* 5

Ingredients:
- 3 potatoes, peeled, chopped
- 2 carrots, chopped
- 1 cup green peas, frozen
- 2 cups of water
- 1 tablespoon tomato paste
- 1 teaspoon salt
- 1 teaspoon cayenne pepper

Directions:
Place carrots, potatoes, and green peas in the instant pot. Then in the separated bowl combine together tomato paste, water, salt, and cayenne pepper. Whisk the liquid until it gets a light red color, and then pour it into the instant pot. Close and seal the lid. Cook the stew on Manual mode for 10 minutes. Then allow natural pressure release for 5 minutes.

Nutrition value/serving: calories 125, fat 0.3, fiber 5.4, carbs 27.5, protein 4.1

Mediterranean Vegan Stew

Prep time: 10 minutes | *Cooking time:* 35 minutes | *Servings:* 4

Ingredients:
- ¼ cup white cabbage, shredded
- 1 potato, chopped
- ½ cup corn kernels
- 1 sweet pepper, chopped
- ½ cup fresh parsley
- 1 cup tomatoes, chopped
- ¼ cup green beans, chopped
- 1 ½ cup water
- 1 teaspoon salt
- 1 tablespoon coconut cream
- 1 teaspoon white pepper

Directions:
Place all the ingredients in the instant pot and mix them up. After this, close the lid and ser Saute mode. Cook the stew for 35 minutes. When the time is over, open the lid and mix the stew well. Check if all the ingredients are cooked and close the lid. Let the stew rest for 10-15 minutes before serving.

Nutrition value/serving: calories 83, fat 1.4, fiber 3.2, carbs 16.8, protein 2.8

Sweet Potato Stew

Prep time: 10 minutes | Cooking time: 35minutes | Servings: 2

Ingredients:
- ¼ cup tomatoes, diced
- 1 tablespoon wheat flour
- 1 cup tomato juice
- ½ onion, diced
- 1 tablespoon olive oil
- 1 tablespoon chives, chopped
- 1 teaspoon salt
- 1 teaspoon curry powder
- 3 sweet potatoes, roughly chopped
- ½ cup of water
- 1 teaspoon sugar

Directions:
Pour olive oil in the instant pot. Add diced onion and sweet potatoes. Sprinkle the vegetables with salt, curry powder, and cook on Saute mode for 10 minutes. After this, whisk together wheat flour and water until smooth. Pour the liquid in the instant pot. Add tomato juice and sugar. Close the lid and cook the stew on Saute mode for 35 minutes. Mix up the stew every 10 minutes. Check if the sweet potatoes are cooked and add chopped chives. Mix up the stew well.

Nutrition value/serving: calories 165, fat 7.4, fiber 3.4, carbs 24.7, protein 2.6

Kuru Fasulye

Prep time: 15 minutes | Cooking time: 20 minutes | Servings: 4

Ingredients:
- 1 cup cannellini beans
- 6 cups of water
- 2 tablespoons tomato paste
- 1 onion, diced
- 1 bell pepper, chopped
- 1 teaspoon coconut oil
- 1 teaspoon chili flakes
- 1 teaspoon ground black pepper
- 1 teaspoon salt
- 1 teaspoon cayenne red pepper

Directions:
Cook diced onion and bell pepper with coconut oil on Saute mode for 3 minutes. Add tomato paste and cannellini beans. Mix up the ingredients and add water, chili flakes, ground black pepper, and red pepper. Close and seal the lid. Set Manual mode (high pressure) and cook the meal for 15 minutes. Then allow natural pressure release for 15 minutes more.

Nutrition value/serving: calories 193, fat 1.8, fiber 13, carbs 34.5, protein 11.9

Rainbow Stew

Prep time: 10 minutes | Cooking time: 30 minutes | Servings: 4

Ingredients:
- 1 eggplant, sliced
- 1 zucchini, sliced
- 2 tomatoes, sliced
- ½ cup corn kernels
- ¼ cup red beans, canned
- 1 cup of water
- 1 tablespoon coconut oil
- 1 teaspoon salt
- 1 teaspoon paprika
- 1 teaspoon cayenne pepper

Directions:
In the mixing bowl combine together sliced eggplant, zucchini, corn kernels, salt, paprika, and cayenne pepper. Shake the mixture well. After this, transfer the vegetables in the instant pot. Add coconut oil, water, and red beans. Close the lead and cook the stew on Saute mode for 30 minutes. Then open the lid, stir the meal gently and let it rest with the opened lid for 5 minutes.

Nutrition value/serving: calories 135, fat 4.3, fiber 7.9, carbs 22, protein 5.6

Irish Stew

Prep time: 20 minutes | Cooking time: 50 minutes | Servings: 4

Ingredients:
- 1 cup baby potatoes
- 1 cup mushrooms, roughly chopped
- 1 oz parsnip, chopped
- 2 cups of water
- 1 tablespoon tomato paste
- 1 tablespoon coconut cream
- 1 teaspoon dried dill
- 1 teaspoon dried coriander
- 1 teaspoon salt
- 1 tablespoon tomato sauce
- 1 teaspoon olive oil
- ¼ cup baby carrot, chopped
- 1 cup beer

Directions:
Cook baby potatoes with olive oil on Saute mode until potatoes are light brown. Then add mushrooms, parsnip, tomato paste, coconut cream, dried dill, coriander, salt, and tomato sauce. Add baby carrots and mix up the stew well. Then add beer and water. Close the lid. Set Saute mode and cook the stew for 50 minutes. When the time is over, switch off the instant pot and let stew rest for 15 minutes.

Nutrition value/serving: calories 85, fat 2.2, fiber 1.5, carbs 11.2, protein 1.8

Fennel Soup

Prep time: 10 minutes | Cooking time: 8 minutes | Servings: 2

Ingredients:
- 1 cup of coconut milk
- ½ cup almond milk
- 8 oz fennel bulb, chopped
- 1 cup cauliflower, chopped
- 1 garlic clove, diced
- 1 tablespoon fresh dill, chopped
- ½ teaspoon chili pepper
- 1 teaspoon salt

Directions:
Pour coconut milk and almond milk in the instant pot. Add chopped fennel bulb, cauliflower, garlic clove, chili pepper, and salt. Close and seal the lid. Cook the soup on High-pressure mode for 8 minutes. Then use quick pressure release. Open the lid and blend the soup until smooth. Ladle it into the soup bowls and sprinkle with fresh dill.

Nutrition value/serving: calories 360, fat 3.2, fiber 7.7, carbs 23.1, protein 6.1

African Stew

Prep time: 20 minutes | Cooking time: 60 minutes | Servings: 4

Ingredients:
- ¼ cup peanuts, chopped
- 3 tablespoons peanut butter
- 1 teaspoon garlic, diced
- 1 teaspoon minced ginger root
- 1 cup collard greens, chopped
- 3 yams, chopped
- 1 white onion, roughly chopped
- 1 teaspoon cumin
- 1 teaspoon ground black pepper
- 1 teaspoon onion powder
- 1 teaspoon cayenne pepper
- 1 teaspoon oregano
- 1 teaspoon cilantro
- 1 bell pepper, chopped
- 2 cups of water
- ½ cup almond milk
- 1 tablespoon almond butter

Directions:
Saute yams, onion, minced ginger root, and diced garlic with almond butter for 5 minutes. Stir the mixture from time to time. Meanwhile, mix up together all the spices; cilantro, oregano, cayenne pepper, onion powder, ground black pepper, and cumin. Add the spice mixture in the instant pot. Then add bell pepper, peanuts, and peanut butter. Add almond milk and water. Check if you add all the ingredients and close the lid. Set saute mode and cook stew for 50 minutes. When the time is over, switch off the instant pot and let the stew stay for at least 15 minutes more.

Nutrition value/serving: calories 288, fat 20.5, fiber 5.8, carbs 22.9, protein 8.6

Thai Curry Soup

Prep time: 10 minutes | Cooking time: 13 minutes | Servings: 2

Ingredients:
- 6 oz firm tofu, cubed
- 1 teaspoon curry paste
- 1 teaspoon curry powder
- ½ cup of coconut milk
- 2 cups of water
- 1 tablespoon fish sauce
- 2 tablespoons soy sauce
- 1 teaspoon paprika
- 2 cups mushroom, chopped
- 1 teaspoon almond butter
- 2 tablespoons lemon juice
- ¼ teaspoon grated lime zest

Directions:
On the saute mode, cook mushrooms with curry powder, curry paste, fish sauce, soy sauce, paprika, and almond butter for 10 minutes. Mix up the mushrooms well. Ten add cubes tofu, coconut milk, and grated lime zest. Close and seal the lid. Cook the soup on high-pressure mode for 3 minutes. Then make quick pressure release and open the lid. Add lemon juice and mix up soup gently.

Nutrition value/serving: calories 150, fat 12.2, fiber 2.3, carbs 6.2, protein 7.1

Garden Stew

Prep time: 10 minutes | Cooking time: 24 minutes | Servings: 3

Ingredients:
- 1 cup green beans, chopped
- 1 potato, chopped
- 4 oz asparagus, chopped
- 1 large tomato, chopped
- 1 cup vegetable broth
- 1 teaspoon ground black pepper
- 1 teaspoon almond butter
- ½ cup kale, chopped
- ¼ cup spinach, chopped

Directions:
Place all the ingredients except spinach and kale in the instant pot and close the lid. Cook the ingredients on Manual mode for 4 minutes. Then allow natural pressure release for 5 minutes. Open the lid and add spinach and kale. Mix up the stew well. Close the lid and keep cooking stew on Saute mode for 10 minutes more. When the time is over, switch off the instant pot and let stew rest for 10 minutes before serving.

Nutrition value/serving: calories 127, fat 3.8, fiber 5, carbs 19.4, protein 6.4

Tom Yum Soup

Prep time: 15 minutes | *Cooking time:* 16 minutes | *Servings:* 4

Ingredients:
- 3 cups of water
- 2 tablespoons Tom Yum paste
- 1 teaspoon lemongrass
- ¼ teaspoon ground ginger
- 1 teaspoon garlic, diced
- 2 tomatoes, chopped
- 4 oz green beans, chopped
- 2 oz celery stalk, chopped
- 1 carrot, chopped
- 1 cup spinach, chopped
- ¼ cup bok choy, chopped

Directions:
In the instant pot combine together water, Tom Yam paste, lemongrass, ground ginger, garlic, and chopped tomatoes. Close and seal the lid. Cook mixture on Manual mode for 4 minutes. Then make a quick pressure release and open the lid. Add green beans, celery stalk, carrot, and bok choy. Mix the soup up and add spinach. Close the lid and cook soup on Saute mode for 16 minutes. Then let the cooked soup rest for 10 minutes with the closed lid.

Nutrition value/serving: calories 62, fat 2.5, fiber 2.5, carbs 8.6, protein 1.6

Coconut Cream Soup

Prep time: 15 minutes | *Cooking time:* 7 minutes | *Servings:* 5

Ingredients:
- 5 cups of coconut milk
- 1 cup of water
- 2 cups carrots
- 1 onion, diced
- 1 teaspoon salt
- 1 teaspoon turmeric
- 1 teaspoon white pepper

Directions:
Peel and chop carrots. Cook the diced onion with salt, turmeric, and white pepper in the instant pot for 2 minutes. Then stir the vegetable carefully and add water, coconut milk, and chopped carrot. Close and seal the lid. Set High-pressure mode and cook soup for 7 minutes. After this, allow natural pressure release for 10 minutes. Open the lid and blend the soup with immersion blender until smooth.

Nutrition value/serving: calories 581, fat 57.3, fiber 7, carbs 20.2, protein 6.2

Hot Pepper Chickpea Stew

Prep time: 15 minutes | Cooking time: 15 minutes | Servings: 3

Ingredients:
- 1 cayenne pepper, chopped
- 1 cup chickpea
- 4 cups of water
- 1 tablespoon almond butter
- 1 onion, chopped
- 2 cups spinach, chopped
- 1 tablespoon coconut yogurt
- 1 teaspoon salt

Directions:
Place almond butter in the instant pot and melt it on saute mode. Add spinach and chopped cayenne pepper. Then add onion and chickpeas. Sprinkle the ingredients with salt and add water. Close and seal the lid. Cook stew on Manual mode for 15 minutes. Then allow natural pressure release for 15 minutes. Transfer the cooked stew in the serving bowls, add coconut yogurt and mix it up.

Nutrition value/serving: calories 297, fat 7.2, fiber 13.4, carbs 45.9, protein 15.1

Summer Stew

Prep time: 15 minutes | Cooking time: 7 minutes | Servings: 6

Ingredients:
- 1 eggplant, chopped roughly
- 1 cup bok choy, chopped
- 1 cup spinach, chopped
- ½ cup fresh cilantro, chopped
- 1 red onion, cut into petals
- 2 sweet peppers, chopped
- ½ cup of rice
- 5 cups vegetable broth
- 1 teaspoon salt
- 1 teaspoon thyme
- 1 teaspoon dried parsley

Directions:
Put eggplant, bok choy, spinach, cilantro, onion, and sweet peppers in the instant pot. Add rice, vegetable broth, salt, thyme, and dried parsley. Mix up the vegetables with the help of the spoon. Close and seal the lid. Set Manual mode (high pressure) and cook the stew for 7 minutes When the time is over, allow natural pressure release for 10 minutes. Mix up the stew before serving.

Nutrition value/serving: calories 131, fat 1.6, fiber 4.2, carbs 22.9, protein 6.9

Texas Stew

Prep time: 10 minutes | Cooking time: 5 minutes | Servings: 2

Ingredients:
- ¼ cup green chili, canned, chopped
- ½ cup tomatoes, canned, diced
- ½ teaspoon salt
- 1/3 cup corn kernels, frozen
- ½ cup potatoes, chopped
- ½ cup kidney beans, canned
- ½ cup almond milk
- 1 teaspoon dried parsley

Directions:
Combine together all the ingredients in the instant pot. Close and seal the lid. Cook stew on Manual mode for 5 minutes. After this, allow natural pressure release for 5 minutes. Chill the stew till the room temperature. Transfer the stew in the serving bowls.

Nutrition value/serving: calories 359, fat 15.2, fiber 10.5, carbs 46, protein 13.6

Soybean Stew

Prep time: 20 minutes | Cooking time: 20 minutes | Servings: 4

Ingredients:
- 1 cup soybeans, soaked
- ¼ cup tomatoes, chopped
- 3 cups of water
- 1 teaspoon mustard
- 1 zucchini, chopped
- 1 tablespoon soy sauce
- 1 jalapeno pepper, sliced
- 3 oz vegan Parmesan, grated

Directions:
Place soybeans and tomatoes in the instant pot. Add mustard, zucchini, soy sauce, jalapeno pepper, and close the lid. Set Manual mode (High pressure) and cook the stew for 20 minutes. Then allow natural pressure release for 20 minutes. Transfer the cooked stew in the serving bowls and top with grated cheese.

Nutrition value/serving: calories 289, fat 9.6, fiber 5.3, carbs 21.2, protein 26.8

Iranian Stew

Prep time: 15 minutes | Cooking time: 6minutes | Servings: 4

Ingredients:
- 1 cup parsley, chopped
- ½ cup fresh cilantro, chopped
- ½ cup spinach, chopped
- ½ cup kale, chopped
- ½ lime
- 1 eggplant, chopped
- 1 yellow onion, chopped
- 1 cup red kidney beans, canned
- 2 cups vegetable broth
- 1 teaspoon harissa
- 2 teaspoons paprika
- 1 tablespoon almond butter

Directions:
Put parsley, cilantro, spinach, kale, and chopped onion in the instant pot. Add red kidney beans, vegetable broth, paprika, harissa, and almond butter. Add eggplant. Close and seal the lid. Cook the stew for 6 minutes in Manual mode. After this, allow natural pressure release for 10 minutes. Open the lid and mix up the stew carefully. It is recommended to serve stew warm.

Nutrition value/serving: calories 259, fat 4.2, fiber 13.4, carbs 42.7, protein 16.2

Ratsherrenpfanne

Prep time: 10 minutes | Cooking time: 10 minutes | Servings: 2

Ingredients:
- 1 cup broccoli florets
- 1 cup portobello mushrooms, chopped
- ½ cup coconut cream
- ½ cup of water
- 1 teaspoon ground black pepper
- 1 teaspoon chili pepper
- 1 teaspoon corn starch
- ½ onion, diced
- 1 teaspoon olive oil

Directions:
Preheat olive oil on saute mode. Add diced onion and cook it for 3-5 minutes or until light brown. Add broccoli florets, chopped mushrooms, water, ground black pepper, chili pepper, and corn starch. Mix up the mixture well. Close and seal the lid. Set Manual mode and cook the stew for 7 minutes. Use quick pressure release. Open the lid and mix up the stew well with the help of the spatula. Chill the stew till the room temperature before serving.

Nutrition value/serving: calories 202, fat 17, fiber 3.8, carbs 12.5, protein 4.2

Main Dishes

Greek Style Stewed Artichokes
Prep time: 8 minutes | Cooking time: 12 minutes | Servings: 4

Ingredients:

- 4 artichokes, trimmed
- ¼ cup lemon juice
- 1 teaspoon minced garlic
- 1 tablespoon olive oil
- 1 teaspoon fresh dill, chopped
- 1 tablespoon vegan mayonnaise
- ½ cup water, for cooking

Directions:
Mix up together minced garlic with lemon juice, and olive oil. Then rub the artichokes with garlic mixture carefully. Let them marinate for 10 minutes. Meanwhile, whisk together vegan mayonnaise and fresh dill. Pour water in the instant pot. Then insert steamer rack. Place the artichokes on the rack and close the lid. Seal the lid and set Steam mode. Cook the vegetables for 12 minutes. When the time is over, use quick pressure release. Open the lid and chill the artichokes till the room temperature. Then sprinkle artichokes with the vegan mayonnaise sauce and transfer on the serving plates.

Nutrition value/serving: calories 120, fat 4.7, fiber 8.9, carbs 18, protein 5.5

Turkish Green Beans
Prep time: 10 minutes | Cooking time: 15 minutes | Servings: 4

Ingredients:

- 1 ½ cup green beans
- ½ onion, diced
- 2 tomatoes, chopped
- 1 teaspoon tomato paste
- 1 teaspoon chili flakes
- 1 teaspoon salt
- 1 cup of water
- 1 tablespoon olive oil

Directions:
Chop the green beans roughly and place in the instant pot. Add diced onion and olive oil. Set saute mode and cook the ingredients for 5 minutes. Stir them from time to time. After this, sprinkle the vegetables with salt, chili flakes, tomato paste. Add water. Close and seal the lid. Set Manual mode and cook green beans for 8 minutes. Then allow natural pressure release for 5 minutes. Open the lid and mix up the green beans carefully.

Nutrition value/serving: calories 61, fat 3.7, fiber 2.5, carbs 6.9, protein 1.5

Nutritious Lasagna
Prep time: 15 minutes | *Cooking time: 9 minutes* | *Servings: 2*

Ingredients:
- 3 oz cashew
- ¼ teaspoon salt
- 1 tablespoon water
- 1 teaspoon sesame oil
- ½ teaspoon lemon juice
- 6 oz tomatoes, diced, canned
- 3 oz kale
- 1 zucchini
- 1 teaspoon dried oregano
- 1 teaspoon Italian seasoning
- 1 onion, grated

Directions:
In the food processor blend together cashew, salt, water, and sesame oil. When the mixture is smooth, transfer it in the mixing bowl. After this, blend lemon juice with diced tomatoes, dried oregano, Italian seasoning, and grated onion. Cut the zucchini lengthwise. The "lasagna" noodles are prepared. Then place little bit tomato mixture in the bottom of the instant pot. Place one zucchini slice and spread it with cashew mixture. Repeat the same steps till you use all the ingredients. Close and seal the lid. Set High-pressure mode and cook the meal for 9 minutes. Then allow natural pressure release for 9 minutes. Open the lid and chill the lasagna till the room temperature.

Nutrition value/serving: calories 348, fat 23.2, fiber 5.5, carbs 30.8, protein 10.4

Vegan Butter "Chicken"
Prep time: 15 minutes | *Cooking time: 6 minutes* | *Servings: 2*

Ingredients:
- ½ teaspoon cornstarch
- 1 teaspoon garam masala
- 1 teaspoon olive oil
- ½ teaspoon chili flakes
- 1-pound firm tofu, cubed
- 4 tablespoons lime juice
- 5 tablespoons tomato sauce
- ½ cup of coconut milk
- 1 teaspoon dried oregano

Directions:
In the mixing bowl, mix up together cornstarch, garam masala, olive oil, and chili flakes. Then cut cubed tofu in the spice mixture and leave for 10 minutes to marinate. Meanwhile, place lime juice, tomato sauce, coconut milk, and dried oregano in the instant pot. Close the lid and cook the sauce for 5 minutes on Saute mode. After this, open the lid, add marinated tofu and mix up the mixture gently. Close the lid and set Manual mode (high pressure) and cook the meal for 1 minute. Use quick pressure release. Chill the butter "chicken" for 5-10 minutes before serving.

Nutrition value/serving: calories 336, fat 26.3, fiber 4.4, carbs 11.9, protein 20.6

Jackfruit Curry

Prep time: 10 minutes | Cooking time: 11 minutes | Servings: 4

Ingredients:
- 1 tablespoon almond butter
- 1 teaspoon curry powder
- 1 teaspoon curry paste
- ½ teaspoon paprika
- ½ teaspoon turmeric
- 1 cup green jackfruit, canned
- 1 cup of water
- 2 potatoes, peeled, chopped
- 1 oz chives, chopped
- 1 onion, diced
- 1 teaspoon thyme
- 1 teaspoon coriander
- 1 teaspoon salt

Directions:

In the instant pot, combine together almond butter, curry powder, curry paste, paprika, turmeric, thyme, coriander, and salt. Then add diced onion, potatoes, and jackfruit. Mix up the mixture. Add water and chives. Mix up the ingredients well. Close and seal the lid of the instant pot. Set manual mode and cook curry for 11 minutes. Then allow natural pressure release. Open the lid and mix up cooked curry gently with the help of the spatula.

Nutrition value/serving: calories 134, fat 3.3, fiber 5.9, carbs 23.5, protein 3.6

Asian Steamed Dumplings

Prep time: 15 minutes | Cooking time: 16 minutes | Servings: 5

Ingredients:
- ¼ cup mushrooms, chopped
- ½ carrot, grated
- ½ onion, diced
- ½ teaspoon ground black pepper
- 1 teaspoon soy sauce
- 1 teaspoon fish sauce
- 1 teaspoon coconut oil
- 5 dumpling wrappers
- 1 cup water, for cooking

Directions:

Preheat instant pot on saute mode and place coconut oil inside. Melt it and add grated carrot, diced onion, and chopped mushrooms. Add soy sauce and fish sauce. Mix up vegetables well and cook them for 10 minutes on saute mode. When the time is over, stir the ingredients with the help of the wooden spatula. Transfer the mixture in the mixing bowl, if it is cooked. Keep cooking for 2-3 minutes more if it wasn't ready yet. Then prepare dumpling wrappers. Brush the edges of the wrappers with water and place the mushroom filling in the center. Wrap the wrappers to make the dumpling shape. Clean instant pot. Pour water inside the instant pot and insert steamer rack. Place dumplings on the steamer rack. Set Steam mode and close the lid. Cook the dumplings for 6 minutes. Make a natural pressure release.

Nutrition value/serving: calories 217, fat 1.4, fiber 2.5, carbs 45, protein 6.4

Portobello Roast

Prep time: 25 minutes | *Cooking time:* 30 minutes | *Servings:* 2

Ingredients:
- 2 Portobello mushrooms
- 1 carrot, chopped
- 1 potato, chopped
- ½ white onion, chopped
- 1 garlic clove, diced
- ½ teaspoon thyme
- ½ teaspoon rosemary
- 1 tablespoon mustard
- ½ cup of water
- 1 teaspoon tomato paste
- 1 teaspoon salt
- 1 teaspoon ground black pepper
- 1 tablespoon coconut oil

Directions:
Wash and trim the mushrooms. Then rub them with salt and ground black pepper generously. Slice the mushrooms and transfer in the instant pot. Add coconut oil. Set saute mode and cook the vegetables for 3-5 minutes. Stir them from time to time. Then sprinkle mushrooms with thyme and rosemary. Add chopped potato, carrot, and diced onion. Add tomato paste, mustard, garlic, and water. Carefully mix up the mixture. Close and seal the lid. Set Manual mode (high pressure) and cook the mushroom roast for 25 minutes. Then allow natural pressure release for 20 minutes. Transfer the cooked roast in the serving bowls and top with the gravy.

Nutrition value/serving: calories 203, fat 8.6, fiber 5.7, carbs 27.4, protein 7

Posole

Prep time: 35 minutes | *Cooking time:* 8 minutes | *Servings:* 4

Ingredients:
- 2 cups hominy
- 1 cup red chili puree
- ½ red onion, sliced
- 2 garlic cloves, peeled, chopped
- 1 cup jackfruit, canned
- 4 cups vegetable broth
- 1 teaspoon almond butter

Directions:
Set Saute mode and preheat instant pot. Toss almond butter and melt it. After this, add sliced onion, chopped garlic, and red chili puree. Cook the mixture for 4 minutes. Stir it carefully. Add jackfruit and cook it for 3 minutes more. With the help of the hand masher, mash the mixture well. Add vegetable broth; close and seal the lid. Cook the meal on Manual mode for 10 minutes. Then allow natural pressure release for 15 minutes. Open the lid, add hominy. Set Manual mode and cook the meal for 1 minute more. Then allow natural pressure release for 20 minutes. Open the lid and mix up the meal carefully.

Nutrition value/serving: calories 189, fat 4.5, fiber 3.4, carbs 29.1, protein 7.8

Lentil Gumbo

Prep time: 10 minutes | *Cooking time:* 23 minutes | *Servings:* 4

Ingredients:
- ½ tablespoon garlic, diced
- ½ tablespoon coconut oil
- 1 bell pepper, chopped
- 1 celery stalk, chopped
- ½ teaspoon thyme
- 1.2 teaspoon coriander
- 1 teaspoon Cajun spices
- ½ teaspoon white pepper
- ½ cup lentils
- 1 ½ cup water
- ½ cup okra, chopped
- ½ cup tomatoes, diced, canned
- 1 teaspoon lemon juice
- 4 oz cauliflower, chopped
- 1 teaspoon salt

Directions:
Preheat instant pot on Saute mode and toss coconut oil inside. Melt it and add bell pepper, garlic, celery stalk, thyme, coriander, and Cajun spices. Mix up the mixture and cook for 10 minutes. Then add all the remaining ingredients except salt. Close and seal the lid. Set Manual mode (high pressure) and cook gumbo for 13 minutes. Then make quick pressure release. Open the lid, add salt and mix up the meal well.

Nutrition value/serving: calories 129, fat 2.2, fiber 9.3, carbs 20.7, protein 7.7

Chana Masala with Spinach

Prep time: 15 minutes | *Cooking time:* 7 minutes | *Servings:* 5

Ingredients:
- 2 cups chickpeas, canned
- 6 cups spinach, chopped
- 2 oz tomato, chopped
- 1 tablespoon olive oil
- 1 white onion, diced
- 1 teaspoon cumin
- 1 teaspoon red chili powder
- 1 teaspoon turmeric
- 1 teaspoon paprika
- 1 teaspoon garam masala
- 1 tablespoon lime juice
- ½ teaspoon Pink salt

Directions:
Put olive oil and diced onion in the instant pot. Set Saute mode and cook the ingredients for 4 minutes. Then make a quick stir and add chopped tomatoes, cumin, red chili powder, turmeric, paprika, garam masala, and Pink salt. Add lime juice and mix the mixture up. Add chickpeas, mix up. Close and seal the lid. Set Manual mode (high pressure) and cook the meal for 3 minutes. Make a quick pressure release. Open the lid and add spinach. Stir it carefully and close the lid. Let the meal rest for 10 minutes before serving.

Nutrition value/serving: calories 341, fat 8.1, fiber 15.8, carbs 53.5, protein 17.1

Potato Tamales

Prep time: 25 minutes | Cooking time: 12 minutes | Servings: 4

Ingredients:
- 1 cup potato mash
- 8 corn husks
- ½ cup green peas, cooked
- ¼ teaspoon minced garlic
- 1 oz onion, diced, fried
- 1 teaspoon Italian seasoning
- ¼ teaspoon ground cinnamon
- ½ cup of coconut oil
- ½ teaspoon baking powder
- ½ cup vegetable stock
- 1 cup masa harina
- 1 cup hot water
- 1 cup water, for cooking

Directions:

Make tamale dough: mash green peas. Combine together mashed green peas, potato mash, minced garlic, fried onion, Italian seasoning, ground cinnamon, baking powder, coconut oil, vegetable stock, and masa harina. Mix up the dough carefully with the help of the wooden spoon. When the mixture is smooth and homogenous, it is cooked. Place corn husks in hot water for 10-15 minutes. Then remove them from water and dry gently with paper towel. Fill the corn husks with the tamale dough and wrap. Pour water in the instant pot and insert steamer rack. Place tamales on the rack, close and seal the lid. Cook the meal on Steam mode for 12 minutes. Then allow natural pressure release for 10 minutes.

Nutrition value/serving: calories 414, fat 30, fiber 3.9, carbs 35.9, protein 5.1

Saag Tofu with Spinach

Prep time: 10 minutes | Cooking time: 16 minutes | Servings: 4

Ingredients:
- 1-pound firm tofu, cubed
- 4 cups spinach, chopped
- 2 cups kale, chopped
- 1 teaspoon olive oil
- 7 tablespoons water
- 1 jalapeno pepper, chopped
- 1 red onion, diced
- 1 teaspoon grated ginger
- 1 teaspoon lemongrass
- 1 tablespoon corn flour
- 4 tablespoons water

Directions:

Pour olive oil in the instant pot. Add diced onion, grated ginger, lemongrass, chopped jalapeno pepper, and cook on the saute mode for 5 minutes. Add chopped spinach and kale. Then add 7 tablespoons of water, mix up the mixture. Cook it for 10 minutes on saute mode. Meanwhile, whisk together water with corn flour. After 10 minutes, add cornflour liquid in the spinach mixture. Stir it well. Blend it with the help of the immersion blender. Add cubed tofu. Mix the meal up and close the lid. Cook it on high-pressure mode for 1 minute. Then make quick pressure release. Open the lid and stir the meal gently.

Nutrition value/serving: calories 133, fat 6.2, fiber 3.1, carbs 11.1, protein 11.7

Tofu Matar

Prep time: 15 minutes | Cooking time: 7 minutes | Servings: 2

Ingredients:

- 8 oz firm tofu, cubed
- 1 teaspoon cumin seeds
- 1 teaspoon turmeric
- 1 teaspoon paprika
- 1 teaspoon ground ginger
- 1 teaspoon chili powder
- 1 teaspoon tomato paste
- 1 tomato, chopped
- 1 teaspoon ground coriander
- 1 teaspoon coconut oil
- 1 teaspoon garlic, diced
- 1 tablespoon almond yogurt
- ½ cup of water
- 1 teaspoon garam masala
- ¼ cup green peas

Directions:

Place coconut oil in the instant pot. Add all the spices, diced garlic, tomato, and green peas. Stir the mixture and cook it on Saute mode for 3-4 minutes. Stir it from time to time. Then add tomato paste and water. Add cubed tofu and close the lid. Cook the meal on High-pressure mode for 2 minutes. Then allow natural pressure release for 5 minutes more. Open the lid, add almond yogurt. Mix up the meal.

Nutrition value/serving: calories 179, fat 10.2, fiber 3.7, carbs 13.8, protein 11.9

Tso's Tofu

Prep time: 15 minutes | Cooking time: 5 minutes | Servings: 2

Ingredients:

- 1-pound firm tofu
- ½ teaspoon corn starch
- ½ teaspoon minced garlic
- ½ teaspoon minced ginger
- 6 tablespoons soy sauce
- 2 tablespoons fish sauce
- 1 teaspoon olive oil
- 1 tablespoon apple cider vinegar
- ½ teaspoon brown sugar
- ½ teaspoon red chili pepper
- ¼ cup of water

Directions:

Cut tofu into the big cubes. Then whisk together water, corn starch, soy sauce, fish sauce, apple cider vinegar, brown sugar, red chili pepper, and minced garlic, and minced ginger. Then place chopped tofu into this mixture. Let the tofu marinate for 15 minutes. Meanwhile, preheat instant pot on Saute mode. Add olive oil. Then place tofu cubes into the instant pot. Cook them for 1 minute each side. Add remaining marinade and close the lid. Set Manual mode (high pressure) and cook a meal for 1 minute. Make a quick pressure release. Transfer the cooked meal into the serving bowls and top with the gravy.

Nutrition value/serving: calories 221, fat 11.9, fiber 2.5, carbs 10.4, protein 22.6

Tofu Cubes in Peanut Sauce
Prep time: 10 minutes | *Cooking time:* 3 minutes | *Servings:* 4

Ingredients:
- 10 oz firm tofu, cubed
- ¼ cup of water
- ½ teaspoon salt
- 1 teaspoon ground black pepper
- 1 tablespoon olive oil
- ½ teaspoon corn flour
- 4 tablespoon peanut butter
- 5 tablespoons almond yogurt
- ½ teaspoon curry powder
- 1 tablespoon soy sauce
- ¼ cup peanuts, chopped
- ½ teaspoon dried rosemary

Directions:
Sprinkle tofu with salt and place in the instant pot. Add water and close the lid. Cook the tofu on High-pressure mode for 1 minute. Then use quick pressure release. Meanwhile, make the sauce: whisk together ground black pepper, corn flour, peanut butter, almond yogurt, curry powder, soy sauce, and dried rosemary. Add chopped peanuts. Transfer the tofu into the bowl and clean the instant pot.и Add olive oil in the instant pot. Then add tofu and peanut sauce. Stir the ingredients gently. Close and seal the lid. Cook the meal for 2 minutes on Manual mode. Then use quick pressure release. Transfer the tofu into the serving plates and top with gravy.

Nutrition value/serving: calories 245, fat 19.8, fiber 2.9, carbs 8.4, protein 12.8

Tempeh
Prep time: 20 hours | *Cooking time:* 16 hours | *Servings:* 10

Ingredients:
- 1 ½ cup soybeans
- 5 cups of water
- 1 tablespoon lemon juice
- 1 teaspoon tempeh starter
- 1 cup water, for cooking

Directions:
Place soybeans and water in the instant pot. Close and seal the lid. Set High-pressure mode and cook soybeans for 45 minutes. Then allow natural pressure release for 30 minutes. Transfer the cooked soybeans in the bowl and sprinkle with lemon juice and tempeh starter. Mix up the soybeans and transfer into the freezer bags. Seal them. Pour 1 cup of water in the instant pot. Add sealed freezer bags with soybeans. Close the lid and set "Yogurt" mode. Cook tempeh for 15 hours. When the time is over, the tempeh should get the white color. Remove the tempeh from the instant pot and let it rest or 20 hours. Slice it into the servings.

Nutrition value/serving: calories 125, fat 5.6, fiber 2.6, carbs 8.4, protein 10.2

Tempeh Tajine

Prep time: 15 minutes | Cooking time: 6 minutes | Servings: 6

Ingredients:

- 3 carrots, chopped
- 1 yellow onion, chopped
- ½ cup prunes, chopped
- ¼ cup apricots, chopped
- 5 oz sweet potato, chopped
- 4 tablespoons lime juice
- 1 tomato, chopped
- 2 cups of water
- 1 teaspoon tamari sauce
- 1 cup vegetable stock
- 2 teaspoons minced garlic
- 10 oz tempeh, chopped
- 1 teaspoon turmeric
- 1 teaspoon ground cumin
- ½ teaspoon ground coriander
- 1 teaspoon salt
- 1 teaspoon chili flakes

Directions:

Mix up together: vegetable stock, minced garlic, tempeh, turmeric, ground cumin, coriander, salt, and chili flakes. Marinate the mixture for 10 minutes. After this, place the chopped carrot, onion, prunes, apricots, sweet potato, lime juice, tomatoes, and water in the instant pot. Add marinated mixture and stir gently. Saute the meal for 4 minutes. Then mix it up, close and seal the lid. Set Manual mode (high pressure) and cook the meal for 2 minutes more. Use the quick pressure release. Open the lid and transfer tajine into the serving bowls.

Nutrition value/serving: calories 178, fat 5.7, fiber 3.3, carbs 25.5, protein 10.4

Aloo Gobi

Prep time: 15 minutes | Cooking time: 5 minutes | Servings: 2

Ingredients:

- 1 large potato, chopped
- 1 tablespoon lime juice
- 1 teaspoon cumin seeds
- 1 teaspoon mango powder
- ¼ teaspoon turmeric
- ¼ teaspoon ground ginger
- 1 onion, diced
- ½ teaspoon garam masala
- 1 cup cauliflower, chopped
- 1 tomato, chopped
- 2 tablespoons water
- 1 tablespoon avocado oil

Directions:

Combine together lime juice, cumin seeds, mango powder, turmeric, ground ginger, garam masala, and avocado oil in the bowl. Whisk it and transfer in the instant pot. Set saute mode and cook spices for 1 minute. After this, add diced onion and water. Then add chopped tomato and cauliflower. Mix the mixture and close the lid. Set manual mode (high pressure) and cook aloo gobi for 4 minutes. Then allow natural pressure release for 10 minutes. Open the lid and shake the mixture well.

Nutrition value/serving: calories 199, fat 1.5, fiber 7.4, carbs 42.9, protein 5.9

Korma

Prep time: 10 minutes | Cooking time: 10 minutes | Servings: 4

Ingredients:
- 10 oz firm tofu, cubed
- 1 teaspoon garam masala
- 2 sweet potatoes, chopped
- 1 teaspoon garlic powder
- 1 tablespoon coconut oil
- ½ cup almond yogurt
- 1 teaspoon ground cardamom
- 1 teaspoon coriander
- 1 teaspoon chili pepper
- 1 teaspoon minced ginger
- 1 teaspoon pumpkin seeds
- ¼ cup of water
- 1 teaspoon diced garlic
- ½ cup fresh cilantro, chopped

Directions:

Toss coconut oil in the instant pot and melt it. Then add cubed tofu. Sprinkle it with garam masala and garlic powder. Saute tofu for 3 minutes. Stir it from time to time. After this, in the separated bowl, mix up together almond yogurt, ground cardamom, salt, coriander, chili pepper, minced garlic, pumpkin seeds, water, and diced garlic. Remove tofu from the instant pot. Place almond yogurt mixture in the instant pot. Saute it for 5 minutes. When the mixture starts to boil, add cooked tofu. Mix it gently. Close the lid and saute for 2 minutes more. Then transfer cooked korma in the serving bowls. Sprinkle it with sauce and garnish with chopped cilantro.

Nutrition value/serving: calories 133, fat 7.9, fiber 2, carbs 10.5, protein 7.1

Cassoulet

Prep time: 10 minutes | Cooking time: 10 minutes | Servings: 4

Ingredients:
- 1 cup cannellini beans, canned
- 1 tablespoon coconut oil
- 1 teaspoon olive oil
- 5 oz leek, chopped
- 5 oz carrot, chopped
- 5 oz celery root, chopped
- 1 cup mushrooms, chopped
- 1 tablespoon garlic, diced
- 1 cup tomatoes, diced
- 5 fl.oz water
- 1 teaspoon ground black pepper
- 1 oz fresh parsley, chopped
- 1 teaspoon fresh rosemary, chopped

Directions:

Place coconut oil in the instant pot and melt it on saute mode. Add chopped leek, carrot, celery root, and mushrooms. Mix up the mixture and cook it for 5 minutes. After this, add diced tomatoes, water, ground black pepper, parsley, and rosemary. Close and seal the lid. Set Manual mode (high pressure) and cook the meal for 4 minutes. Then make quick pressure release. Transfer the meal into the bowl. Then add olive oil and diced garlic in the instant pot. Saute it until light brown. Sprinkle the cooked meal with sauteed garlic.

Nutrition value/serving: calories 263, fat 5.5, fiber 14.9, carbs 43.4, protein 13.6

Stuffed Eggplants

Prep time: 10 minutes | Cooking time: 15 minutes | Servings: 4

Ingredients:
- 2 large eggplants, trimmed
- ½ cup of rice, cooked
- 1 teaspoon tomato paste
- ½ teaspoon dried dill
- 1 teaspoon dried cilantro
- 1 teaspoon dried oregano
- 1 bell pepper, chopped
- 1 teaspoon olive oil
- 1 tomato, chopped
- ½ cup water, for cooking

Directions:

Cut the eggplants into halves. Remove the flesh from the vegetables to get eggplants boats. Then chop the eggplant flesh and transfer it into the instant pot. Add olive oil, dried oregano, cilantro, and dill. Cook it on saute mode for 4 minutes. Then add tomato paste, cooked rice, and chopped tomato. Mix it up and cook for 1 minute more. Then fill the eggplants with the rice mixture and wrap into the foil. Pour water in the instant pot and insert rack. Place eggplants on the rack and close the lid. Set manual (high pressure) mode and cook eggplants for 10 minutes. When the time is over, make quick pressure release. Open the lid, discard foil and transfer eggplants on the serving plates.

Nutrition value/serving: calories 178, fat 2, fiber 10.8, carbs 38, protein 4.9

Herbed Cauliflower Head

Prep time: 10 minutes | Cooking time: 9 minutes | Servings: 6

Ingredients:
- 1-pound cauliflower head
- 1 teaspoon garlic powder
- 1 teaspoon onion powder
- 1 teaspoon ground black pepper
- 1 teaspoon salt
- 1 tablespoon olive oil
- 1 teaspoon chili flakes
- 1 tablespoon lemon juice
- 1 teaspoon coriander
- 1 red onion, roughly chopped
- 1 cup of water
- 1 teaspoon cayenne pepper
- 1 tablespoon wheat flour

Directions:

Make the marinade for cauliflower: mix up together garlic powder, onion powder, ground black pepper, salt, and olive oil. Then rub cauliflower with marinade. After this, pout water in the instant pot. Add chili flakes, lemon juice, coriander, onion, cayenne pepper, and insert steamer rack. Place cauliflower head on the rack and sprinkle with the remaining marinade. Close and seal the instant pot lid. Cook the meal for 5 minutes on high-pressure mode. Then allow natural pressure release for 5 minutes more. Transfer the cooked cauliflower in the bowl. Then remove the rack from the instant pot. Add wheat flour in the instant pot gravy and whisk it until smooth. Cook it on saute mode for 4 minutes. Stir it from time to time. Then the sauce is cooked, pour it over the cooked cauliflower.

Nutrition value/serving: calories 56, fat 2.5, fiber 2.6, carbs 7.8, protein 2.1

Potato Cakes with Filling

Prep time: 10 minutes | *Cooking time:* 15 minutes | *Servings:* 4

Ingredients:
- ¼ cup mushrooms, chopped
- 1 onion, diced
- 1 teaspoon ground black pepper
- 1 cup potato, mashed
- 1/3 cup wheat flour
- 1 tablespoon olive oil

Directions:
In the mixing bowl combine together mashed potato and wheat flour. Make the soft and non-sticky dough. Add more wheat flour if needed. Then pour olive oil in the instant pot. Add chopped mushrooms and diced onion. Cook the vegetables on saute mode for 10 minutes or until they are light brown. Then the mixture till room temperature. Make the medium balls from the potato mixture and fill them with the mushroom mass. Press the balls gently to get the potato cakes. Place them into the preheated instant pot and cook on Saute mode for 2 minutes from each side.

Nutrition value/serving: calories 132, fat 4.4, fiber 1.1, carbs 20.8, protein 3

Norwegian Style Balls

Prep time: 10 minutes | *Cooking time:* 10 minutes | *Servings:* 6

Ingredients:
- 1 cup chickpeas, canned
- ½ cup green peas, frozen
- 1 carrot, chopped
- 1 teaspoon minced garlic
- 4 tablespoons wheat flour
- 1 teaspoon salt
- 1 teaspoon ground black pepper
- ½ cup of coconut milk
- 1 teaspoon cornflour
- 1 teaspoon olive oil
- 1 cup of water

Directions:
Pour water in the instant pot. Add green peas, carrot, and close the lid. Cook the vegetables on high-pressure mode for 4 minutes. Then use quick pressure release. Strain the vegetables and transfer them in the food processor. Add chickpeas, salt, ground black pepper, minced garlic, and wheat flour. Blend the mixture until smooth. Male the medium-size balls from the blended mixture. Pour olive oil in the instant pot. Preheat it on Saute mode. Add prepared vegetable balls and cook them for 2 minutes. Stir them from time to time. After this, transfer the cooked balls in the serving bowl. Pour coconut milk in the instant pot and add corn flour. Whisk it and saute for 4 minutes or until it starts to be thick. Pour the cooked mixture over the balls.

Nutrition value/serving: calories 210, fat 7.7, fiber 7.4, carbs 28.8, protein 8.3

Teriyaki Tofu
Prep time: 20 minutes | Cooking time: 5 minutes | Servings: 2

Ingredients:
- 10 oz firm tofu, cubed
- 1 tablespoon teriyaki sauce
- 1 tablespoon fish sauce
- 1 teaspoon olive oil
- 1 teaspoon dried parsley
- 1 teaspoon tomato paste
- ½ teaspoon chili flakes

Directions:
Whisk together teriyaki sauce, fish sauce, olive oil, dried parsley, tomato paste, and chili flakes. Coat the cubed tofu into the sauce mixture and let it marinate for 15 minutes. After this, preheat instant pot on Saute mode. When the instant pot is hot, place tofu inside and sprinkle with the remaining teriyaki sauce. Cook the meal for 2 minutes from each side. Transfer the cooked tofu in the serving bowls and let it chill till the room temperature.

Nutrition value/serving: calories 133, fat 8.3, fiber 1.4, carbs 4.7, protein 12.8

Broccoli Gnocchi
Prep time: 8 minutes | Cooking time: 18 minutes | Servings: 2

Ingredients:
- ¼ cup green beans, chopped
- ½ cup broccoli, chopped
- 1 cup gnocchi
- 2 cups of water
- 4 oz vegan Parmesan, grated
- ½ cup coconut cream
- 1 teaspoon dried dill
- 1 teaspoon salt

Directions:
Pour 1 cup of water in the instant pot. Add broccoli and green beans. Close and seal the lid. Set Manual mode (high pressure) and cook vegetables for 6 minutes. Then make quick pressure release and drain the water. Place vegetables in the bowl. After this, pour remaining water in the instant pot Add gnocchi and close the lid. Cook them on manual mode (high pressure) for 7 minutes. Then use quick pressure release. Drain water from gnocchi. Add cooked vegetables, dried dill, salt, and vegan Parmesan. Mix up the meal and close the lid. Cook it on Saute mode for 5 minutes.

Nutrition value/serving: calories 433, fat 14.9, fiber 4, carbs 40.7, protein 28.5

Hash Brown Omelette

Prep time: 10 minutes | Cooking time: 15 minutes | Servings: 2

Ingredients:
- 2 white potatoes, peeled, grated
- 1 tablespoon chives, chopped
- ½ teaspoon salt
- 1 tablespoon almond yogurt
- 1 teaspoon ground black pepper
- 1 teaspoon olive oil
- 1 teaspoon
- 1 onion, diced
- 1 sweet red pepper, diced

Directions:
Preheat instant pot on saute mode. Add coconut oil and melt it. Then add diced onion and sweet pepper. Sprinkle the ingredients with ground black pepper and salt. Mix up and cook for 5 minutes. Stir them from time to time. After this, transfer the cooked mixture in the bowl. Add olive oil in the instant pot. Place ½ part of grated potato into the instant pot and flatten it to make the potato layer. After this, place onion mixture over the potato, add chives. Cover it with the remaining grated potato. Close the lid and cook the omelet on saute mode for 4 minutes. Then flip the omelet carefully onto another side and cook for 4 minutes more. When the hash brown omelet is cooked, transfer it onto the serving plate. The meal should be served warm.

Nutrition value/serving: calories 236, fat 5.3, fiber 7.5, carbs 44.4, protein 5.1

Mushroom "Pulled Pork"

Prep time: 10 minutes | Cooking time: 10 minutes | Servings: 5

Ingredients:
- 3-pound Trumpet mushrooms
- 2 tablespoons BBQ sauce
- ½ cup tomato sauce
- 1 onion, diced
- 1 jalapeno pepper, diced
- 1 teaspoon olive oil
- ¼ cup of water

Directions:
Wash and trim mushrooms. Then shred them with the help of the fork or knife. In the instant pot, combine together olive oil, jalapeno pepper, and diced onion. Cook the vegetables on Saute mode for 5 minutes. After this, add shredded mushrooms, BBQ sauce, tomato sauce, and water. Mix up the mixture well. Close and seal the lid. Cook "pulled pork' mushrooms for 5 minutes on manual mode (high pressure). Then allow natural pressure release for 5 minutes more. Open the lid, mix up the meal well and transfer into the serving bowl.

Nutrition value/serving: calories 57, fat 1.6, fiber 6.1, carbs 15.3, protein 4.1

Chipotle Fajitas

Prep time: 10 minutes | *Cooking time:* 15 minutes | *Servings:* 4

Ingredients:

- 2 cups cauliflower florets
- 4 bell peppers
- 1 cup red kidney beans, canned
- 1 teaspoon tomato paste
- ½ teaspoon chili flakes
- 1 chipotle, chopped
- ½ cup cilantro, chopped
- 2 tablespoons lemon juice
- 1 tablespoon coconut oil
- 1 teaspoon salt
- 1 teaspoon taco seasoning
- 4 corn tortillas

Directions:

Melt coconut oil in the instant pot on Saute mode. Cut bell peppers into wedges. Add cauliflower florets and pepper wedges into the instant pot. Sprinkle them with chili flakes, tomato paste, lemon juice, salt, and taco seasoning. Add chipotle and mix up carefully. Close the lid and the ingredients on Saute mode for 10 minutes. Stir the mixture from time to time. Then transfer the cooked mixture on the corn tortillas, add red kidney beans, and chopped cilantro. Transfer fajitas on the serving plates.

Nutrition value/serving: calories 294, fat 5, fiber 11.6, carbs 51.7, protein 14.2

Bibimbap

Prep time: 15 minutes | *Cooking time:* 20 minutes | *Servings:* 2

Ingredients:

- 10 oz firm tofu, cubed
- 1 teaspoon chili paste
- 3 tablespoons soy sauce
- 1/3 cup shiitake mushrooms, chopped
- 1 teaspoon olive oil
- ¼ cup edamame beans, boiled
- ½ cup spinach, chopped
- ½ carrot, grated
- ½ cup of rice, cooked
- 1 teaspoon chives, chopped
- 1 cucumber, sliced

Directions:

Mix up together chili paste, soy sauce, olive oil, and chives in the mixing bowl. Add cubed tofu and mix up. Let it for 10 minutes to marinate. Then place tofu and all marinade in the instant pot. Add shiitake mushrooms, edamame beans, and grated carrot. Saute the mixture for 10 minutes. Stir from time to time. Add spinach, and mix up well. Cook it for 10 minutes more. Then place rice into the serving bowls. Add cooked tofu mixture, chives, and sliced cucumber. Serve the meal warm.

Nutrition value/serving: calories 302, fat 9.6, fiber 4.5, carbs 39.6, protein 18.3

Mushroom Bourguignon

Prep time: 10 minutes | *Cooking time:* 35 minutes | *Servings:* 3

Ingredients:
- ½ cup red wine
- 2 cups mushrooms, chopped
- 1 carrot, chopped
- 1 tablespoon tomato paste
- 1 tablespoon Italian seasoning
- 1 cup vegetable stock
- ½ teaspoon salt
- ¼ teaspoon dried rosemary
- 1 tablespoon olive oil
- 1 onion, chopped
- 1 tablespoon cornstarch

Directions:

In the instant pot, combine together mushrooms, olive oil, dried rosemary, salt, and Italian seasoning. Cook the mixture on Saute mode for 10 minutes. Stir it from time to time. After this, mix up together cornstarch with tomato paste and vegetable stock. Add the liquid into the instant pot. Then add red wine, carrot, and onion. Mix up the ingredients carefully. Close and lid and cook on Saute mode for 25 minutes. When the time is over, mix up the cooked meal well and transfer into the serving bowls.

Nutrition value/serving: calories 138, fat 7, fiber 2, carbs 12.7, protein 2.3

Vegetable Gnocchi

Prep time: 10 minutes | *Cooking time:* 18 minutes | *Servings:* 4

Ingredients:
- 1 ½ cup gnocchi
- 1 tablespoon fresh dill, chopped
- 1 zucchini, diced
- 1 teaspoon salt
- ½ cup almond milk
- ½ teaspoon chili flakes
- ½ teaspoon ground black pepper
- 1 teaspoon olive oil
- 1 cup of water

Directions:

Pour water in the instant pot. Add gnocchi, close and seal the lid. Set Manual mode (high pressure) and cook it for 8 minutes. Make a quick pressure release. Drain water and transfer gnocchi into the bowl. Pour olive oil in the instant pot. Add zucchini, salt, dill, chili flakes, and ground black pepper. Cook vegetables on Saute mode for 5 minutes. Stir them from time to time. Then add gnocchi and almond milk. Mix up the mixture well. Close the lid and saute it for 5 minutes. When the time is over, mix up the cooked meal well and transfer onto serving plates.

Nutrition value/serving: calories 153, fat 8.8, fiber 2.5, carbs 17, protein 3

Cashew Cheese

Prep time: 10 minutes | Cooking time: 4 minutes | Servings: 3

Ingredients:
- 1 cup cashew
- 1 cup of water
- 1 tablespoon lemon juice
- ½ teaspoon lime zest
- ½ teaspoon nutritional yeast
- ½ teaspoon minced garlic
- 1 teaspoon ground black pepper
- ½ teaspoon salt

Directions:
Pour water in the instant pot. Add cashews, close and seal the lid. Cook cashews on Manual mode (high pressure) for 4 minutes. Use quick pressure release. Transfer warm water and cashews in the food processor. Add lemon juice, lime zest, nutritional yeast, minced garlic, ground black pepper, and salt in the food processor. Blend the mixture until you get smooth and soft cheese texture. Place the cooked cheese into the plastic vessel and store it in the fridge up to 5 days.

Nutrition value/serving: calories 268, fat 21.3, fiber 1.8, carbs 16, protein 7.4

Popcorn Cauliflower

Prep time: 10 minutes | Cooking time: 7minutes | Servings: 2

Ingredients:
- ½ cup cauliflower florets
- 1 teaspoon turmeric
- 1 teaspoon curry powder
- ¼ cup wheat flour
- 4 tablespoons coconut cream
- 1 teaspoon salt
- 1 teaspoon chili flakes
- 1 tablespoon bread crumbs
- 1 cup water, for cooking

Directions:
In the mixing bowl combine together turmeric, curry powder, wheat flour, coconut cream, salt, and chili flakes. Whisk the mixture well. Then add cauliflower florets and shake. When all the cauliflower florets are coated, sprinkle them with the bread crumbs. Pour water in the instant pot and insert rack. Place cauliflower florets into the instant pot pan. Transfer the pan on the rack. Close and seal the lid. Cook cauliflower popcorn for 7 minutes on manual mode (high pressure) When the time is over, use quick pressure release. Open the lid and chill the meal till the room temperature.

Nutrition value/serving: calories 153, fat 7.8, fiber 2.4, carbs 18.7, protein 3.5

Lentil Steak

Prep time: 10 minutes | Cooking time: 8 minutes | Servings: 2

Ingredients:
- 1 cup lentils, cooked
- ½ cup bread crumbs
- 3 tablespoons wheat flour
- 1 teaspoon salt
- ½ teaspoon chili pepper
- 1 teaspoon dried oregano
- 1 tablespoon olive oil

Directions:
Place lentils into the mixing bowl and mash them with the help of the fork. After this, add wheat flour, salt, chili pepper, and dried oregano. Mix up the mixture until homogenous. With the help of the fingertips make 2 balls and press them to make steak shape. Preheat instant pot on saute mode. Then add olive oil. Coat lentil steaks in bread crumbs. Put the steaks in the preheated olive oil. Cook them for 3 minutes from each side or until they are light brown.

Nutrition value/serving: calories 551, fat 9.7, fiber 31.2, carbs 86.7, protein 29.7

Ravioli

Prep time: 15 minutes | Cooking time: 10 minutes | Servings: 6

Ingredients:
- 1 cup pumpkin puree
- 3 oz vegan Parmesan, grated
- 1 tablespoon fresh parsley, chopped
- ½ teaspoon ground black pepper
- ½ teaspoon salt
- 1 cup wheat flour
- ¼ cup of water
- 5 tablespoons aquafaba
- 1 cup water, for cooking

Directions:
Make the ravioli filling: in the mixing bowl mix up together pumpkin puree, grated Parmesan, chopped parsley, ground black pepper, and salt. Make ravioli dough: mix up together ¼ cup of water, wheat flour, and aquafaba. Knead soft but mom-sticky dough. Roll up the dough with the help of the rolling pin. Then make the ravioli bags with the help of the cutter. Fill the ravioli bags with pumpkin puree filling and secure the edges. Pour 1 cup of water in the instant pot. Add ravioli. Set Saute mode and cook ravioli until they start to boil (approximately for 6-7 minutes). Then close and seal the lid and set Manual mode. Cook ravioli for 3 minutes more. After this, make quick pressure release. Drain water and transfer ravioli into the serving bowls.

Nutrition value/serving: calories 134, fat 0.3, fiber 1.8, carbs 22.3, protein 8.4

Vegan Pepperoni

Prep time: 15 minutes | Cooking time: 5 minutes | Servings: 4

Ingredients:

- ½ cup wheat flour
- 1 teaspoon salt
- 1 teaspoon paprika
- ½ teaspoon ground cardamom
- 1 teaspoon ground black pepper
- 1 tablespoon tomato paste
- 1 teaspoon soy sauce
- 1 teaspoon olive oil
- 3 tablespoons water
- 1 tablespoon nutritional yeast
- 1 cup water, for cooking

Directions:

In the mixing bowl mix up together all the dry ingredients. Then add tomato paste, soy sauce, water, and mix it. When the mixture is homogenous, add olive and knead it Make the log from the pepperoni dough and wrap it into the foil and parchment. Pour 1 cup of water in the instant pot. Insert rack and place pepperoni log on it/ Close and seal the lid. Set high-pressure mode (manual) and cook it for 5 minutes. Then allow natural pressure release. Open the instant pot lid, discard foil/parchment from the pepperoni log, slice it and transfer on the serving plate.

Nutrition value/serving: calories 83, fat 1.6, fiber 1.6, carbs 14.8, protein 3.2

Vegan Sausages

Prep time: 10 minutes | Cooking time: 6 minutes | Servings: 2

Ingredients:

- 1 teaspoon olive oil
- 1 small onion, chopped
- ¼ teaspoon garlic, diced
- ½ cup chickpeas, cooked
- 1 teaspoon tomato paste
- 1 teaspoon ground cumin
- ½ teaspoon salt
- 1 teaspoon dried parsley
- ¼ teaspoon ground black pepper
- 4 tablespoons oatmeal flour

Directions:

In the food processor, combine together chopped onion, garlic, chickpeas, tomato paste, ground cumin, salt, dried parsley, ground black pepper, and oatmeal flour. Process the mixture until smooth. Then transfer it into the mixing bowl. Preheat instant pot on saute mode. Meanwhile, make the medium size sausages from the chickpea mixture. Pour olive oil in the hot instant pot. Then add prepared sausages and saute them for 2-3 minutes from each side. The cooked sausages should have a light brown color.

Nutrition value/serving: calories 254, fat 6.2, fiber 10.7, carbs 40, protein 11.8

Deli Slices
Prep time: 25 minutes | Cooking time: 17 minutes | Servings: 6

Ingredients:
- 4 oz vegetable stock
- 1 teaspoon tomato paste
- 5 oz firm tofu, chopped
- 7 tablespoons flour
- 2 tablespoons nutritional yeast
- ½ teaspoon minced garlic
- 1 teaspoon paprika
- ½ teaspoon white pepper
- 1 teaspoon coconut oil
- 1 cup water, for cooking

Directions:

In the blender combine together tomato paste, firm tofu, nutritional yeast, minced garlic, paprika, vegetable stock, white pepper, and coconut oil. Blend the mixture until smooth. After this, place flour in the mixing bowl. Add blended mixture. Mix up the mass. Wrap the mass into the foil and make the shape of the log. Pour water in the instant pot. Insert steamer rack. Place wrapped log on the steamer. Close and seal the lid. Set Steam mode and cook the meal for 7 minutes. Use natural pressure release for 10 minutes. Discard the foil from the log and chill it for at least 30 minutes. Slice it.

Nutrition value/serving: calories 72, fat 2.1, fiber 1.6, carbs 9.6, protein 4.6

Mushroom Pie
Prep time: 30 minutes | Cooking time: 30 minutes | Servings: 4

Ingredients:
- 2 cups mushrooms, chopped
- 2 white onions, chopped
- 1 tablespoon coconut oil
- 1 teaspoon salt
- 1 teaspoon ground black pepper
- ½ teaspoon sesame seeds
- 1 teaspoon olive oil
- 7 oz puff pastry
- ½ cup water, for cooking

Directions:

Place mushrooms, onions, and coconut oil in the instant pot. Add ground black pepper and salt. Mix up the ingredients and cook them on Saute mode for 15 minutes. Stir them from time to time. After this, transfer the mushroom mixture in the bowl. Clean the instant pot. Pour water inside. Take the non-sticky instant pot springform pan. Cut puff pastry into halves. Roll up the dough halves. Place 1 puff pastry half in the springform pan, add mushroom mixture, and cover it with the second half of puff pastry. Secure the edges with the fork. Brush the surface of the pie with olive oil and sprinkle with sesame seeds. Cover the pie with the foil and pin small holes. Set steamer rack in the instant pot. Place the pan on the rack. Close and seal the lid. Set manual mode (high pressure) and cook pie for 15 minutes. Allow natural pressure release for 10 minutes. Open the lid, remove the pan with pie from it, discard foil. Transfer the pie on the serving plate and cut it into the slices.

Nutrition value/serving: calories 346, fat 23.8, fiber 2.5, carbs 29.1, protein 5.5

Stuffed Spinach Shells

Prep time: 10 minutes | *Cooking time:* 14 minutes | *Servings:* 2

Ingredients:
- 1 cup pasta shells
- ½ cup tomato sauce
- 2 cup spinach
- 4 oz vegan Parmesan, grated
- 1 teaspoon minced garlic
- ½ teaspoon ground black pepper
- 1 tablespoon olive oil
- ½ onion, diced
- ½ cup of water

Directions:
Pour olive oil in the instant pot. Add diced onion and tomato sauce. Then add water and mix the mixture up. Set Saute mode and it for 5 minutes. Stir it from time to time. Meanwhile, chop the spinach and mix it up with minced garlic, ground black pepper, and grated Parmesan. Fill the pasta shells with the spinach mixture. Transfer the filled pasta shells in the instant pot. Close and seal the lid. Set Manual mode (high pressure) and cook the meal for 9 minutes. Then use quick pressure release. Chill the cooked meal little before serving.

Nutrition value/serving: calories 620, fat 9.3, fiber 4.3, carbs 94.3, protein 33.3

Pumpkin Risotto

Prep time: 10 minutes | *Cooking time:* 12 minutes | *Servings:* 2

Ingredients:
- 1 cup white rice
- 6 tablespoons pumpkin puree
- ½ teaspoon sage
- ½ white onion, diced
- ¼ teaspoon garlic, diced
- 2 cups of water
- 1 teaspoon salt
- 1 teaspoon ground black pepper
- ½ teaspoon paprika
- 1 tablespoon coconut oil

Directions:
Place coconut oil in the instant pot and melt it on Saute mode. Add white rice, sage, salt, and ground black pepper. Saute the rice for 3 minutes. Stir it from time to time. After this, add pumpkin puree, diced onion, garlic, paprika, and water. Mix it gently and close the lid. Set Manual mode (high pressure) and cook risotto for 9 minutes. Then use quick pressure release. Open the lid and mix up the meal carefully.

Nutrition value/serving: calories 428, fat 7.7, fiber 3.7, carbs 81.4, protein 7.6

Strudel

Prep time: 10 minutes | *Cooking time:* 40 minutes | *Servings:* 4

Ingredients:
- 1 cup mushrooms, chopped
- 1 onion, diced
- 1 teaspoon olive oil
- 1 teaspoon ground black pepper
- 1 teaspoon salt
- 7 oz puff pastry, vegan
- ½ cup water, for cooking

Directions:

On the saute mode, cook together for 10 minutes mushrooms, diced onion, olive oil, salt, and ground black pepper. Mix up the mixture from time to time. Meanwhile, roll up the vegan puff pastry with the help of the rolling pin. Transfer the cooked mushroom mixture over the puff pastry and roll it. Secure the edges of the roll and make the shape of strudel. Pin the strudel with the help of a knife. hen pour water in the instant pot. Place strudel in the non-stick instant pot pan and transfer it in the instant pot. You can use a trivet for instant pot too. Close and seal the lid. Cook the strudel on High pressure (manual mode) for 30 minutes. Then use quick pressure release. Chill the strudel till the room temperature and slice it.

Nutrition value/serving: calories 299, fat 20.2, fiber 1.7, carbs 25.9, protein 4.5

Tempeh Ribs

Prep time: 10 minutes | *Cooking time:* 6 minutes | *Servings:* 4

Ingredients:
- 15 oz tempeh
- 1 teaspoon ground black pepper
- 1 teaspoon paprika
- 1 teaspoon turmeric
- 1 teaspoon chili flaked
- 1 teaspoon salt
- ½ teaspoon sugar
- ½ teaspoon garlic powder
- ½ teaspoon onion powder
- 2 tablespoons BBQ sauce
- 1 tablespoon lemon juice
- 1 teaspoon olive oil
- 1 tablespoon chives, for garnish

Directions:

Cut tempeh into the wedges. In the mixing bowl, mix up together paprika, ground black pepper, turmeric, chili flakes, salt, sugar, garlic powder, onion powder, BBQ sauce, and lemon juice. Then rub tempeh wedges with the spice mixture generously. Preheat instant pot on Saute mode. When it is hot, add olive oil and tempeh wedges. Cook them for 3 minutes from each side. The cooked meal should have a light brown color. Then transfer the cooked tempeh ribs onto the serving plate and sprinkle with chives.

Nutrition value/serving: calories 237, fat 12.9, fiber 0.6, carbs 14.9, protein 20

Rainbow Vegetable Pie

Prep time: 15 minutes | Cooking time: 30 minutes | Servings: 6

Ingredients:
- ¼ cup olive oil
- 1 cup wheat flour
- ¼ cup of water
- 1 teaspoon salt
- 1 zucchini, sliced
- 1 tomato, sliced
- 1 red onion, sliced
- 1 carrot, sliced
- 1 teaspoon coconut oil
- 1 teaspoon ground black pepper
- 1 teaspoon paprika
- 1 teaspoon Italian seasoning
- 1 cup water, for cooking

Directions:
Make the dough: mix up together water, oil, and wheat flour. Add salt and knead the non-sticky, soft dough. Cut the dough into 2 parts. Roll up the fist dough part and place it in the pie pan. Then place all vegetables one by one to make the rainbow circle. Sprinkle the pie with coconut oil, ground black pepper, paprika, and Italian seasoning. Roll up the remaining dough and cover vegetables with it. Secure the edges of the pie with the help of the fork. Pour water in the instant pot and insert trivet. Cover the pie with foil and transfer on the trivet. Close and seal the lid. Cook pie for 30 minutes on Manual mode. Then use quick pressure release. Discard foil from the pie and let it chill for 10 minutes. Then transfer pie on the serving plate and slice.

Nutrition value/serving: calories 177, fat 9.8, fiber 1.9, carbs 20.6, protein 3

Stuffed Mini Pumpkins

Prep time: 30 minutes | Cooking time: 60 minutes | Servings: 4

Ingredients:
- 2 mini pumpkin squash, trimmed, cleaned from flesh and seeds
- ½ cup chickpeas, canned
- 1 teaspoon tomato paste
- 1 cup of rice, cooked
- ½ cup fresh parsley, chopped
- 2 tablespoons almond yogurt
- 1 teaspoon chili flakes
- 1 teaspoon salt
- 1 teaspoon peanuts, chopped
- 1 teaspoon olive oil

Directions:
In the mixing bowl combine together tomato paste and almond yogurt. Whisk the mixture. Add chili flakes, salt, peanuts, rice, parsley, and chickpeas. Mix up the mixture well. Fill the pumpkins with rice mixture. Add olive oil and wrap them into the foil. Place the mini pumpkins in the instant pot. Close and seal the lid. Set Manual mode (high pressure) and cook a meal for 60 minutes. Then allow natural pressure release for 20 minutes more. Open the lid, discard foil from the pumpkins and transfer meal on the serving plates.

Nutrition value/serving: calories 511, fat 4.1, fiber 6.3, carbs 41.7, protein 10.8

Nut Loaf
Prep time: 15 minutes | Cooking time: 20 minutes | Servings: 8

Ingredients:
- 1 teaspoon coconut oil
- 1 teaspoon avocado oil
- 3 oz yellow onion, diced
- 3 oz celery stalk, chopped
- 1 teaspoon garlic, diced
- 1 cup mushrooms, chopped
- ½ jalapeno pepper, chopped
- 3 oz carrot, grated
- 1 cup walnuts, chopped
- ½ cup lentils, cooked
- 1 teaspoon salt
- 1 teaspoon flax meal
- 2 tablespoons water
- ½ cup wheat flour
- 1 tablespoon Italian seasoning
- 1 cup water, for cooking

Directions:
Preheat instant po t on saute mode. When it is hot, add avocado oil, diced onion, and mushrooms. Cook the vegetables for 5 minutes, stir them from time to time. Then add a chopped celery stalk and mix up. Cook the mixture for 5 minutes more. Transfer the cooked vegetables into the mixing bowl. Add coconut oil, jalapeno pepper, grated carrot, walnuts, lentils, salt, and flour. Mix it up. In the separated bowl, mix up together flax meal and 2 tablespoons of water. The egg substitutor is cooked. Add the flax meal mixture into the lentils mixture. Then add Italian seasoning and mix up carefully. In the end, you should get soft but a homogenous mixture. Add more wheat flour if needed. Place the loaf mixture in the boiling bag and seal it. Pour water in the instant pot. Add sealed loaf. Close and seal the instant pot lid. Set Manual mode (high pressure) and cook loaf for 6 minutes. Then allow natural pressure release for 10 minutes more. Remove the boiling bag from the instant pot and take loaf. Chill the loaf for 1-2 hours and only after this, slice it.

Nutrition value/serving: calories 193, fat 9.8, fiber 5.8, carbs 17.8, protein 8.3

Fragrant Spring Onions
Prep time: 15 minutes | Cooking time: 5 minutes | Servings: 4

Ingredients:
- 1-pound spring onions
- 1 tablespoon avocado oil
- ½ teaspoon ground cumin
- 1 teaspoon dried cilantro
- ½ teaspoon salt
- 1 tablespoon lemon juice

Directions:
Wash and trim the spring onions. Then cut them lengthwise. Sprinkle them with the dried cilantro, cumin, salt, and lemon juice. Shake well and leave for 10 minutes to marinate. Meanwhile, preheat instant pot on saute mode until hot. Add avocado oil. After this, add spring onions and cook them on Saute mode for 2 minutes from each side. Then sprinkle the vegetables with remaining lemon juice marinade and cook for 1 minute more. The spring onions are cooked when the tender but not soft.

Nutrition value/serving: calories 43, fat 0.8, fiber 3.2, carbs 8.7, protein 2.2

Beet Steaks

Prep time: 10 minutes | Cooking time: 27 minutes | Servings: 2

Ingredients:
- 2 red beets, peeled
- 1 portobello mushroom, chopped
- 1 white onion, sliced
- 1 teaspoon thyme
- 1 teaspoon olive oil
- 2 tablespoons red wine

Directions:
Slice every beet onto 4 slices. Then sprinkle every beet slice with thyme. Preheat instant pot well and pour olive oil inside. Set Saute mode, add mushrooms and sliced onion. Saute the vegetables for 3 minutes. Stir them from time to time. Transfer the cooked vegetables into the mixing bowl. Then add sliced beets in the instant pot. Add red wine and close the lid. Saute the steaks for 15 minutes. After this, add mushrooms and onion. Mix up the ingredients gently. Close the lid and cook for 10 minutes more. When the time is over, switch off the instant pot and open the lid. Transfer the cooked beet steaks on the plates and top with the mushroom and wine sauce.

Nutrition value/serving: calories 110, fat 2.6, fiber 3.9, carbs 17.3, protein 3.9

Stuffed Figs

Prep time: 10 minutes | Cooking time: 20 minutes | Servings: 4

Ingredients:
- 4 figs
- ½ teaspoon brown sugar
- 3 tablespoons water
- ¼ teaspoon ground cinnamon
- 4 teaspoons cashew butter
- 1 pinch ground cardamom
- ½ cup water, for cooking

Directions:
Crosscut the figs and remove a small amount of fig flesh. Then mix up together cashew butter, ground cinnamon, and ground cardamom. Fill the figs with the cashew butter mixture. Then place them in the instant pot pan. Sprinkle the figs with water and sugar. Pour ½ cup of water in the instant pot and insert trivet. Place pan with figs on the trivet. Close and seal the lid. Set Manual mode (high pressure) and cook figs for 2 minutes. Then use quick pressure release. Open the lid and pour the figs with the sweet juice from them. The main dish should be served hot or warm.

Nutrition value/serving: calories 81, fat 2.8, fiber 2.1, carbs 14.1, protein 1.6

Snacks and Appetizers

Boiled Peanuts
Prep time: 15 minutes | Cooking time: 30 minutes | Servings: 8

Ingredients:
- 2 cups green peanuts in shells
- 2 cups of water
- 2 teaspoons salt
- 1 teaspoon cayenne pepper
- 1 teaspoon taco seasoning

Directions:
Place green peanuts, water, salt, cayenne pepper, and taco seasoning in the instant pot. Close the lid and set Manual mode (high pressure). Cook the peanuts for 30 minutes. When the time is over, allow natural pressure release for 10 minutes more. Drain water and transfer peanuts in the serving bowl.

Nutrition value/serving: calories 168, fat 10.6, fiber 0.1, carbs 11.1, protein 7.5

Tempeh Potato Wraps
Prep time: 10 minutes | Cooking time: 5 hours | Servings: 6

Ingredients:
- 1 potato, peeled, chopped
- 8 oz tempeh, chopped
- 1 teaspoon brown sugar
- 1 tablespoon apple cider vinegar
- 1 tablespoon of liquid smoked
- 2 tablespoons tamari
- ½ teaspoon ground black pepper
- 1 tablespoon coconut oil
- 1 cup of water
- 6 corn tortillas

Directions:
Place tempeh and chopped potato in the instant pot. Add brown sugar, apple cider vinegar, liquid smoke, tamari, ground black pepper, coconut oil, and water. Close the lid and set slow cook mode. Cook the mixture for 3 hours. Then open the lid, mix up the ingredients. Fill the tortillas with cooked tempeh mixture and wrap them.

Nutrition value/serving: calories 173, fat 7.1, fiber 2.2, carbs 20.2, protein 9.6

Tofu Wraps

Prep time: 15 minutes | *Cooking time:* 5 minutes | *Servings:* 6

Ingredients:
- 6 lettuce leaves
- 1 teaspoon chili pepper
- 1 tablespoon fish sauce
- 1 teaspoon brown sugar
- 3 tablespoons water
- ½ teaspoon salt
- 8 oz firm tofu, chopped
- 1 teaspoon mustard
- 1 teaspoon olive oil
- 1 oz fresh curly parsley, chopped

Directions:
Make the tofu sauce: whisk together chili pepper, fish sauce, brown sugar, water, salt, mustard, and olive oil. Then combine together tofu and sauce. Let it marinade for 10 minutes. Preheat the instant pot on Saute mode well. Place the tofu and all marinade inside; saute the ingredients for 5 minutes. Stir them from time to time. When the time is over, open the instant pot lid and let tofu chill till the room temperature. Fill the lettuce leaves with chopped parsley and tofu. Before serving, sprinkle tofu wraps with the remaining cooked marinade.

Nutrition value/serving: calories 41, fat 2.6, fiber 0.7, carbs 2, protein 3.6

Pumpkin Hummus

Prep time: 10 minutes | *Cooking time:* 45 minutes | *Servings:* 6

Ingredients:
- ½ cup pumpkin puree
- 1 ½ chickpea, soaked
- 2 teaspoon tahini
- 1 teaspoon harissa
- 4 tablespoons olive oil
- 1 garlic clove, peeled
- 5 cups of water

Directions:
Place chickpeas and water in the instant pot. Add garlic clove. Close and seal the lid. Set Manual mode (high pressure) and cook chickpeas for 25 minutes. When the time is over, allow natural pressure release for 20 minutes. Open the lid and drain the liquid. Transfer the cooked chickpeas and garlic clove in the food processor. Add pumpkin puree, tahini, harissa, and olive oil. Blend the mixture until smooth and homogenous. If the cooked hummus is not soft enough, add water from the cooked chickpeas. Store the cooked hummus in the fridge up to 3 days.

Nutrition value/serving: calories 212, fat 10.1, fiber 7.1, carbs 24.6, protein 7.7

Roasted Nuts
Prep time: 10 minutes | Cooking time: 15 minutes | Servings: 4

Ingredients:
- 1 cup pecans
- ¼ cup brown sugar
- 1 teaspoon vanilla extract
- ¼ teaspoon ground cardamom
- ½ teaspoon ground clove
- ¼ cup of water

Directions:
Mix up together pecans, brown sugar, vanilla extract, ground cinnamon, and ground clove. Shake the mixture well and transfer it into the instant pot. Set Saute mode and cook pecans for 5 minutes. Stir them constantly. Then add water and mix up carefully. Set manual mode and close the lid. Cook pecans for 8 minutes. Then use quick pressure release. Meanwhile, preheat oven to 365F. Line the tray with baking paper. Drain the water from pecans and transfer nuts on the tray. Place them in the preheated oven and cook for 2-3 minutes. Chill the pecans and store them in the paper bags.

Nutrition value/serving: calories 57, fat 2, fiber 0.3, carbs 9.6, protein 0.4

Spicy Edamame Snack
Prep time: 10 minutes | Cooking time: 11 minutes | Servings: 6

Ingredients:
- 1 cup edamame beans
- 1 teaspoon minced garlic
- 1 tablespoon almond butter
- ½ teaspoon cayenne pepper
- 1 tablespoon sesame seeds
- ¼ cup of soy sauce
- ¼ teaspoon salt
- ½ teaspoon brown sugar
- 1 cup water, for cooking

Directions:
Pour water in the instant pot. Add edamame beans and salt. Close and seal the lid. Set Manual mode and cook beans for 6 minutes. Then use quick pressure release. Meanwhile, mix up together minced garlic, cayenne pepper, sesame seeds. brown sugar, and soy sauce. Transfer cooked edamame beans in the bowl. Toss almond butter in the instant pot and melt it on Saute mode. Add soy sauce mixture and bring to boil it (approximately 5 minutes). Then open the lid and chill the sauce to room temperature. Pour the sauce over the edamame beans and mix up well.

Nutrition value/serving: calories 89, fat 4.3, fiber 2.6, carbs 7.5, protein 5.6

Vegan Nuggets
Prep time: 10 minutes | Cooking time: 6 minutes | Servings: 8

Ingredients:
- ½ cup panko bread crumbs
- 1 tablespoon turmeric
- 4 oz rolled oats
- 1 onion, diced
- 1 tablespoon olive oil
- ½ teaspoon black pepper
- 1 teaspoon salt
- 1 tablespoon coconut milk
- 1 cup chickpeas, canned
- 1 tablespoon tomato sauce
- ½ cup water for cooking

Directions:
Preheat instant pot on Saute mode. When it is hot, add olive oil and diced onion. Cook it for 3-4 minutes, stir from time to time. When the onion is soft, transfer it in the food processor. Add rolled oats, ground black pepper, salt, coconut milk, canned chickpeas, and tomato sauce. Blend the mixture until smooth. In the separated bowl, mix up together turmeric and panko bread crumbs. Make the medium size nuggets from the chickpea mixture. Then coat nuggets in the panko bread mixture. Pour water in the instant pot and insert rack. Place instant pot pan on the rack and put nuggets inside it. Close and seal the lid. Set manual mode (high pressure) and cook "nuggets" for 3 minutes. Then use quick pressure release. Chill the cooked snack till the room temperature.

Nutrition value/serving: calories 200, fat 5.1, fiber 6.7, carbs 31.7, protein 7.9

Crunchwrap Supreme
Prep time: 15 minutes | Cooking time: 10 minutes | Servings: 4

Ingredients:
- 5 oz tofu, chopped
- 1 tablespoon olive oil
- 1 teaspoon taco seasoning
- 1 tablespoon salsa sauce
- 2 tablespoons queso sauce
- 4 burrito size tortillas
- 1/3 cup tortilla chips
- ½ cup black beans, canned
- 1 avocado, peeled, cored
- 1 tomato, chopped
- 1 teaspoon coconut oil

Directions:
Pour olive oil in the instant pot and preheat it on Saute mode. Add chopped tofu and sprinkle it with taco seasoning. Cook it on saute mode for 2 minutes. Stir it. Then mash the avocado. Spread the burrito tortillas with mashed avocado. After this, add salsa sauce, cooked tofu, chopped tomatoes, and black beans. Repeat the same steps with all burrito tortillas. Place tortilla chips on the top of black beans and wrap burrito tortillas. Toss coconut oil in the instant pot, melt it on Saute mode and add wrapped burrito tortillas. Cook them for 3 minutes from each side.

Nutrition value/serving: calories 518, fat 26.1, fiber 9.6, carbs 58.4, protein 14.4

Spring Rolls
Prep time: 15 minutes | Cooking time: 4 minutes | Servings: 6

Ingredients:
- ¼ cup red cabbage, shredded
- 2 oz fresh parsley, chopped
- 1 cup mushrooms, chopped
- 1 carrot, cut into wedges
- 1 tablespoon fish sauce
- 1 teaspoon paprika
- 1 tablespoon lemon juice
- ¼ teaspoon lime zest
- ½ teaspoon chili flakes
- 6 spring roll wraps
- 1 cup water, for cooking

Directions:
In the mixing bowl, mix up together shredded red cabbage, fresh parsley, chopped mushrooms, carrot, fish sauce, paprika, lemon juice, lime zest, and chili flakes. Fill the spring roll wraps with cabbage mixture. Wrap the spring roll wraps. Pour water in the instant pot, insert steamer rack inside. Place prepared spring rolls on the steamer rack. Close and seal the lid. Set Manual mode (high pressure) and cook the meal for 4 minutes. Then allow natural pressure release for 5 minutes.

Nutrition value/serving: calories 22, fat 0.2, fiber 1.9, carbs 4.5, protein 2

Delicious Lettuce Wraps
Prep time: 10 minutes | Cooking time: 4 minutes | Servings: 4

Ingredients:
- 4 lettuce leaves
- 3 oz vegan Parmesan, grated
- 1 cucumber, chopped
- 1 tablespoon chives, chopped
- 8 oz tempeh, chopped
- 1 tablespoon Italian seasoning
- 3 tablespoons tomato sauce
- ¼ cup tomato juice
- 1 teaspoon brown sugar
- 1/3 cup turnip, chopped

Directions:
In the instant pot, combine together chopped tempeh, Italian seasoning, tomato sauce, tomato juice, brown sugar, and turnip. Mix up the mixture, close and seal the instant pot lid. Cook it on Manual for 4 minutes; use quick pressure release. After this, mix up together grated Parmesan chopped cucumber, and chives. Place the mixture on the lettuce leaves. Chill the tempeh mixture till the room temperature. Transfer it over the vegetables and wrap the lettuce leaves.

Nutrition value/serving: calories 209, fat 7.3, fiber 0.9, carbs 15.7, protein 20.1

Garlic Toasts

Prep time: 5 minutes | *Cooking time:* 2 minutes | *Servings:* 4

Ingredients:
- 4 grey bread slices
- 1 tablespoon minced garlic
- 1 tablespoon olive oil

Directions:
Preheat instant pot. When it is hot, add olive oil. Then add bread slices and cook them on Saute mode for 1 minute from each side. Remove the bread slices from the instant pot and rub with minced garlic from each side. Serve the toasts warm.

Nutrition value/serving: calories 153, fat 8, fiber 0, carbs 17.7, protein 3.1

Quinoa Sandwich

Prep time: 10 minutes | *Cooking time:* 5 minutes | *Servings:* 2

Ingredients:
- 4 bread slices
- ¼ cup quinoa
- ½ cup of water
- 1 teaspoon salt
- 1 tablespoon vegan mayonnaise
- ½ teaspoon paprika
- 1 oz micro greens

Directions:
Place water, salt, and quinoa in the instant pot. Close and seal the lid. Set manual mode and cook quinoa for 5 minutes. Then allow natural pressure release. Open the lid and transfer it in the mixing bowl. Add paprika and vegan mayonnaise. Mix it up. Spread 2 bread slices with quinoa mixture. Add microgreens and cover with the remaining bread slices to get sandwiches.

Nutrition value/serving: calories 148, fat 3.7, fiber 2.7, carbs 24.1, protein 5

Crispy Chickpea

Prep time: 10 minutes | *Cooking time:* 57 minutes | *Servings:* 4

Ingredients:
- 7 oz chickpeas
- 4 cups of water
- 1 teaspoon salt
- 1 tablespoon Taco seasoning
- 1 tablespoon olive oil
- 1 teaspoon ground black pepper

Directions:
Place chickpeas, salt, and water in the instant pot. Close and seal the lid. Cook the chickpeas on Manual mode (high pressure) for 50 minutes. Then use quick pressure release and open the lid. Drain water and dry the chickpeas with the help of the paper towel. Then add olive oil, Taco seasoning, and ground black pepper. Mix the mixture up. Cook it on Saute mode for 7 minutes. Stir it from time to time. Chill the cooked chickpeas little bit and transfer in the serving bowl.

Nutrition value/serving: calories 219, fat 6.5, fiber 8.8, carbs 31.9, protein 9.6

Turkish Vegan Borek

Prep time: 10 minutes | Cooking time: 16 minutes | Servings: 6

Ingredients:
- 3 cups spinach, chopped
- 1 tablespoon coconut oil
- 1 teaspoon salt
- 1 teaspoon ground black pepper
- 4 oz phyllo dough

Directions:
Place spinach, salt, and coconut oil in the instant pot. Cook the ingredients on Saute mode for 10 minutes. Stir them from time to time. Then transfer spinach on the phyllo dough and roll it. Place the rolled dough in the instant pot and cook it for 3 minutes from each side on Saute mode. The cooked borek should have a light brown color. When borek is cooked, cut it into the serving pieces.

Nutrition value/serving: calories 80, fat 3.5, fiber 0.8, carbs 10.7, protein 1.8

Vegan Jerky

Prep time: 20 minutes | Cooking time: 3 hours | Servings: 2

Ingredients:
- 5 oz tempeh, cut into wedges
- 1 teaspoon BBQ sauce
- 1 teaspoon soy sauce
- 1 teaspoon lemon juice
- 1 teaspoon chili pepper
- ½ teaspoon brown sugar
- 1 teaspoon olive oil

Directions:
Make the marinade: in the bowl whisk together BBQ sauce, soy sauce, lemon juice, chili pepper, brown sugar, and olive oil. Place tempeh wedges in the marinade and marinate them for 15 minutes. After this, dry the tempeh wedges with the help of the paper towel and transfer in the instant pot. Close the lid and cook jerky on slow cooker mode for 3 hours.

Nutrition value/serving: calories 167, fat 10, fiber 0.2, carbs 8.9, protein 13.4

Carrot "Dogs"

Prep time: 15 minutes | Cooking time: 4 minutes | Servings: 4

Ingredients:
- 4 hot dog buns
- 4 teaspoons mustard
- 4 teaspoon ketchup
- 4 carrots, peeled
- 1 tablespoon fish sauce
- 1 teaspoon liquid smoke
- 2 cups of water

Directions:
Pour water in the instant pot. Add carrots, fish sauce, and liquid smoke. Close and seal the lid. Cook carrots on Manual mode for 4 minutes. Then make quick pressure release. Open the lid and let carrots stay in liquid for at least 10 minutes. Then fill hot dog buns with carrots, add ketchup and mustard.

Nutrition value/serving: calories 187, fat 3, fiber 2, carbs 33.6, protein 4.6

Gyros

Prep time: 15 minutes | *Cooking time:* 15 minutes | *Servings:* 4

Ingredients:
- 1 cucumber, grated
- 6 oz firm tofu, chopped
- 2 tablespoons lime juice
- 1 teaspoon minced garlic
- 1 teaspoon rice vinegar
- 1 tablespoon dried dill
- 1 cup lettuce, chopped
- 1 red onion, sliced
- 4 pitas or corn tortillas
- 4 Portobello mushrooms
- 1 tablespoon olive oil
- 1 teaspoon ground black pepper
- ½ teaspoon chili pepper
- ½ teaspoon ground coriander
- 1 tablespoon liquid smoke

Directions:
Cut Portobello mushrooms into the wedges and sprinkle them with olive oil, ground black pepper, chili pepper, ground coriander, and liquid smoked. Transfer the mushrooms in the instant pot. Cook them on Saute mode for 15 minutes. Stir them from time to time. Meanwhile, put in the blender: tofu, cucumber, lime juice, minced garlic, rice vinegar, and dried dill. Blend the ingredients until you get a smooth mixture. Spread pitas with the smooth tofu mixture, add lettuce, and sliced red onion. When the mushrooms are cooked, transfer them over the red onion. Wrap pitas.

Nutrition value/serving: calories 275, fat 6.2, fiber 4.1, carbs 44.2, protein 13.1

Herbed Tomato

Prep time: 5 minutes | *Cooking time:* 20 minutes | *Servings:* 4

Ingredients:
- 4 tomatoes
- 1 oz fresh cilantro, chopped
- 3 garlic cloves, peeled
- 1 teaspoon ground black pepper
- ½ teaspoon salt
- 1 teaspoon oregano
- 1 tablespoon apple cider vinegar
- 1/3 cup water

Directions:
Cut tomatoes into the halves and place in the instant pot. Add fresh cilantro, garlic cloves, ground black pepper, salt, oregano, apple cider vinegar, and water. Close the lid and cook the meal on Saute mode for 20 minutes. Stir it from time to time. Chill the tomatoes to the room temperature and transfer into the serving bowl.

Nutrition value/serving: calories 30, fat 0.4, fiber 2, carbs 6.4, protein 1.5

Lentils Crackers

Prep time: 10 minutes | Cooking time: 10 minutes | Servings: 8

Ingredients:
- 1 cup green lentils, cooked
- ½ cup flax meal
- 1 teaspoon ground black pepper
- 1 teaspoon salt
- 1 teaspoon dried parsley
- 4 teaspoons coconut oil

Directions:
Blend lentils until you get the smooth mixture and transfer them in the mixing bowl. Add flax meal, ground black pepper, salt, dried parsley, and coconut oil. Mix it up and knead the non-sticky dough. Roll up the lentils dough with the help of the rolling pin. Then make medium size crackers from the dough. Use the cracker cutter for this step. Preheat instant pot on Saute mode. Place the layer of the crackers inside and cook them for 1.5-2 minutes from each side or until they start to be crunchy. Repeat the same step with all prepared crackers. Chill the crackers well and store them in the paper bags.

Nutrition value/serving: calories 135, fat 5, fiber 9.4, carbs 16.6, protein 7.7

Eggplant Rolls

Prep time: 10 minutes | Cooking time: 10 minutes | Servings: 4

Ingredients:
- 1 large eggplant, trimmed
- 1 tablespoon minced garlic
- ½ cup arugula, chopped
- 1 tablespoon olive oil
- 1 tablespoon vegan ricotta
- 1 tablespoon peanuts, chopped

Directions:
Cut eggplants lengthwise slices. Sprinkle them with salt if desired. Then preheat instant pot on Saute mode well. Add olive oil. Place eggplant slices in the instant pot and cook them for 2 minutes from each side. Meanwhile, mix up together vegan ricotta, peanuts, arugula, and minced garlic. Chill the eggplant slices well. Then spread them with ricotta mixture and roll. Secure rolls with the toothpicks.

Nutrition value/serving: calories 99, fat 6.8, fiber 4.4, carbs 9, protein 2.6

Mushroom Bruschetta

Prep time: 10 minutes | Cooking time: 15 minutes | Servings: 5

Ingredients:
- 5 bruschetta bread slices
- 1 cup mushrooms, sliced
- 1 yellow onion, sliced
- ½ cup coconut cream
- 1 teaspoon olive oil
- 1 teaspoon salt

Directions:
Place sliced onion and mushrooms in the instant pot. Add olive oil and salt. Cook the vegetables on Saute mode for 5 minutes. Mix them up from time to time. After this, add coconut cream. Mix up again and close the lid. Cook the mushroom mixture for 10 minutes on Saute mode. When the time is over, open the lid and chill the cooked meal little. Place mushrooms mixture over the bruschetta bread slices.

Nutrition value/serving: calories 255, fat 16.7, fiber 1.1, carbs 19.8, protein 6.2

BBQ Cauliflower Florets

Prep time: 15 minutes | Cooking time: 15 minutes | Servings: 2

Ingredients:
- 1 cup cauliflower florets
- 4 tablespoons BBQ sauce
- 1 teaspoon turmeric
- 1 teaspoon paprika
- 1 teaspoon cayenne pepper
- ¼ cup of water
- 1 teaspoon olive oil

Directions:
Place cauliflower florets in the bowl. Add BBQ sauce, turmeric, paprika, cayenne pepper, olive oil, and water. Carefully mix up the cauliflower and leave it for 5-10 minutes to marinate. Then transfer it in the instant pot, add all the remaining BBQ sauce mixture. Saute the cauliflower for 10-15 minutes or until it is cooked. Stir it time to time with the help of the wooden spatula. Chill the cooked snack till the room temperature and then transfer in the serving bowl or serve in the closed glass vessel in the fridge up to 2 days.

Nutrition value/serving: calories 89, fat 2.9, fiber 2.3, carbs 15.8, protein 1.3

Asparagus Pastries

Prep time: 15 minutes | Cooking time: 10 minutes | Servings: 8

Ingredients:
- 8 oz vegan puff pastry
- 11 oz asparagus
- 1 tablespoon olive oil
- ½ teaspoon salt
- 1 teaspoon dried oregano
- 1 cup water, for cooking

Directions:
Roll up the puff pastry with the help of the rolling pin. Then cut it into the strips. Mix up together salt, dried oregano, and olive oil. Spread the puff pastry strips with the oregano mixture. Then wrap the strips around the asparagus. Pour water in the instant pot. Insert steamer rack Line it with the baking paper. Place wrapped asparagus over it. Close and seal the lid. Set Manual mode (high pressure) and cook pastries for 10 minutes. Then use quick pressure release. Chill the cooked pastries well before serving.

Nutrition value/serving: calories 182, fat 12.7, fiber 1.3, carbs 14.6, protein 3

Cocktail Balls

Prep time: 10 minutes | Cooking time: 10 minutes | Servings: 4

Ingredients:
- 1 cup mashed potato
- ¼ cup panko bread crumbs
- 1 teaspoon salt
- 3 tablespoons flax meal
- 1 tablespoon fresh parsley, chopped
- ½ onion, grated
- 1 tablespoon avocado oil

Directions:
Mix up together mashed potato, panko bread crumbs, salt, flax meal, parsley, and grated onion. When you get a homogenous mixture, make medium size balls. Do it with the help of 2 spoons or fingertips. Preheat avocado oil in the instant pot. Add potato balls and roast them on Saute mode for 2 minutes from each side. Dry the cooked balls with the help of the paper towel and transfer on the serving plate. Put the toothpicks inside.

Nutrition value/serving: calories 119, fat 4.9, fiber 3.1, carbs 16.8, protein 3.3

Arugula Puffs

Prep time: 15 minutes | Cooking time: 4 minutes | Servings: 4

Ingredients:
- 7 oz phyllo dough
- 1 teaspoon olive oil
- 5 oz vegan Cheddar cheese, grated
- ½ cup arugula, chopped
- ½ teaspoon thyme

Directions:
Cut phyllo dough into 4 equal squares. Then in the center of every phyllo square put grated cheese, chopped arugula, and thyme. Wrap the phyllo squares in such a way to get the envelopes – arugula puffs. Pour olive oil in the instant pot. Preheat it well on Saute mode. Then place phyllo envelopes in the instant pot and cook them 3 minutes. After this, flip the meal onto another side and cook for 1 minute. Serve the arugula puffs warm.

Nutrition value/serving: calories 263, fat 10.5, fiber 2.6, carbs 33.2, protein 4.5

Beetroot Fold-Overs

Prep time: 15 minutes | Cooking time: 30 minutes | Servings: 6

Ingredients:
- 2 beetroots, trimmed
- 2 cups of water
- 6 oz vegan Parmesan, grated
- 1 teaspoon minced garlic
- 1 tablespoon scallions, chopped
- 1 tablespoon almond yogurt
- ¼ teaspoon smoked paprika
- 1/3 cup fresh parsley, chopped

Directions:
Place beetroots in the instant pot. Add water and close the lid. Cook beetroots on Manual mode (high pressure) for 30 minutes. Then allow natural pressure release for 10 minutes. Chill and peel the cooked beetroots. In the mixing bowl, mix up together grated Parmesan, minced garlic, scallions, almond yogurt, smoked paprika, and chopped parsley. Slice the beetroots. Fill the beetroot slices with the cheese mixture and fold over every slice.

Nutrition value/serving: calories 106, fat 0.2, fiber 0.9, carbs 9.8, protein 12.3

Sweet Apple Wedges

Prep time: 15 minutes | Cooking time: 5 minutes | Servings: 4

Ingredients:
- 3 apples
- ¼ cup maple syrup
- ½ teaspoon ground ginger
- ½ teaspoon ground cinnamon
- ½ teaspoon cardamom
- 1 tablespoon brown sugar
- 1 tablespoon coconut oil

Directions:
Cut the apples into the halves and remove seeds. Then cut the apples into 2 wedges more. Preheat instant pot and toss coconut oil inside. Add maple syrup, ground ginger, brown sugar, ground cinnamon, and ground cardamom. Stir the mixture until homogenous. Add apple wedges and coat them well. Saute the fruits for 3 minutes. Then switch off the instant pot and let apple wedges rest for at least 10 minutes before serving.

Nutrition value/serving: calories 179, fat 3.8, fiber 4.3, carbs 39.1, protein 0.5

Candied Pecans

Prep time: 5 minutes | Cooking time: 5 minutes | Servings: 5

Ingredients:
- 1 cup pecans
- ¼ cup of water
- ¾ cup maple syrup
- 1 teaspoon ground cinnamon
- 1 tablespoon brown sugar
- 3 tablespoons white sugar
- ¼ teaspoon salt

Directions:
Cut the pecans into halves. Then place them in the instant pot. Add maple syrup, ground cinnamon, and brown sugar. Mix up the pecans and cook them on Saute mode 3 minutes. Stir them constantly. When sugar is melted, switch off the instant pot. Add salt and white sugar. Mix up pecans well. Place the cooked pecans in the paper envelopes for snacks.

Nutrition value/serving: calories 359, fat 21.1, fiber 2.9, carbs 44.9, protein 2.7

Buffalo Brussels Sprouts

Prep time: 10 minutes | Cooking time: 10 minutes | Servings: 4

Ingredients:
- 1 cup Brussels sprouts
- 5 tablespoons vegan Buffalo sauce
- 1 teaspoon olive oil
- 1 cup water, for cooking

Directions:
Pour water in the instant pot. Add Brussels sprouts, close and seal the lid. Cook the vegetables on Manual mode (high pressure) for 4 minutes. Then use quick pressure release. Drain water. Pour olive oil in the instant pot. Add Buffalo sauce and mix up well. Cook Brussels sprouts on saute mode for 5 minutes. Stir them from time to time. Chill the cooked appetizer to the room temperature before serving.

Nutrition value/serving: calories 29, fat 1.3, fiber 1.6, carbs 3.5, protein 0.8

Mushroom Pate

Prep time: 10 minutes | Cooking time: 12 minutes | Servings: 6

Ingredients:
- 1 shallot, diced
- 2 cups mushrooms, chopped
- 2 tablespoons almond butter
- 1 tablespoon avocado oil
- 1 teaspoon ground black pepper
- ½ teaspoon chili pepper
- 1 teaspoon salt
- 1 cup water, for cooking

Directions:
Put mushrooms and pour water in the instant pot. Close and seal the lid. Cook mushrooms on manual mode for 8 minutes. Then use quick pressure release. Open the lid and drain water. Transfer the mushrooms in the food processor. After this, pour avocado oil in the instant pot. Preheat it on Saute mode. Add diced shallot, ground black pepper chili pepper, and salt. Saute shallot for 4 minutes or until it is light brown. Then transfer it in the food processor too. Add almond butter and blend the mixture well until you get soft pate. Transfer cooked pate in the serving bowl.

Nutrition value/serving: calories 44, fat 3.4, fiber 1, carbs 2.7, protein 2

Cardamom Pineapple Sticks

Prep time: 15 minutes | *Cooking time:* 5 minutes | *Servings:* 4

Ingredients:
- 1 teaspoon ground cardamom
- 10 oz pineapple, cut into the sticks
- 2 tablespoon lemon juice
- ½ teaspoon brown sugar
- 1 tablespoon water
- ¼ teaspoon lime zest

Directions:

In the mixing bowl, mix up together ground cardamom, lemon juice, brown sugar, water, and lime zest. Then place pineapple sticks in the cardamom liquid and coat well. Let them marinate for 10 minutes. Meanwhile, preheat the instant pot on Saute mode well. Place the pineapple sticks in the instant pot and roast them on Saute mode for 1.5 minutes from each side. Chill the cooked snack.

Nutrition value/serving: calories 40, fat 0.2, fiber 1.2, carbs 10.2, protein 0.5

Appetizer Quinoa Balls

Prep time: 15 minutes | *Cooking time:* 15 minutes | *Servings:* 6

Ingredients:
- 1 cup quinoa
- 3 tablespoons flax meal
- 1 teaspoon dried oregano
- ¼ cup onion, diced
- 1 teaspoon ground black pepper
- 2 tablespoons wheat flour
- ½ cup vegetable stock
- 1 teaspoon tomato paste
- 1 teaspoon salt
- ½ teaspoon chili flakes
- 1 cup of water

Directions:

Place quinoa and water in the instant pot. Close and seal the lid. Cook the quinoa on Manual mode for 5 minutes. Then use quick pressure release. Transfer the quinoa in the mixing bowl. Then place diced onion in the instant pot. Add dried oregano, salt, tomato paste, chili flakes. Saute the onions for 3 minutes. Mix up the onions and add them in the quinoa bowl. Add flax meal, wheat flour, and ground black pepper. Mix up the mixture. Make the medium size bowls from quinoa mixture. Then pour vegetable stock in the instant pot. Insert trivet. Place quinoa balls in the instant pot pan. Place the pan on the trivet. Close and seal the lid. Cook the quinoa balls for 5 minutes. Use quick pressure release. Place the meal on the serving plate and sprinkle with the small amount of vegetable stock.

Nutrition value/serving: calories 135, fat 3.4, fiber 3.4, carbs 22.5, protein 5.2

Tofu Strips

Prep time: 5 minutes | Cooking time: 5 minutes | Servings: 4

Ingredients:
- 9 oz firm tofu
- 1 teaspoon miso paste
- 1 teaspoon tahini paste
- ¼ cup of water
- 1 teaspoon soy sauce
- 1 tablespoon balsamic vinegar
- 1 teaspoon olive oil
- 1 tablespoon fresh parsley, chopped

Directions:
Cut firm tofu into strips. In the mixing bowl, mix up together miso paste, tahini paste, water, soy sauce, balsamic vinegar, and olive oil. Coat tofu strips into the miso paste mixture. Then preheat instant pot on Saute mode. Place tofu stick and cook them for 1 minute from each side. Transfer the tofu sticks on the serving plate and sprinkle with fresh parsley.

Nutrition value/serving: calories 67, fat 4.6, fiber 0.8, carbs 1.9, protein 5.7

Chickpea Slices

Prep time: 10 minutes | Cooking time: 60 minutes | Servings: 4

Ingredients:
- 4 flour tortillas
- ½ cup chickpeas, soaked
- 2 cups of water
- 1 teaspoon salt
- 1 tablespoon vegan mayonnaise
- 1 bell pepper, chopped

Directions:
Place tortillas and chickpeas in the instant pot. Close and seal the lid. Cook the chickpeas on Manual mode for 35 minutes. Use quick pressure release. Drain the water and transfer the chickpeas in the blender. Add salt, vegan mayonnaise, and bell pepper. Blend the mixture. Spread the flour tortillas with the blended chickpeas and roll them. Slice the tortillas into small pieces and secure with toothpicks.

Nutrition value/serving: calories 162, fat 3.1, fiber 6.3, carbs 28.4, protein 6.5

Crunchy Oyster Mushrooms

Prep time: 15 minutes | Cooking time: 15 minutes | Servings: 3

Ingredients:
- 7 oz oyster mushrooms
- 1 tablespoon olive oil
- 1 teaspoon chili flakes
- ¼ cup bread crumbs
- 1 teaspoon apple cider vinegar
- 1 cup water, for cooking

Directions:
Place oyster mushrooms in instant pot pan. Pour water in the instant pot and insert trivet. Place pan with oyster mushrooms on the trivet and close the lid. Seal the lid and cook mushrooms for 10 minutes. After this, use quick pressure release. Open the lid and drain water. Chop the oyster mushrooms roughly and sprinkle with olive oil, chili flakes, and apple cider vinegar. Mix up the mushrooms and let them for 10 minutes to marinate. Then preheat instant pot on Saute mode. Add oyster mushrooms and cook them for 4 minutes. Stir the vegetables and sprinkle with bread crumbs. Mix up the mushrooms well. Transfer them in the serving bowl.

Nutrition value/serving: calories 312, fat 5.2, fiber 7.5, carbs 44.3, protein 20.1

Jackfruit Coated Bites

Prep time: 15 minutes | Cooking time: 5 minutes | Servings: 4

Ingredients:
- 1 cup jackfruit, canned, drained
- ½ cup wheat flour
- 2 tablespoons soy sauce
- 2 tablespoons maple syrup
- 4 tablespoons agave syrup
- 1 teaspoon ground cumin
- ½ teaspoon salt
- 1 teaspoon paprika
- ½ teaspoon ground black pepper
- 1 teaspoon dried cilantro
- 1 teaspoon turmeric
- ½ cup olive oil

Directions:
In the mixing bowl, mix up together soy sauce, maple syrup, agave syrup, ground cumin, salt, and paprika. Whisk the mixture. Place canned jackfruit in the soy mixture and mix up well. Leave it for 10 minutes to marinate. Meanwhile, pour olive oil in the instant pot and preheat it on Saute mode. In the separated bowl, combine together wheat flour, ground black pepper, cilantro, and turmeric. Coat the jackfruit into the wheat mixture. Place the coated pieces of jackfruit in the hot olive oil and cook them for 1 minute from each side or until light brown. Dry the snack with the paper towel and transfer on the serving bowl.

Nutrition value/serving: calories 412, fat 257., fiber 1.,6 carbs 47, protein 3

Sofritas Tofu

Prep time: 5 minutes | *Cooking time:* 4 minutes | *Servings:* 4

Ingredients:
- 8 oz firm tofu, chopped
- ½ teaspoon cayenne pepper
- 1 teaspoon ground black pepper
- 1 teaspoon smoked paprika
- 1 teaspoon chili flakes
- ½ teaspoon salt
- ½ teaspoon brown sugar
- 1 tablespoon avocado oil
- 5 tablespoons vegan Adobo sauce

Directions:
Pour avocado oil in the instant pot. Add chopped tofu. Cook it on Saute mode for 1 minute. Sprinkle tofu with cayenne pepper, ground black pepper, smoked paprika, chili flakes, and salt. Mix up well and add sugar. Stir it carefully and cook for 2 minutes. Then add vegan Adobo sauce and mix up the meal well. Cook it for 2 minutes more. Transfer cooked sofritas tofu in the serving bowl.

Nutrition value/serving: calories 99, fat 2.9, fiber 1.1, carbs 13.6, protein 4.9

Garlic Pumpkin Seeds

Prep time: 5 minutes | *Cooking time:* 10 minutes | *Servings:* 6

Ingredients:
- 1 ½ cup pumpkin seeds
- 3 teaspoons garlic powder
- ½ teaspoon chipotle chili pepper
- 1 teaspoon salt
- 1 tablespoon olive oil

Directions:
Place pumpkin seeds in the instant pot. Set Saute mode and cook them for 5 minutes. Stir pumpkin seeds every 1 minute. After this, sprinkle the seeds with olive oil, chipotle chili pepper, salt, and garlic powder. Mix up well and cook for 4 minutes more. Then switch off the instant pot and let seeds rest for 1 minute.

Nutrition value/serving: calories 212, fat 18.2, fiber 1.6, carbs 7.3, protein 8.7

Flatbread

Prep time: 10 minutes | *Cooking time:* 5 minutes | *Servings:* 5

Ingredients:
- 1 cup wheat flour
- 1 teaspoon salt
- ¼ cup of water
- ¾ cup olive oil

Directions:
In the mixing bowl mix up together salt, water, and wheat flour. Add olive oil and knead the soft and non-sticky dough. Preheat instant pot on Saute mode well. Meanwhile, cut dough into 5 buns and roll them up to make rounds. Roast dough rounds in the instant pot for 1 minute from each side. Cover cooked flatbreads with the cloth towel till serving.

Nutrition value/serving: calories 350, fat 30.5, fiber 0.7, carbs 19.1, protein 2.6

Polenta Fries
Prep time: 15 minutes | Cooking time: 10 minutes | Servings: 10

Ingredients:
- 1 cup polenta
- 3 cups almond milk
- 1 teaspoon salt
- 1 teaspoon ground black pepper
- 1 teaspoon dried cilantro
- ½ teaspoon ground cumin
- 1 tablespoon almond butter
- 1 tablespoon olive oil

Directions:
Place polenta in the instant pot. Add almond milk and salt. Then add ground black pepper, dried cilantro, and ground cumin. Mix it up. Close and seal the lid. Cook polenta for 6 minutes on High-pressure mode. Allow natural pressure release for 10 minutes. Open the lid and add almond butter. Mix up it well. Transfer the polenta into the square pan and flatten well. Let it chill until solid. Then cut solid polenta onto 10 sticks. Brush every stick with the olive oil. Clean and preheat instant pot on Saute mode until hot. Then cook polenta sticks for 1 minute from each side or until light brown. Chill the snack before serving.

Nutrition value/serving: calories 244, fat 19.6, fiber 2.2, carbs 16.7, protein 3.2

Green Croquettes
Prep time: 15 minutes | Cooking time: 5 minutes | Servings: 4

Ingredients:
- 2 sweet potatoes, peeled, boiled
- 1 cup fresh spinach
- 1 tablespoons peanuts
- 3 tablespoons flax meal
- 1 teaspoon salt
- 1 teaspoon ground black pepper
- 1 tablespoon olive oil
- ½ teaspoon dried oregano
- ¾ cup wheat flour

Directions:
Mash the sweet potatoes and place them in the mixing bowl. Add flax meal salt, dried oregano, and ground black pepper. Then blend the spinach with peanuts until smooth. Add the green mixture in the sweet potato. Mix up the mass. Make medium size croquettes and coat them in the wheat flour. Preheat instant pot on Saute mode well. Add olive oil. Roast croquettes for 1 minute from each side or until golden brown. Dry the cooked croquettes with a paper towel if needed.

Nutrition value/serving: calories 155, fat 6.8, fiber 2.7, carbs 20.6, protein 4.4

Cigar Borek

Prep time: 10 minutes | Cooking time: 5 minutes | Servings: 6

Ingredients:
- 6 oz phyllo dough
- 8 oz vegan Parmesan, grated
- 1 tablespoon vegan mayonnaise
- 1 teaspoon minced garlic
- 1 tablespoon avocado oil

Directions:
In the mixing bowl, mix up together grated Parmesan, vegan mayonnaise, and minced garlic. Then cut phyllo dough into triangles. Spread the triangles with cheese mixture and roll in the shape of cigars. Preheat avocado oil in the instant pot on Saute mode. Place rolled "cigar" in the instant pot and cook them for 1-2 minutes or until they are golden brown.

Nutrition value/serving: calories 210, fat 2.6, fiber 0.7, carbs 23.1, protein 17.5

Flaked Clusters

Prep time: 10 minutes | Cooking time: 4 minutes | Servings: 4

Ingredients:
- 3 oz chia seeds
- ½ cup pumpkin seeds
- 1 cup coconut flakes
- 1/3 cup maple syrup
- 1 cup water, for cooking

Directions:
In the mixing bowl mix up together chia seeds, pumpkin seeds, coconut flakes, and maple syrup. Then line the trivet with the baking paper. Pour water in the instant pot. Insert lined trivet. With the help of 2 spoons make medium size clusters (patties) from the coconut mixture and put them on the trivet. Close and seal the lid. Cook clusters for 4 minutes on High. Then use quick pressure release and open the lid. Transfer the cooked clusters on the plate and let them chill well.

Nutrition value/serving: calories 336, fat 21.2, fiber 9.8, carbs 32.7, protein 8.4

Chickpea Crackers

*Prep time: 10 minutes | **Cooking time:** 5 minutes | **Servings:** 4*

Ingredients:
- 1 cup chickpeas, cooked
- 1 teaspoon ground coriander
- 1 teaspoon cumin
- 1 teaspoon salt
- ½ teaspoon sesame seeds
- ¼ cup wheat flour
- 1 cup water, for cooking

Directions:
Put chickpeas, ground coriander, cumin, and salt in the blender. Blend the mixture until smooth and transfer it in the mixing bowl. Add wheat flour and sesame seeds. Mix it up with the help of a spoon. Then line instant pot baking pan with baking paper. Put chickpea mixture in the pan and flatten it well to get a thin layer. Cut into square pieces. Pour water in the instant pot and insert rack. Place pan with chickpeas mixture on the rack. Close and seal the lid. Cook the crackers for 3 minutes on High-pressure mode. Then use quick pressure release. Open the lid, transfer crackers in the serving bowl and chill well.

Nutrition value/serving: calories 215, fat 3.4, fiber 9, carbs 36.6, protein 10.6

Eggplant Fries

*Prep time: 15 minutes | **Cooking time:** 5 minutes | **Servings:** 4*

Ingredients:
- 1 large eggplant
- 1 teaspoon salt
- 2 tablespoons wheat flour
- ½ teaspoon garlic powder
- 1 teaspoon ground black pepper
- 1 cup water, for cooking

Directions:
Trim the eggplant and cut it into wedges. Then sprinkle with salt, garlic powder, and ground black pepper. Shake the vegetables well and leave for 5 minutes. After this, coat every eggplant wedge with wheat flour. Pour water in the instant pot, insert trivet. Place pan on the trivet. Transfer eggplant wedges in the pan. Close and seal the instant pot lid. Cook eggplants for 5 minutes on Manual mode (high pressure). Use quick pressure release. Dry the eggplant wedges with the paper towel gently.

Nutrition value/serving: calories 45, fat 0.3, fiber 4.3, carbs 10.3, protein 1.6

Crunchy Artichoke Hearts

Prep time: 15 minutes | Cooking time: 10 minutes | Servings: 2

Ingredients:
- 1/3 cup artichoke hearts, canned
- ½ cup panko bread crumbs
- ¼ cup almond milk
- 1 tablespoon flax meal
- 1 teaspoon paprika
- 2 tablespoons sesame oil

Directions:
Whisk together almond milk and flax meal. Add paprika and stir well. Then dip artichoke hearts into the almond milk mixture and coat in the panko bread crumbs. Pour sesame oil in the instant pot. Preheat it on saute mode. Place coated artichoke hearts in the instant pot and cook them for 2 minutes from each side.

Nutrition value/serving: calories 329, fat 23.7, fiber 5.8, carbs 26.2, protein 6

Scallion Pancakes

Prep time: 10 minutes | Cooking time: 5 minutes | Servings: 4

Ingredients:
- ½ cup scallions, chopped
- 2 tablespoons flax meal
- 4 tablespoons water
- 1 teaspoon salt
- 1 potato, peeled, boiled
- 1 tablespoon olive oil
- 1 teaspoon ground black pepper

Directions:
Mix up together flax meal and water. Whisk it. Add chopped scallions, salt, and ground black pepper. After this, mash potato and add it in the scallions mixture. Stir it well. Make the balls from the mixture and press them to get pancake shape. Pour olive oil in the instant pot. Preheat it on Saute mode. Add scallions pancakes and cook them for 2 minutes from each side.

Nutrition value/serving: calories 83, fat 4.8, fiber 2.4, carbs 9.7, protein 1.9

Mushroom Arancini

Prep time: 10 minutes | Cooking time: 6 minutes | Servings: 8

Ingredients:
- ½ cup mushrooms, chopped, fried
- ½ cup of rice, cooked
- ½ onion, minced
- ¼ teaspoon minced garlic
- 4 oz vegan Parmesan, grated
- 3 tablespoons flax meal
- 5 tablespoons almond milk
- ¼ cup olive oil
- 1 cup bread crumbs

Directions:
Put chopped mushrooms, rice, minced onion, garlic, and grated cheese in the blender. Blend the mixture for 30 seconds. After this, transfer it in the mixing bowl. In the separated bowl whisk together almond milk and flax meal. Add the flax meal mixture in the rice mixture and stir well. Pour olive oil in the instant pot and bring it to boil on Saute mode. Meanwhile, make balls from the rice mixture and coat them in the bread crumbs well. Place the mushroom balls in the hot olive oil and cook for 3 minutes or until light brown. Dry the snack with the paper towel.

Nutrition value/serving: calories 230, fat 10.3, fiber 1.9, carbs 23.9, protein 9.4

Coated Heart of Palm

Prep time: 10 minutes | Cooking time: 25 minutes | Servings: 4

Ingredients:
- 1 cup heart of palm
- ¼ cup wheat flour
- ½ teaspoon salt
- 1 teaspoon maple syrup
- ½ teaspoon paprika
- ½ teaspoon soy sauce
- ¼ cup coconut flakes
- 2 tablespoon sesame oil

Directions:
Mix up together wheat flour, salt, paprika, and coconut flakes. In the separated bowl, mix up together the heart of palm, maple syrup, and soy sauce. Stir gently. Toss the heart of palm in the coconut flakes mixture and coat well. Pour sesame oil in the instant pot and preheat it on Saute mode. Cook coated heart of palm in the hot oil for 2 minutes. Then dry with the help of the paper towel. Serve the snack with your favorite vegan sauce.

Nutrition value/serving: calories 122, fat 8.8, fiber 1.7, carbs 9.7, protein 2

Sweet Tofu Cubes

Prep time: 10 minutes | *Cooking time:* 40 minutes | *Servings:* 2

Ingredients:
- 6 oz firm tofu, cubed
- 1 teaspoon mustard
- 1 teaspoon olive oil
- 1 teaspoon apple cider vinegar
- ½ teaspoon maple syrup

Directions:
Place tofu in the instant pot. Sprinkle it with mustard, olive oil, apple cider vinegar, and maple syrup. Mix up the mixture well. Close and seal the lid. Cook tofu cubes for 2 minutes on High-pressure mode. Then use quick pressure release. Transfer the tofu cubes on the serving plate and sprinkle with the remaining gravy. Insert a toothpick in every tofu cube.

Nutrition value/serving: calories 92, fat 6.4, fiber 1, carbs 3.2, protein 7.4

Sauces and Fillings

Vegan Gravy

Prep time: 10 minutes | Cooking time: 15 minutes | Servings: 4

Ingredients:
- ½ teaspoon cornstarch
- 1 cup almond milk
- 1 tablespoon olive oil
- 1 yellow onion, diced
- 1 cup mushrooms, chopped
- 1 teaspoon ground black pepper
- 1 teaspoon salt
- 1 teaspoon chili flakes
- 1 teaspoon oregano
- 1 teaspoon cilantro
- 1 teaspoon garlic, diced
- ¼ cup white wine
- ½ teaspoon miso paste
- 1 tablespoon soy sauce

Directions:
Preheat olive oil on Saute mode well. Add diced onion, mushrooms, and garlic. Stir well and saute the vegetables for 5 minutes. After this, add ground black pepper, salt, chili flakes, oregano, cilantro, and soy sauce. Stir well. Add miso paste and white wine. Saute the mixture until it starts to boil. Then add almond milk and cornstarch. Mix it well. Close and seal the lid. Cook the gravy on manual mode (high pressure) for 2 minutes. Then make quick pressure release. Chill the cooked gravy little.

Nutrition value/serving: calories 203, fat 18, fiber 2.5, carbs 8.5, protein 2.7

Samosa Filling

Prep time: 20 minutes | Cooking time: 30 minutes | Servings: 6

Ingredients:
- 1 cup chickpeas, soaked
- 3 cups of water
- 1 oz beetroot, chopped
- 1 garlic clove
- 1 tablespoon tahini paste
- 1 teaspoon salt
- ½ teaspoon harissa
- 2 tablespoons olive oil

Directions:
Place the soaked chickpeas and water in the instant pot. Ad beetroot and garlic clove. Close and seal the lid. Cook the ingredients for 30 minutes on manual mode (high pressure). After this, allow natural pressure release for 10 minutes. Place 4 tablespoons of the liquid from cooked chickpeas in the blender. Add cooked chickpeas, garlic clove, and beetroot. Blend the mixture until smooth. Add tahini paste, salt, harissa, and olive oil. Blend the mixture well.

Nutrition value/serving: calories 180, fat 8.1, fiber 6.1, carbs 21.6, protein 7

Cacao Spread

Prep time: 10 minutes | Cooking time: 5 minutes | Servings: 3

Ingredients:
- 1 tablespoon nuts
- ½ cup cashew milk
- 1 tablespoon raw cacao powder
- ¼ cup of sugar
- 1 teaspoon almond butter

Directions:
Blend together raw cacao powder and cashew milk. Pour the liquid in the instant pot. Add sugar and almond butter. Cook the mixture on Saute mode for 5 minutes. Stir it from time to time. Add nuts and mix up well. Close the lid. Switch off the instant pot and let it rest for 10 minutes.

Nutrition value/serving: calories 142, fat 5.3, fiber 2.6, carbs 22.9, protein 2.5

Mexican Rice Filling

Prep time: 10 minutes | Cooking time: 4 minutes | Servings: 3

Ingredients:
- ½ cup black beans, canned
- 2 cups of water
- 1 cup fresh cilantro, chopped
- ½ cup corn kernels, frozen
- 1 cup of rice
- 1 teaspoon salt
- 1 tablespoon olive oil
- ½ teaspoon paprika
- 1 teaspoon chili flakes

Directions:
Place rice and water in the instant pot. Add salt and corn kernels. Close and seal the lid. Set rice mode (high pressure) and cook rice for 4 minutes. Use quick pressure release. Meanwhile, in the mixing bowl mix up together canned black beans, olive oil, paprika, chili flakes, and chopped cilantro. Mix up the mixture well. When the rice and corn are cooked, chill them to the room temperature and add in the beans mixture. Mix up well.

Nutrition value/serving: calories 200, fat 2.9, fiber 3.4, carbs 37.4, protein 6.2

Cauliflower Sauce

Prep time: 10 minutes | Cooking time: 10 minutes | Servings: 3

Ingredients:
- 7 oz cauliflower
- 1 cup of water
- ½ cup almond milk
- 1 teaspoon salt
- 1 teaspoon ground black pepper
- 1 tablespoon wheat flour

Directions:
Place cauliflower and water in the instant pot. Close and seal the lid. Cook the vegetable on Manual mode (high pressure) for 7 minutes. Then make quick pressure release and open the lid. Drain the water and mash cauliflower with the help of the fork Add salt, ground black pepper, wheat flour, and almond milk. Mix up the mixture well. Cook it on Saute mode for 3 minutes more. The cooked sauce shouldn't be smooth.

Nutrition value/serving: calories 120, fat 9.7, fiber 2.8, carbs 8.2, protein 2.6

Vegan French Sauce

Prep time: 10 minutes | Cooking time: 6 minutes | Servings: 3

Ingredients:
- 1 cup mushrooms, chopped
- ½ cup vegetable stock
- 1 teaspoon salt
- 4 oz firm tofu
- 1 tablespoon olive oil
- 1 teaspoon ground black pepper
- 1 tablespoon almond yogurt
- 1 teaspoon potato starch

Directions:
Pour vegetable stock in the instant pot. Add mushrooms, salt, tofu, olive oil, ground black pepper, almond yogurt, and close the lid. Cook the dip on manual mode (high pressure) for 6 minutes. Then make quick pressure release. Open the lid and add potato starch. Blend the mixture with the help of the hand blender until smooth. The sauce is cooked.

Nutrition value/serving: calories 51, fat 4.3, fiber 0.5, carbs 2.4, protein 2.4

Pumpkin Butter

Prep time: 5 minutes | *Cooking time:* 3 minutes | *Servings:* 4

Ingredients:
- ½ cup pumpkin puree
- 3 tablespoons orange juice
- 1 tablespoon sugar
- 1 tablespoon almond butter
- ¾ teaspoon salt
- 1 teaspoon pumpkin pie spices

Directions:
Put pumpkin puree, orange juice, sugar, almond butter, and salt in the instant pot. Sprinkle the mixture with pumpkin pie spices and stir well. Close and seal the lid. Cook the butter for 3 minutes on Manual mode (high pressure). Then make quick pressure release. Open the lid and transfer the meal in the bowl. Chill it for 20-30 minutes before serving.

Nutrition value/serving: calories 53, fat 2.4, fiber 1.4, carbs 7.7, protein 1.3

Cranberry Sauce

Prep time: 10 minutes | *Cooking time:* 2 minutes | *Servings:* 6

Ingredients:
- 8 oz cranberries
- 3 oz maple syrup
- 1 tablespoon lemon juice
- ¾ teaspoon dried oregano

Directions:
Place cranberries, maple syrup, lemon juice, and dried oregano in the instant pot. Stir gently. Close and seal the lid. Cook the sauce on manual mode for 2 minutes. When the time is over, allow natural pressure release for 5 minutes more. Stir the sauce gently before serving.

Nutrition value/serving: calories 59, fat 0.1, fiber 1.5, carbs 13.1, protein 0

Spinach Dip

Prep time: 10 minutes | *Cooking time:* 10 minutes | *Servings:* 4

Ingredients:
- 1 teaspoon onion powder
- 2 cups spinach, chopped
- ½ cup artichoke hearts, canned, chopped
- 1 tablespoon olive oil
- 1 teaspoon ground black pepper
- 1 teaspoon salt
- ½ cup of coconut yogurt
- 1 teaspoon cornstarch
- 4 oz vegan Parmesan, grated

Directions:
Preheat the instant pot on Saute mode. Then pour olive oil inside. Add chopped spinach and chopped artichoke hearts. Sprinkle the greens with ground black pepper and salt. Stir it well. Close the lid and cook on Saute mode for 5 minutes. After this, add coconut yogurt, onion powder, and cornstarch. Add grated Parmesan and mix up the mixture well. Cook it for 5 minutes more.

Nutrition value/serving: calories 150, fat 4.1, fiber 1.6, carbs 11.5, protein 13.3

Red Kidney Beans Sauce

Prep time: 10 minutes | Cooking time: 35 minutes | Servings: 4

Ingredients:
- ½ cup red kidney beans, soaked
- 2 cups of water
- 1 tablespoon tomato paste
- 1 bell pepper, chopped
- 1 teaspoon salt
- 1 teaspoon chili flakes
- ½ teaspoon white pepper
- 1 tablespoon corn flour
- ¼ cup fresh dill, chopped

Directions:
In the instant pot, combine together red kidney beans, water, tomato paste, chopped bell pepper, salt, chili flakes, white pepper, and dill. Mix up the mixture well. Close and seal the instant pot lid. Set manual mode and cook the ingredients for 30 minutes. Then use quick pressure release and open the lid. Add corn flour and mix up the sauce well. Close the lid. Saute the sauce for 5 minutes on Saute mode. Then stir it well and let chill till the room temperature.

Nutrition value/serving: calories 105, fat 0.6, fiber 4.7, carbs 20.4, protein 6.4

Cayenne Pepper Filling

Prep time: 5 minutes | Cooking time: 15 minutes | Servings: 2

Ingredients:
- 1 sweet potato, peeled, chopped
- 1 cayenne pepper, chopped
- ½ cup of water
- 1 tablespoon almond yogurt
- 1 teaspoon olive oil
- 1 carrot, grated
- 1 teaspoon mustard

Directions:
Pour olive oil in the instant pot and preheat it on Saute mode. Add chopped sweet potato and cayenne pepper. Saute the vegetables for 5 minutes. Add grated carrot and stir it well. Then pour water in the instant pot and add mustard and almond yogurt. Mix up the mixture. Close and seal the lid. Cook the filling on Manual mode (high pressure) for 5 minutes. Then make a quick pressure release and transfer the meal in the serving plate.

Nutrition value/serving: calories 103, fat 3.2, fiber 3.5, carbs 17, protein 1.9

Vegan Cheese Sauce

Prep time: 10 minutes | Cooking time: 6 minutes | Servings: 4

Ingredients:

- 1 white potato, peeled, chopped
- 1 sweet potato, peeled, chopped
- 1 carrot, chopped
- ½ cup peanuts, chopped
- 1 tablespoon lime juice
- 1 teaspoon salt
- 1 teaspoon onion powder
- 1 teaspoon ground black pepper
- 1 teaspoon chili flakes
- ½ teaspoon dried oregano
- 1 teaspoon dried basil
- 1 ½ cup water
- 1 tablespoon apple cider vinegar
- ¾ cup of coconut milk
- 1 teaspoon nutritional yeast

Directions:

Put in the instant pot: chopped white potato, sweet potato, carrot, and peanuts. Add water. Close and seal the lid. Cook the vegetables on manual mode (high pressure) for 6 minutes. Then allow natural pressure release. Open the lid. Transfer the contents of the instant pot in the food processor. Add lime juice, salt, onion powder, ground black pepper, chili flakes, dried oregano, dried basil, apple cider vinegar, coconut milk, and nutritional yeast. Blend the mixture until smooth and homogenous. Transfer the cooked cheese sauce in the serving bowl.

Nutrition value/serving: calories 280, fat 19.9, fiber 5.3, carbs 21.9, protein 7.9

Beetroot Garlic Filling

Prep time: 20 minutes | Cooking time: 10 minutes | Servings: 4

Ingredients:

- 1 cup beetroot, cubed
- 1 tablespoon garlic, diced
- 1 tablespoon olive oil
- 1 tablespoon lime juice
- ¼ teaspoon lime zest
- 1 tablespoon fresh parsley, chopped
- 1 cup of water

Directions:

Put beetroot and water in the instant pot. Close and seal the lid. Cook the vegetables for 10 minutes on Manual mode (high pressure). Then allow natural pressure release for 10 minutes more. Drain water and transfer beetroot in the bowl. Add garlic, lime juice, olive oil, lime zest, and chopped parsley. Stir the filling carefully and let for 10 minutes to marinate.

Nutrition value/serving: calories 53, fat 3.6, fiber 1, carbs 5.3, protein 0.9

Avocado Pesto

Prep time: 10 minutes | Cooking time: 5 minutes | Servings: 7

Ingredients:
- 2 cups spinach, chopped
- 1 tablespoon olive oil
- 1 teaspoon minced garlic
- 1 tablespoon fresh basil
- 1 tablespoon lemon juice
- 1 avocado, peeled, chopped
- ¼ cup sesame oil
- 1 teaspoon salt
- ½ teaspoon cayenne pepper

Directions:
Place chopped spinach and olive oil in the instant pot. Add lemon juice and salt. Stir well. Cook the greens on saute mode for 5 minutes. Transfer the cooked spinach in the blender. Add minced garlic, fresh basil, avocado, sesame oil, and cayenne pepper. Blend the mixture until smooth. Pour the cooked pesto sauce in the sauce bowl.

Nutrition value/serving: calories 148, fat 15.5, fiber 2.2, carbs 3, protein 0.9

Pear Filling

Prep time: 15 minutes | Cooking time: 10 minutes | Servings: 4

Ingredients:
- 2 cups pears, chopped
- 1 teaspoon ground cinnamon
- ½ teaspoon ground clove
- 1 tablespoon maple syrup
- 2 tablespoons brown sugar

Directions:
Place pears in the instant pot. Sprinkle them with ground cinnamon, clove, maple syrup, and brown sugar. Mix up the fruits well and let them rest for 5-10 minutes or until they start to give juice. After this, cook filling on Saute mode for 10 minutes. Stir it from time to time. Chill the filling well.

Nutrition value/serving: calories 79, fat 0.2, fiber 2.9, carbs 20.7, protein 0.3

Mushroom Sauce

Prep time: 5 minutes | Cooking time: 4 minutes | Servings: 4

Ingredients:
- 1 cup mushrooms, grinded
- 1 onion, grinded
- 1 cup of coconut milk
- 1 teaspoon salt
- 1 teaspoon white pepper
- ¼ teaspoon ground thyme

Directions:
Place grinded mushrooms and onion in the instant pot. Add salt, white pepper, and ground thyme. After this, add coconut milk and mix up the mixture well. Close the lid and set manual mode. Cook the sauce for 4 minutes. Then use quick pressure release. Open the lid and mix up the cooked sauce well.

Nutrition value/serving: calories 154, fat 14.4, fiber 2.3, carbs 6.9, protein 2.3

White Bean Sauce

Prep time: 10 minutes | Cooking time: 35 minutes | Servings: 4

Ingredients:
- ½ cup white beans, soaked
- 1 ½ cup water
- ½ cup almond milk
- 1 tablespoon smoked paprika
- 1 teaspoon salt
- 1 cup fresh parsley, chopped
- 5 oz vegan Parmesan, grated

Directions:
Place white beans, water, almond milk, smoked paprika, salt, and chopped parsley in the instant pot. Close and seal the lid. Cook the beans on Manual mode (high pressure) for 35 minutes. Then use the quick pressure release. Open the lid and add grated cheese. Mix up the sauce well until cheese is melted.

Nutrition value/serving: calories 272, fat 7.7, fiber 5.7, carbs 26, protein 21.8

Caramel Pumpkin Sauce

Prep time: 5 minutes | Cooking time: 3 hours | Servings: 6

Ingredients:
- 6 oz pumpkin puree
- 8 oz almond milk
- 1 cup of sugar
- 1 teaspoon ground cinnamon
- 1 teaspoon coconut oil

Directions:
Put all the ingredients in the instant pot and mix up them well. Close the lid and cook the sauce on Low-pressure mode for 3 hours.

Nutrition value/serving: calories 229, fat 9.9, fiber 1.9, carbs 38, protein 1.2

Ravioli Sauce

Prep time: 10 minutes | Cooking time: 18 minutes | Servings: 5

Ingredients:
- 1 cup tomatoes, canned, chopped
- ½ cup tomato juice
- 2 tablespoons almond yogurt
- 1 teaspoon chili pepper
- 1 teaspoon chili flakes
- 1 teaspoon salt
- ½ teaspoon paprika
- ½ teaspoon ground oregano
- ½ teaspoon ground ginger
- 1 onion, diced
- 1 teaspoon olive oil

Directions:
Preheat instant pot on Saute mode. Add olive oil and diced onion. Saute it for 3 minutes. After this, add chopped canned tomatoes, tomato juice, chili pepper, chili flakes, salt, paprika, ground oregano, ground ginger, and stir the sauce well. Close the lid and cook it on Saute mode for 15 minutes. Then switch off the instant pot, add almond yogurt, mix it up, and chill the sauce till the room temperature.

Nutrition value/serving: calories 34, fat 1.3, fiber 1.3, carbs 5.4, protein 0.9

Queso Sauce

***Prep time:** 5 minutes | **Cooking time:** 3 minutes | **Servings:** 4*

Ingredients:
- ½ can chilies, chopped, drained
- 6 oz cashew
- ½ teaspoon taco seasoning
- ½ red onion, diced
- 1 teaspoon olive oil
- 1 teaspoon paprika
- ¼ cup of water

Directions:
Pour olive oil in the instant pot. Set Saute mode and preheat it. Add red onion and saute it until it is soft. Then transfer the cooked onion in the food processor. Add cashew, chopped chilies, paprika, water, and taco seasoning. Blend the mixture until you get a smooth sauce. Store the sauce in the fridge in the closed container up to 2 days.

Nutrition value/serving: calories 265, fat 21, fiber 1.9, carbs 16.4, protein 6.8

Basil Cream Sauce

***Prep time:** 10 minutes | **Cooking time:** 2 minutes | **Servings:** 6*

Ingredients:
- 1 cup coconut cream
- ½ cup of water
- 1 cup fresh basil, chopped
- 1 garlic clove, peeled
- 1 teaspoon salt
- 1 teaspoon Italian spices
- 1 teaspoon nutritional yeast

Directions:
Place fresh basil in the instant pot. Add water and coconut cream. Sprinkle the greens with salt and Italian seasoning. Close and seal the lid. Cook basil for 2 minutes on high-pressure mode. Use quick pressure release. Open the lid and add garlic clove. Blend the mixture until smooth. When the mixture gets to room temperature, add nutritional yeast and mix up well. Transfer the sauce in the serving bowl.

Nutrition value/serving: calories 96, fat 9.6, fiber 1.1, carbs 2.8, protein 1.3

Creamy Green Peas Filling

***Prep time:** 10 minutes | **Cooking time:** 5 minutes | **Servings:** 4*

Ingredients:
- 2 cups green peas, frozen
- 2 cups of water
- ½ cup coconut cream
- 1 teaspoon tahini paste
- 1 oz fresh dill, chopped

Directions:
Place green peas and water in the instant pot. Close and seal the lid. Cook green peas for 5 minutes on manual mode. After this, use quick pressure release. Open the lid and drain the water. Then transfer the green peas in the food processor. Add coconut cream, tahini paste, and chopped dill. Blend it until homogenous. Store the filling in the closed container in the fridge up to 4 days.

Nutrition value/serving: calories 153, fat 8.4, fiber 5.4, carbs 16.4, protein 6.3

Tomato Sauce
Prep time: 10 minutes | Cooking time: 10 minutes | Servings: 4

Ingredients:
- 1 tablespoon tomato paste
- 1 cup of water
- 1 tablespoon coconut cream
- 1 tablespoon onion, diced
- 1 teaspoon cornstarch
- 1 teaspoon ground black pepper
- ½ teaspoon chili pepper

Directions:
In the instant pot mix up together tomato paste and water. When the mixture changes color to red, add coconut cream, diced onion, ground black pepper, and chili pepper. Close and seal the lid. Cook the sauce for 10 minutes. Use quick pressure release. After this, open the lid and add cornstarch. Stir the sauce until it gets the homogenous texture. Chill it well before serving.

Nutrition value/serving: calories 17, fat 0.9, fiber 0.5, carbs 2.2, protein 0.4

Alfredo Sauce
Prep time: 10 minutes | Cooking time: 8 minutes | Servings: 4

Ingredients:
- 1 teaspoon minced garlic
- 1 tablespoon avocado oil
- 2 cups cauliflower, chopped
- 3 tablespoons cashews, chopped
- 1 cup of water
- 1 cup of coconut milk
- 1 teaspoon salt

Directions:
Pour water and coconut milk in the instant pot. Add chopped cauliflower, salt, and minced garlic. Then add avocado oil. Close and seal the lid. Cook the mixture for 8 minutes on High-pressure mode (manual mode). Then use quick pressure release and open the lid. Add cashews and blend the mixture with the help of the hand blender. When the sauce gets a smooth texture, it is cooked.

Nutrition value/serving: calories 193, fat 17.8, fiber 2.9, carbs 8.5, protein 3.4

Spaghetti Sauce

Prep time: 15 minutes | Cooking time: 10 minutes | Servings: 2

Ingredients:
- 1 white onion, peeled
- 1 cup tomatoes, chopped
- ½ carrot, chopped
- 1 teaspoon salt
- 1 teaspoon ground black pepper
- 1 garlic clove
- ½ teaspoon sugar
- 1 teaspoon tomato paste

Directions:
Put all the ingredients in the instant pot. Close and seal the lid. Cook mixture on Manual mode (high pressure) for 10 minutes. Then allow natural pressure release for 10 minutes. Open the lid and blend the mixture with the help of the hand blender. Transfer the cooked sauce in the bowl and chill little.

Nutrition value/serving: calories 55, fat 0.3, fiber 3.1, carbs 12.8, protein 1.9

Marinara Sauce

Prep time: 15 minutes | Cooking time: 10 minutes | Servings: 4

Ingredients:
- 1 tablespoon onion, minced
- 3 oz bell pepper, chopped
- 1 teaspoon ground black pepper
- ½ teaspoon dried oregano
- ½ teaspoon apple cider vinegar
- ½ cup tomatoes, chopped
- ½ teaspoon tomato paste
- ¼ teaspoon minced garlic
- ¾ cup red wine
- 1/3 teaspoon salt
- ½ teaspoon sugar
- 1 oz mushrooms, chopped
- ¾ cup of water

Directions:
On the saute mode, cook minced onion bell pepper, and tomato paste for 3-4 minutes. Stir it. Add ground black pepper, dried oregano, apple cider vinegar, chopped tomatoes, minced garlic, red wine, salt, and sugar. Then add water and mushrooms. Mix up the mixture. Close and seal the lid. Cook the sauce on manual mode for 5 minutes. Then allow natural pressure release for 10 minutes. Chill the sauce well before serving.

Nutrition value/serving: calories 77, fat 0.3, fiber 1.8, carbs 10.5, protein 1.5

Tomato Bean Pate

Prep time: 10 minutes | *Cooking time:* 35 minutes | *Servings:* 4

Ingredients:
- 1 cup red kidney beans, soaked
- 1 teaspoon tomato paste
- 1 teaspoon coconut oil
- 3 cups of water
- 1 teaspoon salt
- 1 carrot, peeled
- 1 teaspoon ground black pepper

Directions:

Place red kidney beans, water, and carrot in the instant pot. Close and seal the lid. Cook beans on high-pressure mode for 35 minutes. Then use quick pressure release. Open the lid and drain water. Transfer beans and carrot in the blender. Add tomato paste, coconut oil, salt, and ground black pepper. Blend the mixture until it gets a soft and smooth texture. Transfer the cooked pate in the bowl.

Nutrition value/serving: calories 173, fat 1.7, fiber 7.6, carbs 30.3, protein 10.6

Mint Filling

Prep time: 5 minutes | *Cooking time:* 4 minutes | *Servings:* 2

Ingredients:
- ¼ cup of rice
- 1 cup of water
- 1 teaspoon almond butter
- 1 tablespoon dried mint
- ½ cup corn kernels, frozen
- 1 teaspoon salt

Directions:

Place rice and water in the instant pot. Add dried mint and corn kernels. Add salt. Close and seal the lid. Set manual mode and cook filling for 4 minutes. Use quick pressure release. Open the lid and transfer filling in the mixing bowl. Add almond butter and mix up well.

Nutrition value/serving: calories 168, fat 5.1, fiber 2.3, carbs 27.5, protein 4.7

Artichoke Sandwich Filling

Prep time: 10 minutes | *Cooking time:* 15 minutes | *Servings:* 4

Ingredients:
- ½ cup artichoke petals
- 1 cup almond milk
- 3 oz vegan Parmesan, grated
- 1 teaspoon cayenne pepper
- 1 tablespoon cashew butter
- 1 teaspoon olive oil

Directions:

Pour almond milk in the instant pot. Add artichoke petals, cayenne pepper, cashew butter, and olive oil. Close the lid and cook the mixture on saute mode for 15 minutes. When the time is over, add grated cheese and let the mixture stay for 10 minutes more. Stir the filling well before serving.

Nutrition value/serving: calories 246, fat 17.6, fiber 2.4, carbs 10.6, protein 11.3

Caramel Sauce for Vegetables
Prep time: 10 minutes | Cooking time: 2.5 hours | Servings: 4

Ingredients:
- ½ cup of sugar
- ½ cup applesauce
- ¾ cup of water
- 1 tablespoon lemon juice
- 1 teaspoon ground coriander

Directions:
Preheat instant pot well. Add applesauce, water, lemon juice, and ground coriander. Bring the mixture to boil. After this, add sugar and stir well. Close the lid and set low-pressure mode. Cook the sauce for 2.5 hours. Chill the cooked sauce well.

Nutrition value/serving: calories 108, fat 0.1, fiber 0.4, carbs 28.5, protein 0.1

Spinach Sauce
Prep time: 10 minutes | Cooking time: 6 minutes | Servings: 4

Ingredients:
- 1 cup broccoli
- 2 cups spinach, chopped
- 2 cups of water
- 1 teaspoon olive oil
- 1 teaspoon sriracha
- 1 tablespoon lime juice
- 2 oz avocado, chopped
- 1 tablespoon peanuts

Directions:
Chop broccoli and place in the instant pot. Add water and close the lid. Cook broccoli on manual mode for 6 minutes. Then use quick pressure release. Drain ½ part of water. Place broccoli and remaining water in the food processor. Add spinach, olive oil, sriracha, lime juice, chopped avocado, and peanuts. Blend the sauce mixture until smooth. Transfer the cooked sauce in the glass jar and close the lid. Stor it in the fridge for up to 2 days.

Nutrition value/serving: calories 65, fat 5.2, fiber 2.1, carbs 4.2, protein 1.9

Coconut Filling
Prep time: 5 minutes | Cooking time: 3 minutes | Servings: 5

Ingredients:
- 1 cup coconut shred
- 1 cup pumpkin puree
- ½ teaspoon ground cardamom
- 1 teaspoon almond butter
- 1 teaspoon sugar

Directions:
Place coconut shred, pumpkin puree, and sugar in the instant pot. Add almond butter and ground cardamom. Stir it. Close and seal the lid. Cook the filling for 3 minutes. Then use quick pressure release. Chill the filling well.

Nutrition value/serving: calories 133, fat 8.6, fiber 2.6, carbs 14.4, protein 1.8

Ginger Sauce

Prep time: 10 minutes | Cooking time: 8 minutes | Servings: 4

Ingredients:
- ½ cup of water
- ¾ cup soy sauce
- 1 tablespoon rice vinegar
- 1 teaspoon sesame seeds
- 1 teaspoon minced garlic
- 1 tablespoon minced ginger
- ½ tablespoon sugar
- 1 teaspoon olive oil

Directions:
Preheat instant pot on saute mode well. Transfer in the instant pot water, soy sauce, rice vinegar, sugar, and olive oil. Bring the mixture to boil. After this, pour it in the glass bottle. Add sesame seeds, minced garlic, and minced ginger. Close the bottle and shake it well. Leave it for 10 minutes to rest.

Nutrition value/serving: calories 53, fat 1.6, fiber 0.7, carbs 6.5, protein 3.3

Tahini Sauce with Orange Juice

Prep time: 5 minutes | Cooking time: 5 minutes | Servings: 2

Ingredients:
- 1/3 cup orange juice
- 3 oz tahini
- ½ teaspoon minced garlic
- 1 teaspoon olive oil

Directions:
Set saute mode and pour orange juice in the instant pot. Add minced garlic and olive oil. Preheat the mixture until it hot but doesn't start to boil. Transfer the orange juice mixture in the jar. Add tahini and whisk well. Chill it.

Nutrition value/serving: calories 293, fat 25.3, fiber 4, carbs 13.5, protein 7.6

Sriracha Sauce

Prep time: 7 minutes | Cooking time: 4 hours | Servings: 4

Ingredients:
- 1 cup red chili peppers, chopped
- 1/3 cup water
- ½ cup apple cider vinegar
- 1 teaspoon sugar
- ½ teaspoon salt

Directions:
Blend the chili peppers in the blender and transfer the mixture in the instant pot. Add water, apple cider vinegar, sugar, and salt. Mix it up. Close the lid. Cook sauce on low-pressure mode for 4 hours.

Nutrition value/serving: calories 40, fat 0.5, fiber 2.7, carbs 7.7, protein 1

Chimichurri Sauce

Prep time: 15 minutes | Cooking time: 11 minutes | Servings: 2

Ingredients:
- 2 tablespoons wine vinegar
- 1 oz fresh parsley, chopped
- 1 teaspoon dried oregano
- ½ teaspoon garlic, diced
- ¼ teaspoon chili flakes
- ½ teaspoon ground black pepper
- ¼ cup olive oil

Directions:
Pour oil in the instant pot and preheat it on Saute mode. Add dried oregano, chili flakes, and ground black pepper. Stir the mixture and cook it for 1 minute. After this, add wine vinegar and chopped parsley. Stir it well. Switch off the instant pot and let sauce chill till the room temperature.

Nutrition value/serving: calories 231 fat 25.4, fiber 1.9, carbs 21, protein 0.6

Guacamole with Broccoli

Prep time: 10 minutes | Cooking time: 2 minutes | Servings: 2

Ingredients:
- 1 cup broccoli florets
- ½ cup almond yogurt
- 1 cup of water
- 1 teaspoon salt
- ½ jalapeno, chopped
- ½ red onion, diced
- 2 tablespoons lemon juice
- 1 teaspoon fresh cilantro, chopped
- ¼ cup tomatoes, chopped
- ¼ teaspoon ground black pepper

Directions:
Cook broccoli: put broccoli florets and water in the instant pot. Close and seal the lid; cook broccoli for 2 minutes on high-pressure mode. Use quick pressure release. Drain water and transfer broccoli in the blender. Add salt, chopped jalapeno, almond yogurt, diced onion, lemon juice, cilantro, and ground black pepper. Blend the mixture well. Transfer it in the bowl and mix up with the chopped tomatoes.

Nutrition value/serving: calories 116, fat 1.9, fiber 3.8, carbs 23.7, protein 2.5

Miso Butter

Prep time: 10 minutes | *Cooking time:* 7 minutes | *Servings:* 4

Ingredients:
- 1 cups carrot, chopped
- 4 teaspoon tahini paste
- 2 teaspoons maple syrup
- 1 tablespoon miso paste
- 3 tablespoons water
- 1 cup water, for cooking

Directions:

Place carrot and 1 cup of water in the instant pot. Close and seal the lid. Cook carrot on high-pressure mode for 7 minutes. Allow natural pressure release for 10 minutes. Drain the water and transfer hot carrot in the blender. Add tahini paste, maple syrup, miso paste, and 3 tablespoons of water. Blend the mixture until you get the smooth buttery texture. Transfer it in the bowl for butter.

Nutrition value/serving: calories 58, fat 3, fiber 1.4, carbs 7.1, protein 1.6

Vegan Buffalo Dip

Prep time: 10 minutes | *Cooking time:* 4 minutes | *Servings:* 3

Ingredients:
- 1 cup cauliflower, chopped
- 1 cup of water
- ½ cup chickpeas, canned
- 1/3 cup almond milk
- 1 teaspoon salt
- 4 teaspoons hot sauce
- 1 tablespoon lemon juice
- 1 teaspoon garlic powder

Directions:

Place cauliflower and water in the instant pot. Close and seal the lid; cook the vegetable for 4 minutes on manual mode. Then use quick pressure release. Open the lid and drain water. Transfer cauliflower in the blender. Add chickpeas, almond milk, salt, hot sauce, lemon juice, and garlic powder. Blend it until smooth. Transfer cooked Buffalo dip in the serving bowl.

Nutrition value/serving: calories 196, fat 8.5, fiber 7.4, carbs 24.4, protein 7.9

Oregano Onion Dip

Prep time: 10 minutes | *Cooking time:* 10 minutes | *Servings:* 5

Ingredients:
- 3 cups onions, chopped
- 2 cups of coconut milk
- 1 teaspoon coconut butter
- 1 teaspoon salt
- 1 teaspoon white pepper
- 1 teaspoon paprika
- 1 teaspoon wheat flour
- 1 tablespoon dried oregano

Directions:

Toss coconut butter in the instant pot and melt it on Saute mode. Add chopped onions and sprinkle them with salt, white pepper, paprika, and dried oregano. Stir well and cook on saute mode for 5 minutes. After this, add wheat flour and coconut milk. Mix up the mixture. Close and seal the lid. Cook the onion dip on manual mode for 4 minutes. Then allow natural pressure release for 5 minutes more. Chill the cooked meal to room temperature.

Nutrition value/serving: calories 262, fat 23.7, fiber 4.4, carbs 13.5, protein 3.3

Baba Ganoush

Prep time: 10 minutes | Cooking time: 10 minutes | Servings: 8

Ingredients:
- 2 eggplants
- ¼ cup fresh cilantro, chopped
- ¾ cup lime juice
- ½ teaspoon garlic, diced
- 4 teaspoons tahini
- ½ teaspoon salt
- 1 cup water, for cooking

Directions:
Pour water in the instant pot. Insert rack. Peel the eggplants and place them on the rack. Close the lid and cook vegetables on Steam mode for 10 minutes. When the time is over, transfer the eggplants in the blender. Add lime juice, garlic, tahini, and salt. Blend the mixture until smooth. Add fresh cilantro and pulse the mixture for 5 seconds more. Transfer the cooked meal in the serving bowl.

Nutrition value/serving: calories 56, fat 1.7, fiber 5.2, carbs 10.7, protein 1.9

Chili Sauce

Prep time: 8 minutes | Cooking time: 8 minutes | Servings: 4

Ingredients:
- 2 chili peppers
- 1 cup tomatoes
- ½ teaspoon tomato paste
- ¼ cup of water
- 1 teaspoon diced garlic
- 1 date, chopped
- 1 tablespoon rice vinegar
- 1 cup water, for cooking

Directions:
Pour 1 cup of water in the instant pot and insert rack. Place chili peppers and tomatoes on the rack. Close and seal the lid. Cook the vegetables on Steam mode for 8 minutes. Transfer the cooked peppers and tomatoes in the blender. Add tomato paste, ¼ cup water, diced garlic, chopped date, and rice vinegar. Blend the sauce until it reaches the desired structure.

Nutrition value/serving: calories 19, fat 0.1, fiber 0.8, carbs 3.8, protein 0.6

Walnut Sauce

Prep time: 7 minutes | Cooking time: 4 minutes | Servings: 2

Ingredients:
- 1/3 cup walnuts, chopped
- 1 white onion, peeled
- ½ teaspoon minced garlic
- 1 tablespoon olive oil
- 1 teaspoon ground black pepper
- ½ teaspoon salt
- ½ cup water, for cooking

Directions:
Place onion and water in the instant pot. Close and seal the lid. Cook onion for 4 minutes on Manual mode. Use quick pressure release. Drain water from the instant pot and transfer the onion in the blender. Add walnuts, minced garlic, olive oil, ground black pepper, and salt. Blend the sauce well.

Nutrition value/serving: calories 214, fat 19.4, fiber 2.9, carbs 8.1, protein 5.8

Green Sauce

Prep time: 10 minutes | Cooking time: 2 minutes | Servings: 4

Ingredients:
- 6 oz avocado, mashed
- 2 cups spinach, chopped
- 1 teaspoon wine vinegar
- 1 tablespoon lemon juice
- 1 cup fresh parsley, chopped
- 3 oz scallions, chopped
- ½ garlic clove, diced
- 1 teaspoon salt
- 1 teaspoon chili pepper
- ½ cup water, for cooking

Directions:
In the instant pot combine together ½ cup of water and spinach. Close and seal the lid. Cook spinach for 2 minutes. Use quick pressure release. After this, transfer the water and spinach in the blender. Add avocado mash, wine vinegar, lemon juice, chopped parsley, scallions, garlic clove, salt, and chili pepper. Blend the mixture until smooth. Stir the sauce in the closed glass jar up to 2 days.

Nutrition value/serving: calories 106, fat 8.6, fiber 4.6, carbs 11.8, protein 2.2

Herbed Lemon Sauce

Prep time: 5 minutes | Cooking time: 5 minutes | Servings: 3

Ingredients:
- 1 teaspoon lemon juice
- 1 tablespoon almond butter
- 1 teaspoon cornstarch
- ½ cup of water
- 2 teaspoons sugar
- ½ teaspoon salt
- ¼ teaspoon lemon zest

Directions:
Pour water in the instant pot and preheat it on Saute mode. Add cornstarch and stir carefully until homogenous. After this, add lemon juice, almond butter, sugar, salt, and lemon zest. Whisk the mixture well and bring it to boil. Then switch off the instant pot and chill the sauce.

Nutrition value/serving: calories 47, fat 3, fiber 0.6, carbs 4.6, protein 1.1

Roasted Pepper Salsa

Prep time: 10 minutes | Cooking time: 5 minutes | Servings: 4

Ingredients:
- 1-pound sweet pepper, seeded
- 1 cup tomatoes, chopped
- 1 oz fresh basil
- 1 teaspoon salt
- 1 teaspoon ground black pepper
- 1 garlic clove, chopped
- 1 tablespoon balsamic vinegar
- 2 tablespoons olive oil
- 1 cup water, for cooking

Directions:
Pour water in the instant pot. Insert the trivet. Place sweet peppers on the trivet and close the lid. Cook them on Manual mode (high pressure) for 5 minutes. Then use quick pressure release. Open the lid and transfer the peppers in the blender. Add tomatoes, fresh basil, salt, ground black pepper, garlic, balsamic vinegar, and olive oil. Blend the mixture for 1 minute. Transfer the cooked salsa in the serving bowl.

Nutrition value/serving: calories 82, fat 7.2, fiber 1.2, carbs 4.8, protein 1

Arugula Hummus

Prep time: 25 minutes | Cooking time: 25 minutes | Servings: 4

Ingredients:
- 1 cup garbanzo beans, soaked
- 3 cups of water
- 2 cups arugula
- 1 teaspoon salt
- 1 teaspoon harissa
- 1 tablespoon olive oil
- 1 teaspoon lemon juice
- ½ teaspoon tahini

Directions:
Cook garbanzo beans: place water and beans in the instant pot. Close and seal the lid; cook the beans for 25 minutes, then allow natural pressure release for 20 minutes more. After this, transfer beans and 1/3 cup of bean water in the blender. Add arugula, salt, harissa, olive oil, lemon juice, and tahini. Blend the mixture until smooth. Transfer arugula hummus in the serving bowl.

Nutrition value/serving: calories 223, fat 7.2, fiber 8.9, carbs 31.4, protein 10.1

Edamole

Prep time: 10 minutes | *Cooking time:* 8 minutes | *Servings:* 4

Ingredients:
- 1 cup green soybeans, soaked
- 4 cups of water
- 1 garlic clove, chopped
- ½ teaspoon ground cumin
- 1 tablespoon hot sauce

Directions:
Place water and soybeans in the instant pot. Close and seal the lid. Cook soybeans on manual mode for 30 minutes. Then use quick pressure release. Drain water and transfer soybeans in the blender. Add garlic clove, ground cumin, and hot sauce. Blend the mixture for 1-2 minutes. Transfer edamole in the serving bowl.

Nutrition value/serving: calories 210, fat 9.3, fiber 4.4, carbs 14.5, protein 17.1

Pizza Sauce

Prep time: 5 minutes | *Cooking time:* 6 minutes | *Servings:* 6

Ingredients:
- ½ cup tomato juice
- ¼ cup almond yogurt
- 1 teaspoon minced garlic
- 1 teaspoon dried dill
- 1 teaspoon Italian seasoning
- 1 teaspoon maple syrup
- 1 teaspoon chili pepper
- 1 teaspoon olive oil

Directions:
Pour olive oil in the instant pot. Preheat it on Saute mode. Add chili pepper, Italian seasoning, dried dill, and minced garlic. Cook the mixture for 2 minutes. Stir it. Then add maple syrup, tomato juice, and almond yogurt. Mix up the mixture. Close the lid and saute sauce for 4 minutes. Then open the lid, mix up the sauce one more time and transfer it in the bowl.

Nutrition value/serving: calories 24, fat 1.4, fiber 0.2, carbs 2.8, protein 0.4

Garlic Dip

Prep time: 15 minutes | *Cooking time:* 5 minutes | *Servings:* 2

Ingredients:
- ½ cup almond milk
- ¼ cup garlic, minced
- 1 teaspoon salt
- ½ teaspoon ground black pepper
- 1 teaspoon corn flour

Directions:
Pour almond milk in the instant pot. Preheat it on Saute mode. Add corn flour and whisk well. Then add minced garlic, salt, and ground black pepper. Keep whisking dip for 3 minutes more. Then switch off the instant pot and close the lid. Let the dip rest for 10-15 minutes before serving.

Nutrition value/serving: calories 169, fat 14.5, fiber 1.9, carbs 10.2, protein 2.6

Desserts
Black Beans Cookies
Prep time: *15 minutes* | ***Cooking time:*** *13 minutes* | ***Servings:*** *6*

Ingredients:
- 1 cup black beans, canned
- 1 tablespoon almond butter
- 1 teaspoon ground flax seeds
- 2 tablespoons water
- ½ teaspoon baking powder
- 1 tablespoon lemon juice
- 1 oz vegan dark chocolate, chopped
- 1 tablespoon cocoa powder
- 1/3 cup wheat flour
- 2 tablespoons sugar
- ½ cup of water

Directions:
lace the black beans in the food processor. Blend them until you get soft and smooth mass. After this, mix up together blended black beans with almond butter, ground flax seeds, water, baking powder, lemon juice, and cocoa powder. Add wheat flour and sugar. Mix it up. Microwave chocolate until it is melted and transfer it into the black bean mixture. Make the cookie dough with the help of the wooden spoon. Let the prepared mixture rest for 10 minutes. After this, make the medium size balls from the black bean dough and press them gently to get the cookies. Line the instant pot pan with the baking pepper. Pour the water in the instant pot and insert the pan. Place the cookies into the pan, close and seal the lid. Set High pressure (manual mode) and cook cookies for 8 minutes. When the time is over, allow natural pressure release for 5 minutes. Open the lid and chill the cookies well before serving.

Nutrition value/serving: calories 197, fat 3.7, fiber 5.9, carbs 33.6, protein 8.9

Bean Cookie Dough
Prep time: *15 minutes* | ***Cooking time:*** *55minutes* | ***Servings:*** *3*

Ingredients:
- ½ cup white beans, soaked
- 2 cups of water
- ¼ teaspoon salt
- 2 tablespoons brown sugar
- 1 teaspoon vanilla extract
- 2 tablespoons coconut milk
- 1 tablespoon coconut oil
- 1 tablespoon peanut butter
- 2 tablespoons chocolate chips

Directions:
Place water and white beans in the instant pot. Close and seal the lid. Set Manual mode (high pressure) and cook beans for 30 minutes. Then allow natural pressure release for 20 minutes. Drain water from the white beans and transfer them in the food processor. Process the beans until they get a smooth texture. After this, add salt, brown sugar, vanilla extract, coconut milk, coconut oil, and peanut butter. lend the mixture for 1 minute more. Transfer the bean mixture in the bowl and add chocolate chips. Stir the blend until homogenous. Place the cooked dessert in the fridge and let it there for at least 20 minutes.

Nutrition value/serving: calories 270, fat 12, fiber 5.9, carbs 32.1, protein 10

Navy Beans Biscuits
Prep time: 10 minutes | Cooking time: 12 minutes | Servings: 8

Ingredients:
- 6 oz navy beans, cooked
- 1 cup wheat flour
- 1 teaspoon vanilla extract
- 3 teaspoons brown sugar
- 2 tablespoons coconut oil
- ½ cup flax meal flour
- ¾ teaspoon salt
- ½ teaspoon ground cinnamon
- ¼ cup walnuts, chopped
- 1 cup of water

Directions:
Mash the navy beans with a fork or pulse them in the blender. Then transfer the beans in the mixing bowl; add wheat flour, vanilla extract, brown sugar, coconut oil, flax meal flour, salt, and ground cinnamon. With the help of the spoon stir the mixture until you get a smooth dough. Then add chopped walnuts and knead the dough. Make the log from the dough and cut it into 8 pieces. Make the balls from the dough pieces. Pour water in the instant pot and insert rack. Line the rack with parchment. Place dough balls on the rack. Close and seal the lid. Set Manual mode (high pressure) and cook biscuits for 12 minutes. Use quick pressure release. Chill the cookies well before serving.

Nutrition value/serving: calories 223, fat 8.7, fiber 8, carbs 29, protein 8.8

Chickpea Chocolate Hummus
Prep time: 10 minutes | Cooking time: 55 minutes | Servings: 5

Ingredients:
- 2 cups chickpeas, soaked
- 5 cups of water
- 2 tablespoons tahini
- 4 tablespoons maple syrup
- 1 teaspoon vanilla extract
- 1 tablespoon cocoa powder

Directions:
Put the chickpeas and water in the instant pot. Close and seal the lid. Cook the chickpeas on High-pressure mode for 35 minutes. Allow natural pressure release for 20 minutes. Place tahini, maple syrup, vanilla extract, and cocoa powder in the blender. Drain water from the chickpeas and transfer them in the blender too. Blend the mixture until it is smooth. Transfer the cooked hummus in the serving bowl. Add 1-2 teaspoons of boiled water if the cooked meal is not soft enough.

Nutrition value/serving: calories 373, fat 8.2, fiber 14.8, carbs 61.2, protein 16.7

White Beans Blondies

Prep time: 15 minutes | *Cooking time:* 13 minutes | *Servings:* 4

Ingredients:
- ½ cup white beans, canned
- 4 tablespoons wheat flour
- 1/3 teaspoon baking soda
- 1 teaspoon lemon juice
- 1 tablespoon cashew butter
- ½ teaspoon vanilla extract
- 1 tablespoon peanuts, chopped
- ¾ cup vegan chocolate chips
- ½ teaspoon olive oil
- 1 tablespoon sugar

Directions:
In the bowl of food processor combine together white beans, wheat flour, baking soda, lemon juice, cashew butter, vanilla extract, and sugar. Blend the mixture until you get soft dough texture. Spray the instant pot springform pan with olive oil. Transfer the bean dough in the instant pot, flatten it gently and add chocolate chips. Press the chocolate chips inside the dough with the help of the spatula or hand palm. Cover the blondies with foil and secure the edges. Pin the foil to make small holes. Pour water in the instant pot and insert springform pan. Close and seal the lid. Cook the blondies on Manual mode (high pressure) for 13 minutes. Then allow natural pressure release. Open the lid and discard the foil from the dessert. Chill it well and cut into the servings.

Nutrition value/serving: calories 227, fat 7, fiber 5.1, carbs 33.3, protein 8.8

Cranberry Cake

Prep time: 15 minutes | *Cooking time:* 30 minutes | *Servings:* 6

Ingredients:
- 8 oz wheat flour
- ¼ teaspoon ground cinnamon
- ½ teaspoon ground cardamom
- ½ teaspoon baking powder
- ½ cup of coconut milk
- ½ cup of sugar
- 4 oz cranberries, chopped
- Cooking spray
- 1 cup water, for cooking

Directions:
In the mixing bowl mix up together wheat flour, ground cinnamon, cardamom, baking powder, coconut milk, and sugar. When the mixture is homogenous, add chopped cranberries and stir it carefully. Spray the bundt pan with the cooking spray from inside and transfer the mixed dough. Flatten it gently with the help of the spatula. Cover the pan with the parchment or foil. Secure the edges. Pour water in the instant pot. Insert bundt pan and close the lid. Set Manual mode (high pressure) and cook cake for 30 minutes. Allow natural pressure release for 20 minutes. When the cake is cooked, discard the foil parchment from it and chill it till the room temperature. Slice it.

Nutrition value/serving: calories 258, fat 5.2, fiber 2.3, carbs 48.8, protein 4.4

Apple Crumble

Prep time: 20 minutes | *Cooking time:* 14 minutes | *Servings:* 4

Ingredients:
- ¼ cup coconut flakes
- 1 cup rolled oats
- ¼ cup wheat flour
- 3 tablespoons cashew butter
- 1 teaspoon vanilla extract
- 1 cup apples, chopped
- 1 tablespoon brown sugar
- 1 tablespoon maple syrup
- ¾ cup of soy milk
- Cooking spray
- ½ cup of water

Directions:

In the mixing bowl combine together coconut flakes, rolled oats, wheat flour, cashew butter, vanilla extract, brown sugar, and soy milk. Add maple syrup and stir it until homogenous. Spray the pan with the cooking spray. Make the crumble: place 1 tablespoon of the coconut flake dough in the pan, flatten it well to make the layer, then add chopped apples, after this repeat the steps till you use all the ingredients. Cover the pan with the foil. Pour water in the instant pot and insert pan. Close and seal the lid. Cook the crumble on High-pressure mode for 14 minutes. Then use quick pressure release. Discard the foil from the crumble and let it chill for 10 minutes.

Nutrition value/serving: calories 273, fat 9.9, fiber 4.6, carbs 40.2, protein 7.4

Gajar Halwa

Prep time: 10 minutes | *Cooking time:* 15 minutes | *Servings:* 2

Ingredients:
- 2 teaspoons coconut oil
- 1 oz cashew, chopped
- ½ oz raisins
- 1 ½ cup carrot, grated
- 4 tablespoons coconut milk
- ¾ teaspoon cardamom powder
- ¾ teaspoon ground cinnamon
- 1 tablespoon semolina
- Cooking spray

Directions:

Preheat instant pot well on Saute mode. Then add chopped cashews and raisins. Cook them on Saute mode for 3 minutes. Stit from time to time. After this, add grated carrot, cardamom powder, and ground cinnamon. Add coconut milk. Mix up the ingredients well. Close the lid and cook the mixture on Manual mode for 2 minutes. Then make a quick pressure release and open the lid. Add all the remaining ingredients and stir well. Saute the meal for 10 minutes. Stir it from time to time. Then chill the cooked halwa gently and transfer into the bowl.

Nutrition value/serving: calories 268, fat 18.4, fiber 4.3, carbs 25, protein 4.5

Chocolate Cake

Prep time: 40 minutes | Cooking time: 40 minutes | Servings: 6

Ingredients:
- 1 cup wheat flour
- 2 tablespoons cocoa powder
- 1 teaspoon vanilla extract
- 1 teaspoon baking powder
- 1 teaspoon apple cider vinegar
- ½ cup cashew milk
- 1 cup coconut cream
- 2 tablespoons dark chocolate, melted
- Cooking spray
- 1 cup water for cooking

Directions:
In the mixing bowl, mix up together all dry ingredients. Then add apple cider vinegar, vanilla extract, and cashew milk. Mix up the chocolate batter until homogenous. Spray the springform pan with the cooking spray and pour chocolate batter inside. Pour water in the instant pot. Cover the pan with foil and secure edges. Place it in the instant pot. Close and seal the instant pot lid. Cook the cake on High-pressure mode (manual mode) for 40 minutes. Then allow natural pressure release for 15 minutes. Meanwhile, whisk together melted chocolate and coconut cream. Transfer the cake on the plate and chill it well. Cut it into 2 cake layers. Spread every cake layer with the coconut cream mixture. Combine the cake layers in the cake. Place it in the fridge for 30 minutes then cut it into servings.

Nutrition value/serving: calories 196, fat 11.2, fiber 2.1, carbs 21.8, protein 3.7

Pumpkin Muffins

Prep time: 15 minutes | Cooking time: 10 minutes | Servings: 4

Ingredients:
- 4 teaspoons pumpkin puree
- 4 tablespoons wheat flour
- 1 teaspoon baking powder
- 1 teaspoon apple cider vinegar
- 1 teaspoon ground cinnamon
- 1 tablespoon coconut oil
- 2 teaspoons sugar
- ½ cup water, for cooking

Directions:
In the mixing bowl, mix up together pumpkin puree, wheat flour, baking powder, apple cider vinegar, ground cinnamon, and sugar. Then add coconut oil and stir it until smooth. The muffin batter is cooked. Pour water in the instant pot and set steamer rack. Then fill ½ of every muffin mold with muffin batter and transfer them on the steamer rack. Close and seal the lid. Set Manual mode (high pressure) and cook muffins for 10 minutes. Then allow natural pressure release for 10 minutes more. Open the lid and transfer the cooked muffins on the serving plate.

Nutrition value/serving: calories 70, fat 3.5, fiber 0.7, carbs 9.4, protein 0.9

Vanilla Custard
Prep time: 15 minutes | Cooking time: 10 minutes | Servings: 3

Ingredients:
- 1 cup almond milk
- 1 tablespoon cornstarch
- 2 teaspoons vanilla extract
- 2 tablespoons sugar
- ½ teaspoon ground cinnamon
- 1 tablespoon almond butter

Directions:

Preheat instant pot on Saute mode. When it is hot, pour almond milk inside. Saute it until it starts to boil. Add vanilla extract, sugar, and ground cinnamon. Stir it well and cook until sugar is dissolved. Then add cornstarch and whisk the liquid with the help of the hand whisker for 3-4 minutes or until it starts to be thick. Then add almond butter and mix it. Transfer the custard into the serving bowls and let chill for 10-15 minutes or at least till the room temperature.

Nutrition value/serving: calories 266, fat 22.1, fiber 2.5, carbs 16.5, protein 3

Vanilla Caramel Cream
Prep time: 10 minutes | Cooking time: 10 minutes | Servings: 2

Ingredients:
- 1 cup brown sugar
- 1 teaspoon coconut oil
- ½ cup coconut cream
- 1 tablespoon vanilla extract

Directions:

Preheat instant pot on Saute mode. Then add brown sugar and start to melt it. Do not stir it for the first 2 minutes. When the sugar starts to melt, add vanilla extract, coconut oil, and coconut cream. Stir it slowly and gently until homogenous. Cook the caramel for 5 minutes. Then pour the dessert into the mason jars and let it chill till the room temperature.

Nutrition value/serving: calories 452, fat 16.6, fiber 1.3, carbs 75.3, protein 1.5

Strawberry Gummies
Prep time: 10 minutes | Cooking time: 10 minutes | Servings: 8

Ingredients:
- ½ cup strawberry syrup
- 3 cups of water
- 1 teaspoon citrus pectin
- 3 tablespoons gelatins

Directions:

Combine together gelatin with a ½ cup of water and stir. Let it rest until gelatin soaks all water. Meanwhile, place strawberry syrup and all remaining water in the instant pot. Preheat it on saute mode and add citrus pectin. Stir it well and don't let it boil. Then microwave the gelatin mixture for 2-3 seconds. Add melted gelatin in the hot strawberry liquid. Stir it until homogenous. Pour the liquid into the silicone gummy molds. Chill the gummies until they are solid (approximately 2-3 hours.) Store the gummies in the cold place or in the fridge.

Nutrition value/serving: calories 88, fat 0, fiber 0, carbs 13, protein 9

Carrot Cake

Prep time: 10 minutes | *Cooking time:* 35 minutes | *Servings:* 6

Ingredients:
- 1 cup wheat flour
- 1 cup almond flour
- ½ cup carrot, grated
- 1 tablespoon vanilla extract
- 1 teaspoon ground cinnamon
- 1 teaspoon ground nutmeg
- ½ teaspoon ground clove
- ½ cup walnuts, chopped
- 4 tablespoons brown sugar
- 1 tablespoon coconut oil
- 1 teaspoon baking powder
- 1 tablespoon lemon juice
- ½ cup of coconut milk
- 1 cup coconut cream
- ¼ cup maple syrup
- Cooking spray
- 1 cup water, for cooking

Directions:
In the cooking machine: combine together wheat flour and almond flour. Add vanilla extract, ground cinnamon, nutmeg, ground clove, brown sugar, coconut oil, baking powder, lemon juice, and coconut milk. Start to mix up the dough. When it gets homogenous texture, add grated carrot and walnuts. Mix up the dough. Pour water in the instant pot and insert trivet. Spray the springform pan with cooking pray from inside and transfer the dough. Flatten it gently with the help of a spatula. Then cover it with foil, secure edges, and pin the surface to get tiny holes. Transfer the pan on the trivet and close the lid. Seal the lid and set Manual mode (high pressure). Cook the cake for 35 minutes. After this, use quick pressure release. Open the lid, discard the foil and chill the cake till the room temperature. Meanwhile, whisk together coconut cream and maple syrup. When the cream is smooth and fluffy – it is cooked. Spread the coconut cream over the carrot cake and cut it into the servings.

Nutrition value/serving: calories 481, fat 24, fiber 2.9, carbs 62.2, protein 6.9

Pumpkin Spice Pie
Prep time: 20 minutes | Cooking time: 16 minutes | Servings: 4

Ingredients:
- 3 tablespoons buckwheat flour
- 1 cup wheat flour
- 1 tablespoon vanilla extract
- 1 teaspoon pumpkin spices
- 4 tablespoons pumpkin puree
- 1 teaspoon coconut oil
- 1/3 cup sugar
- ¼ cup almond milk
- 1 cup of water

Directions:
Combine together all dry ingredients in the mixing bowl. After this, start to add wet ingredients: vanilla extract, pumpkin puree, coconut oil, and almond milk. Mix up the mixture to get the homogenous liquid dough. Pour water and insert trivet in the instant pot. Then transfer the liquid dough in the non-sticky pie pan. Place the pan on the trivet and cover it with foil. Close and seal the lid. Cook the pie for 16 minutes. Then allow natural pressure release for 10 minutes. Open the lid and discard foil, transfer the cake on the serving plate, chill it till room temperature and slice.

Nutrition value/serving: calories 255, fat 5.3, fiber 2.2, carbs 47.3, protein 4.5

Lemon Curd
Prep time: 10 minutes | Cooking time: 10 minutes | Servings: 2

Ingredients:
- ½ cup lemon juice
- 1 cup of coconut milk
- 1 teaspoon lemon zest
- 1 tablespoon vanilla extract
- 1 tablespoon cornstarch
- ¾ cup brown sugar

Directions:
Preheat instant pot on Saute mode. Meanwhile, whisk together lemon juice and cornstarch. Then pour coconut milk in the preheated instant pot. Add lemon juice mixture, lemon zest, and vanilla extract. Whisk it gently to make the homogenous liquid. Then add sugar and start to stir it constantly until the liquid is thick. The curd is cooked. Strain it with the help of colander and transfer in the serving bowls.

Nutrition value/serving: calories 532, fat 29.1, fiber 3, carbs 66, protein 3.3

Brownies

Prep time: 20 minutes | Cooking time: 15 minutes | Servings: 4

Ingredients:
- 1 teaspoon baking powder
- 1 teaspoon apple cider vinegar
- 1 cup wheat flour
- 1 tablespoon cocoa powder
- ¼ cup walnuts, chopped
- 3 tablespoons coconut oil
- 1 teaspoon vanilla extract
- 2 tablespoons brown sugar
- 1 cup water, for cooking

Directions:
In the food processor mix up together all the ingredients. Pour the brownie batter in the non-stick pan. Pour water in the instant pot and insert the trivet. Place the pan with a brownie on the trivet and cover with the foil. Close and seal the lid. Set Manual mode (High pressure) and cook brownies for 15 minutes. After this, allow natural pressure release for 10 minutes. Open the lid, discard the foil and transfer brownies on the chopping board. Cut the brownies into the square bars.

Nutrition value/serving: calories 275, fat 15.3, fiber 1.8, carbs 30.5, protein 5.4

Dulce de Leche

Prep time: 15 minutes | Cooking time: 2 hours | Servings: 4

Ingredients:
- 1 teaspoon vanilla extract
- 1 cup of sugar
- 1 cup of coconut milk

Directions:
Pour coconut milk in the instant pot. Add sugar and vanilla extract. Cook it on Saute mode for 15 minutes. Stir it from time to time. After this, close the lid and cook the dessert on Low-pressure mode for 2 hours. Chill cooked dulce de leche and pour into the mason jars.

Nutrition value/serving: calories 329, fat 14.3, fiber 1.3, carbs 53.5, protein 1.4

Cheesecake

Prep time: 40 minutes | Cooking time: 10 minutes | Servings: 6

Ingredients:
- 2 tablespoons coconut oil
- 1 cup vegan cookies
- 5 oz cashew, soaked
- 6 oz firm tofu
- 7 oz coconut cream
- 1 teaspoon lemon zest
- 3 tablespoons sugar
- 1 teaspoon vanilla extract
- 1 cup water, for cooking
- Cooking spray

Directions:

For the cake crust: crush the vegan cookies until you get crumbs and mix them up with the coconut oil. Then place the mixture in the cheesecake form, press it well to get the cookies layer (crust). After this, put cashew and firm tofu in the food processor. Blend the mixture until smooth. Add coconut cream, lemon zest sugar, and vanilla extract. Blend it well for 3-5 minutes. Pour the coconut cream mixture over the cookies crust and flatten gently with the help of the silicone spatula. Pour water in the instant pot. Insert the trivet and place cheesecake on it. Cover the dessert with the foil and secure the edges. Make the small holes in the foil with the help of the toothpick. Then close and seal the lid. Cook the cheesecake on High-pressure mode for 10 minutes. Then allow natural pressure release for 15 minutes. Open the lid and remove the cheesecake pan from it. Discard the foil and chill the dessert till the room temperature. After this, chill it in the fridge for 30 minutes. Slice it.

Nutrition value/serving: calories 340, fat 27, fiber 2.2, carbs 20.9, protein 7.2

Flan Mini Cakes

Prep time: 30 minutes | Cooking time: 10 minutes | Servings: 4

Ingredients:
- 4 tablespoons caramel topping
- 2 cups soy cream
- 1 oz cornstarch
- ¾ cup maple syrup
- 1 teaspoon vanilla extract

Directions:

Set instant pot on Saute mode and pour 1 cup of soy cream inside. Start to preheat it. In the mixing bowl, mix up together cornstarch and remaining soy cream. Add vanilla extract and whisk it. Then take 4 ramekins. Place 1 tablespoon of caramel topping inside every dish. Mix up together hot soy cream and cornstarch mixture in the instant pot. Whisk it well for 5 minutes or until it thickens. Then transfer the thick soy cream mixture in the ramekins with caramel topping. Place them in the fridge and chill for 30 minutes. Place the chilled ramekins on the serving plates and turn upside down.

Nutrition value/serving: calories 302, fat 2.3, fiber 1, carbs 67.4, protein 4.3

Creme Brulee

Prep time: 15 minutes | Cooking time: 10 minutes | Servings: 6

Ingredients:
- 4 cups cashew milk
- 2 oz cornstarch
- 1 tablespoon vanilla extract
- ½ cup of sugar
- 6 teaspoon brown sugar

Directions:
In the blender, blend together cashew milk, cornstarch, vanilla extract, and sugar. Meanwhile, preheat the instant pot on Saute mode. Pour the blended liquid into the preheated instant pot. Saute it for 10 minutes. Stir it from time to time. The liquid is cooked when it starts to be thick. Then transfer the thick cashew milk mixture in the creme brulee ramekins. Let it chill for at least 30 minutes. Sprinkle the surface of mixture with brown sugar. Caramelize it with the blow torch.

Nutrition value/serving: calories 133, fat 1.3, fiber 0.1, carbs 29.2, protein 0

Maple Syrup Apples

Prep time: 15 minutes | Cooking time: 10 minutes | Servings: 3

Ingredients:
- 3 Granny Smith apples
- ½ cup maple syrup
- 1 cup of water
- 1 teaspoon ground cinnamon

Directions:
Trim the apples and cut them into the halves. Pour maple syrup and water in the instant pot. Cook the liquid on Saute mode for 5 minutes. Then add ground cinnamon, stir it. Add apple halves. Coat them carefully in the syrup mixture and close the lid. Saute the apples for 5 minutes more. Then switch off the instant pot and let the apples for 10 minutes.

Nutrition value/serving: calories 255, fat 0.5, fiber 5.8, carbs 66.6, protein 0.6

Pear Pudding

Prep time: 10 minutes | Cooking time: 10 minutes | Servings: 4

Ingredients:
- ½ cup pear puree
- 2 cups of soy milk
- 4 tablespoons brown sugar
- 1 tablespoon wheat flour
- 1 teaspoon cornflour
- 1 teaspoon almond butter
- 1 tablespoon almond flakes

Directions:
Mix up together pear puree and wheat flour. Add soy milk, brown sugar, corn flour, and almond butter. Stir it well. Preheat instant pot on Saute mode well. Transfer the pear puree mixture in the preheated instant pot and bring it to boil. Then pour the cooked pudding into the serving bowls and sprinkle with almond flakes. It is recommended to chill the dessert until the room temperature before serving.

Nutrition value/serving: calories 225, fat 5.7, fiber 1.5, carbs 37, protein 5.6

Rhubarb Bars

Prep time: 20 minutes | Cooking time: 35 minutes | Servings: 3

Ingredients:
- ¼ cup rhubarb, chopped
- 1 cup wheat flour
- 1 teaspoon vanilla extract
- 1 tablespoon flax meal
- 4 tablespoons water
- 3 oz sugar
- 1 tablespoon coconut oil
- 1/3 cup soy milk
- 1 teaspoon baking powder
- 1 teaspoon lemon juice
- 1 cup water, for cooking

Directions:

Mix up together wheat flour, vanilla extract, sugar, coconut oil, milk, baking powder, and lemon juice. Make the homogenous batter. Then take the separated bowl and whisk water with flax meal in it. Add the liquid into the batter and stir it well. After this, add chopped rhubarb and stir gently. Pour water in the instant pot. Insert trivet. Place the cake form on the trivet and line it with baking paper. Pour rhubarb batter in the cake form and close the lid. Cook the dessert on high-pressure mode for 35 minutes. Then allow natural pressure release for 15 minutes. Chill the cooked meal well and only after this cut it into the bars.

Nutrition value/serving: calories 330, fat 6.3, fiber 2.2, carbs 64, protein 5.8

Pumpkin Pudding

Prep time: 5 minutes | Cooking time: 10 minutes | Servings: 1

Ingredients:
- ¼ teaspoon pumpkin pie spices
- ¾ cup maple syrup
- ½ cup pumpkin puree
- ¾ cup of coconut milk
- ½ teaspoon cornstarch

Directions:

Mix up together cornstarch and pumpkin puree. Add maple syrup and coconut milk. Whisk it. Pour the pumpkin mixture in the instant pot. Add pumpkin pie spices and saute the pudding for 10 minutes. Stir it every 1 minute. Then transfer the pudding in the serving ramekin and chill.

Nutrition value/serving: calories 675, fat 0.9, fiber 5.4, carbs 171.8, protein 2

Sweet Potato Pie

Prep time: 30 minutes | *Cooking time:* 20 minutes | *Servings:* 8

Ingredients:
- 1 cup vegan chocolate cookies, crushed
- 4 tablespoons almond butter
- 3 tablespoons brown sugar
- ½ cup coconut cream
- 9 oz sweet potato, cooked, mashed
- ½ teaspoon ground cinnamon
- ½ teaspoon ground clove
- 1 teaspoon vanilla extract
- 2 tablespoons cashew butter
- ½ teaspoon orange zest
- ¾ cup white sugar
- 1 cup water, for cooking

Directions:
For the pie crust: mix up together vegan chocolate cookies, brown sugar, and almond butter. Place the mixture in the cake form and press it with the help of the spoon to get the pie crust. Transfer the cake from with pie crust in the freezer. fter this, put in the food processor: coconut cream, mashed potato, ground cinnamon, vanilla extract, cashew butter, and white sugar. Blend it until smooth. Get the form with pie crust from the freezer. Pour the mashed sweet potato mixture over the pie crust. Cover the pie into foil and secure the edges. Pour water in the instant pot. nsert trivet and place cake form on it. Close and seal the lid. Cook the pie on High-pressure mode for 20 minutes. Then allow natural pressure release for 20 minutes. Open the lid and transfer the form with pie on the chopping board or rack. iscard the foil. Transfer the pie on the serving plate, chill well, and cut into the servings.

Nutrition value/serving: calories 401, fat 19.2, fiber 3.4, carbs 55.4, protein 5.4

Soda Cake

Prep time: 15 minutes | *Cooking time:* 20 minutes | *Servings:* 6

Ingredients:
- 1 cup of sugar
- 1 cup flour
- ½ cup almond milk
- 3 tablespoons coconut oil
- 1 teaspoon vanilla extract
- 1 tablespoon coconut flakes
- 1 teaspoon baking soda
- 1 tablespoon apple cider vinegar
- 1 cup water, for cooking
- Cooking spray

Directions:
Combine together all the dry ingredients: sugar, flour, coconut flakes, and baking soda. Then start to add wet ingredients: almond milk, coconut oil, vanilla extract, and apple cider vinegar. With the help of the hand mixer, blend the mixture until smooth. Spray the cake form with the cooking spray and pour batter inside. latten the surface gently. Pour water in the instant pot. Insert the trivet. Place the cake pan on the trivet and cover it with foil. Close and seal the lid. Set manual mode (high pressure) and cook cake for 20 minutes. After this, allow natural pressure release for 10 minutes more.

Nutrition value/serving: calories 311, fat 12.1, fiber 1.1, carbs 50.6, protein 2.6

Poached Peaches
Prep time: 10 minutes | Cooking time: 3 minutes | Servings: 4

Ingredients:
- 1 cup of water
- 1 cup apple juice
- 5 tablespoons brown sugar
- 1 cinnamon stick
- 1-pound peaches

Directions:
Cut the peaches into halves and remove pits. Place them in the instant pot. In the mixing bowl, combine together apple juice, brown sugar, and water. Then pour the liquid over the peaches. Add cinnamon stick. Close and seal the lid. Set high-pressure mode and cook peaches for 3 minutes. Then allow natural pressure release for 5 minutes. Place the cooked peaches in the bowls and pour them with the apple juice syrup (from the instant pot).

Nutrition value/serving: calories 111, fat 1.4, fiber 0.7, carbs 24.5, protein 0.9

Date Bars
Prep time: 10 minutes | Cooking time: 4 minutes | Servings: 4

Ingredients:
- 1 cup dates, pitted
- 1 cup rolled oats
- 3 tablespoons brown sugar
- 1 teaspoon vanilla extract
- 1 tablespoon lemon juice
- 1/3 cup wheat flour
- 3 tablespoons almond butter
- ½ cup of water

Directions:
Place the dates in the bowl and mash them with the help of the fork. When the fruits are smooth, add rolled oats, brown sugar, vanilla extract, lemon juice, and wheat flour. Stir the mixture little and add almond butter. Mix it up carefully. Then place the mixture on the parchment and roll it up. Cut it into the medium size bars. Cover them with the second sheet of parchment and make the "envelope". Pour water in the instant pot. Insert the trivet. Place the envelope with date bars on the trivet. Close and seal the lid. Cook the dessert for 4 minutes on High-pressure mode. Then use the quick pressure release. Open the lid, transfer the bars on the plate and chill well.

Nutrition value/serving: calories 344, fat 8.4, fiber 7.1, carbs 64.3, protein 7.5

Banana Cream Tart

Prep time: 15 minutes | *Cooking time:* 8 minutes | *Servings:* 4

Ingredients:
- 5 oz instant banana pudding
- 1 cup of soy milk
- 1 banana, sliced
- 1 teaspoon lemon juice
- 3 oz rice vegan crackers
- 2 tablespoons almond butter

Directions:
Mix up together soy milk and instant banana pudding. Pour the liquid in the instant pot. Cook it on saute mode for 5-8 minutes. Stir it from time to time. The cooked pudding should be thick. Meanwhile, chop the crackers into the tiny pieces and mix up with the almond butter. Line the springform pan with the parchment. Place the cracker mixture inside the springform pan and distribute it evenly to get the pie crust shape. Pour the cooked pudding over the pie crust. Then place sliced banana over the pudding. Sprinkle it with lemon juice (it will protect from black spots on the fruits.)

Nutrition value/serving: calories 332, fat 8.9, fiber 2, carbs 54.5, protein 8.9

Cookie Cake

Prep time: 15 minutes | *Cooking time:* 15 minutes | *Servings:* 6

Ingredients:
- 1 cup wheat flour
- 1 teaspoon baking powder
- 1 teaspoon apple cider vinegar
- ½ cup of sugar
- ¼ cup vegan chocolate chips
- 3 tablespoons cashew butter, melted
- 1 cup coconut cream
- 2 tablespoons cocoa powder
- ½ cup walnuts, chopped
- 1 cup water, for cooking

Directions:
In the mixing bowl make the cookie batter: in the spoon mix up together apple cider vinegar and baking powder. Transfer the mixture in the mixing bowl. Add wheat flour, sugar, cashew butter, and stir it well until you get the batter texture. Then add vegan chocolate chips and mix up gently. Transfer the batter in the cake pan. Pour water in the instant pot. After this, insert the trivet. Put the cake pan with batter in the trivet and cover it with foil. Close and seal the lid. Cook the cake for 15 minutes on manual mode(high pressure). Then allow natural pressure release for 10 minutes. Meanwhile, make the cake frosting: whisk together coconut cream, walnuts, and cocoa powder. When the mixture is fluffy, it is cooked. ransfer the cooked cookie on the serving plate. Spread it with the coconut cream frosting.

Nutrition value/serving: calories 360, fat 20.8, fiber 3, carbs 41.1, protein 7.5

Chocolate Pudding

Prep time: 5 minutes | Cooking time: 3 hours | Servings: 2

Ingredients:
- ½ cup of coconut milk
- ½ cup cashew milk
- 1 teaspoon cornflour
- 1 teaspoon vanilla extract
- 1/3 cup peanuts, chopped
- 1 tablespoon cocoa powder
- 2 teaspoons brown sugar

Directions:
Put in the food processor: coconut milk, cashew milk, cornflour, vanilla extract, cocoa powder, and brown sugar. Blend it until homogenous. Pour the liquid in the instant pot. Add chopped peanuts. Close the lid. Set low-pressure mode and cook pudding for 3 hours. Then stir it well and place into the serving glasses.

Nutrition value/serving: calories 310, fat 27.2, fiber 4.3, carbs 13.1, protein 8.2

Chia Seeds Cookies

Prep time: 15 minutes | Cooking time: 5 minutes | Servings: 10

Ingredients:
- 1 cup almonds
- ½ cup chia seeds
- 3 oz dates, pitted
- 1 cup of rice flour
- 1 tablespoon coconut oil
- 5 tablespoons maple syrup
- 1 cup of water

Directions:
Blend the almonds in the food processor until you get almond flour. After this, combine almond flour with rice flour, and chia seeds. Blend the dates until you get date puree. Add them in the flour mixture. Add coconut oil and maple syrup. nead the non-sticky dough. Add more coconut oil if needed. Then make 10 balls from the date mixture. Pres them gently. Pour water in the instant pot. Insert trivet. Line the trivet with baking paper. Place the date cookies on it. Close the instant pot lid. Cook the cookies on High-pressure mode for 5 minutes. Allow natural pressure release for 5 minutes more. Chill the cookies well.

Nutrition value/serving: calories 230, fat 9.9, fiber 6.1, carbs 32.6, protein 5

Orange-Pineapple Cake

Prep time: 35 minutes | Cooking time: 20 minutes | Servings: 6

Ingredients:
- 1 cup pineapple, canned, chopped
- 1 orange, peeled, sliced
- ½ teaspoon nutritional yeast
- 1 cup almond milk
- 1 ½ cup wheat flour
- 1 teaspoon vanilla extract
- 1 tablespoon ground cinnamon
- 2 tablespoons brown sugar
- ½ cup maple syrup
- Cooking spray

Directions:

Mix up together nutritional yeast, maple syrup, and almond milk. Add ½ cup of wheat flour and stir until smooth. Leave the liquid at a warm place for 20 minutes. Then add all the remaining wheat flour and vanilla extract. Mix it. The cake batter is cooked. Spray the instant pot with cooking spray from inside. Then pour the batter. After this, add chopped pineapples and sliced oranges. Close and seal the lid. Cook the cake for 20 minutes on High-pressure mode or manual mode (it depends on the type of your instant pot). Then use quick pressure release. Open the instant pot, chill the cake until warm. Cut it into the pieces.

Nutrition value/serving: calories 320, fat 10, fiber 3.5, carbs 55, protein 4.8

Almond Cookies

Prep time: 10 minutes | Cooking time: 7 minutes | Servings: 4

Ingredients:
- 4 almonds
- ½ cup wheat flour
- 3 tablespoons almond butter
- ½ teaspoon baking powder
- 4 teaspoons sugar
- ½ teaspoon vanilla extract
- ½ cup water, for cooking

Directions:

In the cooking machine mix up together almond butter, wheat flour, baking powder, and sugar. Add vanilla extract. Then knead the dough with the help of the fingertips. When the dough is smooth and soft, make the log from it. Cut the log into 4 pieces and roll them into the balls. Press every ball gently and place an almond in the center to get the cookie shape. Pour water and insert trivet in the instant pot. Place almond cookies in the pan and place it on the trivet. Close and seal the lid. Cook the cookies for 9 minutes on high-pressure mode. Then use quick pressure release. Chill the cookies well before serving.

Nutrition value/serving: calories 154, fat 7.5, fiber 1.8, carbs 18.8, protein 4.4

Gingerbread Pie

Prep time: 15 minutes | *Cooking time:* 20 minutes | *Servings:* 6

Ingredients:
- 1 teaspoon ground clove
- 1 teaspoon ground cinnamon
- ½ teaspoon ground ginger
- 1 teaspoon vanilla extract
- ½ cup maple syrup
- ½ cup of sugar
- 4 tablespoons coconut butter
- 1 cup flour
- ½ cup almond flour
- 1 tablespoon sugar, powdered

Directions:

Mix up together ground clove, ground cinnamon, ginger, vanilla extract, maple syrup, sugar, and coconut butter. Then add flour and almond flour. Stir the mixture gently. Then knead it until homogenous and non-sticky. Place the dough in the instant pot pie pan and flatten with the help of the fingertips. Pour water and insert trivet in the instant pot. Put the pie pan on the trivet. Close and seal the lid. Cook the pie for 20 minutes on manual mode (high pressure). Then make quick pressure release. Transfer the pie on the serving plate and sprinkle with powdered sugar.

Nutrition value/serving: calories 332, fat 11, fiber 3.6, carbs 56.6, protein 4.9

Apple Upside Down Cake

Prep time: 30 minutes | *Cooking time:* 20 minutes | *Servings:* 6

Ingredients:
- 2 bananas, mashed
- 1 teaspoon vanilla extract
- 1 teaspoon turmeric
- 2 apples, chopped
- ½ cup apple juice
- 1 teaspoon baking soda
- 1 tablespoon lemon juice
- 2 cups wheat flour
- ½ cup of coconut milk
- 1 teaspoon almond butter
- ½ cup of sugar
- 1 cup water, for cooking

Directions:

In the mixing bowl, mix up together mashed bananas, vanilla extract, turmeric, apple juice, baking soda, lemon juice, wheat flour, coconut milk, and sugar. Stir it carefully until smooth. Leave the mixture for 10 minutes to rest. Pour water and insert the trivet in the instant pot. Rub the instant pot pan with the almond butter generously. Then place the chopped apples in the bottom of the pan. Add prepared dough (batter). Flatten it with the help of the spatula. Cover the cake with foil and secure the edges. Pin some holes on the surface. Place the pan on the trivet. Close and seal the lid. Cook the cake on High-pressure mode (manual mode) for 20 minutes. Then allow natural pressure release for 10 minutes. Chill the cooked cake and flip it on the serving plate. Slice it.

Nutrition value/serving: calories 364, fat 7, fiber 4.8, carbs 72, protein 6

Snickerdoodle Bars

Prep time: 25 minutes | Cooking time: 15 minutes | Servings: 4

Ingredients:
- ¼ cup maple syrup
- 1 tablespoon applesauce
- ½ teaspoon vanilla extract
- 2 tablespoons coconut flour
- 1 cup wheat flour
- 1 teaspoon baking powder
- 1 tablespoon candied oranges, chopped
- 2 tablespoons brown sugar
- 1 tablespoon ground cinnamon
- ¼ teaspoon ground cardamom
- ½ cup of water

Directions:
In the big mixing bowl, mix up together maple syrup, applesauce, vanilla extract, coconut flour, wheat flour, and baking powder. Mix up the mixture well with the help of the spoon. Then add candied oranges and knead the soft dough. Line the instant pot pan with the baking paper. Pour water and insert trivet in the instant pot. Put the dough in the prepared pan and flatten it. Then sprinkle it with ground cinnamon, cardamom, and brown sugar. Cover the pan with foil and transfer on the trivet. Close and seal the lid. Cook the dessert for 15 minutes on high-pressure mode. Then allow natural pressure release for 10 minutes. Chill the dessert and cut into bars.

Nutrition value/serving: calories 219, fat 0.8, fiber 3.4, carbs 49.8, protein 3.8

Walnut Sweets

Prep time: 5 minutes | Cooking time: 5 minutes | Servings: 4

Ingredients:
- 1 cup walnuts kernels
- 4 oz vegan raw chocolate, chopped
- ¾ cup almond milk

Directions:
Preheat instant pot on Saute mode until hot. Add chopped raw chocolate and cook it for 2 minutes. When it is melted, add almond milk and whisk until homogenous. Then coat the walnut kernels in the chocolate mixture. Line the tray with the baking paper. Transfer the coated chocolate walnuts on the prepared tray. Let the sweets dry. Store the walnut sweets in the closed paper box.

Nutrition value/serving: calories 459, fat 40.3, fiber 12.2, carbs 19.8, protein 9.6

Cinnamon Swirls
Prep time: 60 minutes | Cooking time: 25 minutes | Servings: 6

Ingredients:
- 1 teaspoon nutritional yeast
- 1 cup of soy milk
- ½ cup of water
- ¾ teaspoon salt
- 2 tablespoons white sugar
- 1 ½ cup wheat flour
- ½ cup of rice flour
- 2 tablespoons ground cinnamon
- 2 tablespoons brown sugar
- 2 tablespoons coconut oil
- 1 cup water, for cooking

Directions:
Set Saute mode and preheat the soy milk little bit. Then mix up together white sugar, nutritional yeast, and ½ cup wheat flour. Cover the mixture and leave it in a warm place for 20 minutes. After this, add salt, water, remaining wheat flour, rice flour, and coconut oil. Knead the soft dough. If the dough is sticky – add olive oil. Leave the dough for 20 minutes in warm place. Then pour water in the instant pot. Insert the rack inside. Line the springform pan with baking paper. In the separated bowl, mix up together brown sugar and ground cinnamon. Roll up the dough and sprinkle the surface of it with the ground cinnamon mix. Roll the dough to get the long log. Cut the log into 6 buns and press them gently. Place the buns (swirls) in the prepared springform pan and cover with foil. Secure the edges of the foil and pin small holes on the surface. Transfer the pan on the rack. Close and seal the lid. Cook the cinnamon swirls for 25 minutes on High-pressure mode. Then allow natural pressure release for 10 minutes.

Nutrition value/serving: calories 257, fat 5.8, fiber 2.8, carbs 46, protein 5.7

Turmeric Loaf
Prep time: 35 minutes | Cooking time: 25 minutes | Servings: 8

Ingredients:
- 6 oz coconut flakes
- 1 cup almond milk
- 1 cup wheat flour
- 1 teaspoon vanilla extract
- ¾ cup of sugar
- 1 teaspoon ground cinnamon
- 2 tablespoons turmeric
- 2 bananas, chopped
- 1 teaspoon baking soda
- 1 tablespoon apple cider vinegar
- 1 cup of water

Directions:
In the blender: blend together coconut flakes, almond milk, vanilla extract, sugar, and ground cinnamon. Pour the blended liquid in the mixing bowl. Add wheat flour, turmeric, baking soda, and apple cider vinegar. Mix up the loaf batter with the help of the spoon. Pour the batter in the loaf mold. Pour water in the instant pot, insert the trivet. Place loaf mold on the trivet, close and seal the lid. Cook the turmeric loaf for 25 minutes. Then allow natural pressure release for 20 minutes. Transfer the loaf on the plate and slice.

Nutrition value/serving: calories 306, fat 14.7, fiber 4.3, carbs 43.7, protein 3.5

Semolina Halwa

Prep time: 10 minutes | Cooking time: 8 minutes | Servings: 4

Ingredients:
- 2 teaspoons olive oil
- 1 cup semolina
- ½ cup peanuts, chopped
- 4 dates, pitted, chopped
- 4 tablespoons brown sugar
- 1 cup of water
- ½ teaspoon ground cinnamon
- ½ teaspoon ground cardamom
- ¼ teaspoon ground cloves
- ¼ cup dried cranberries, chopped

Directions:
Pour olive oil in the instant pot. Add semolina, peanuts, and pitted dates. Start to cook ingredients for 3-4 minutes on Saute mode. Stir them from time to time. After this, add brown sugar, ground cinnamon, cardamom, and ground cloves. Mix up well. Add water and cranberries. With the help of the wooden spatula, mix up semolina mixture very well. Close and seal the instant pot lid. Cook halwa for 4 minutes. Allow natural pressure release for 10 minutes. Open the lid, mix up cooked halwa well and transfer into the small serving ramekins.

Nutrition value/serving: calories 337, fat 11.8, fiber 4.4, carbs 49.5, protein 10.3

Pecan Pie

Prep time: 15 minutes | Cooking time: 15 minutes | Servings: 4

Ingredients:
- ½ cup wheat flour
- ½ cup coconut butter
- 2 tablespoons brown sugar
- 1 cup pecans, chopped
- ½ cup white sugar
- ¼ cup almond milk
- 1 cup water, for cooking

Directions:
Make the sable: mix up together wheat flour, coconut butter, and brown sugar. Knead the soft dough. After this, place the dough in the cake mold and flatten the dough to get the shape of pie crust. Pour water in the instant pot and insert trivet. Place the mold with pie crust on the trivet and close the lid. Set manual mode (high pressure) and cook pie crust for 5 minutes. Allow natural pressure release for 10 minutes. Then open the lid, transfer the mold with pie crust on the chopping board and let it chill. After this, clean the instant pot and discard the trivet. Place inside the instant pot white sugar and almond milk. Melt the mixture on Saute mode. When the sugar mass starts to boil, add chopped pecans and stir well. Switch off the instant pot. Remove the pie crust from the mold. Place the cooked sugar pecans on it and flatten gently. Chill it little.

Nutrition value/serving: calories 441, fat 27.2, fiber 6.5, carbs 50.2, protein 4.7

Warm Aromatic Lassi

Prep time: 5 minutes | *Cooking time:* 5 minutes | *Servings:* 2

Ingredients:
- ½ cup almond yogurt
- ½ cup of water
- 2 tablespoons white sugar
- 1 pinch saffron
- ¾ teaspoon ground cardamom
- 1 tablespoon pistachios, chopped

Directions:
Preheat instant pot on saute mode. Then add water and boil it. Then add sugar and stir it until dissolved. Pour sweet water in the glass jar. After this, mix up together almond yogurt and water. Whisk the mixture carefully to get homogenous liquid. Sprinkle the liquid with ground cinnamon and saffron. Add ground cardamom. Stir it. Sprinkle the lassi with pistachios and pour into the serving glasses.

Nutrition value/serving: calories 100, fat 3.2, fiber 0.9, carbs 17.8, protein 1.5

Toffee

Prep time: 10 minutes | *Cooking time:* 5 minutes | *Servings:* 2

Ingredients:
- ¼ cup almond butter
- ¼ cup brown sugar
- 1 tablespoon peanuts, chopped
- ½ teaspoon vanilla extract
- 3 oz vegan chocolate chips

Directions:
Place sugar and almond butter in the instant pot. Melt the mixture on Saute mode. Line the tray with parchment. Pour the melted mixture on the parchment and spread it. Then sprinkle it with chopped peanuts and chocolate chips. Place the parchment in the freezer for 5-10 minutes. Then remove it from the freezer break into medium size pieces.

Nutrition value/serving: calories 337, fat 14.7, fiber 3.4, carbs 47.4, protein 4.5

Pear Compote

Prep time: 10 minutes | *Cooking time:* 6 minutes | *Servings:* 4

Ingredients:
- 4 pears, trimmed
- 1 cup of water
- 1 cinnamon stick
- ¼ teaspoon ground ginger
- 1 tablespoon sugar

Directions:
Cut the pears into halves and remove seeds. Chop the fruits. Place them in the instant pot. Add cinnamon stick, ground ginger, water, and sugar. Close and seal the lid. Set Manual mode and cook compote for 6 minutes. Then use quick pressure release. Open the lid and pour the cooked dessert into 4 bowls. Chill well.

Nutrition value/serving: calories 265, fat 0.6, fiber 13, carbs 69.8, protein 1.5

Cream Pie Pudding

Prep time: 15 minutes | Cooking time: 10 minutes | Servings: 5

Ingredients:
- 2 cups cashew milk
- 1 tablespoon vanilla extract
- 1 tablespoon corn flour
- 1 teaspoon cornstarch
- 4 oz vegan raw chocolate, chopped
- ½ cup of coconut milk
- 1/3 cup sugar
- 2 tablespoons coconut flakes

Directions:
Mix up together cashew milk, vanilla extract, corn flour, cornstarch, and sugar. Pour the liquid in the blender and blend it for 15 seconds. Preheat the instant pot on Saute mode until hot. Pour cashew milk mixture in the instant pot. Boil the liquid until it thickens. Then pour the pudding in the bowl. After this, clean the instant pot and place raw chocolate inside. Add coconut milk and saute the mixture until homogenous. Then make the last preparations of the dessert: take the glass jars and pour small inside of the cashew milk pudding inside. Then add melted chocolate mixture. Repeat the steps until you use all the mixtures. Chill the pudding.

Nutrition value/serving: calories 267, fat 16.2, fiber 8.1, carbs 28.6, protein 1.5

Banana Cake

Prep time: 15 minutes | Cooking time: 7 minutes | Servings: 4

Ingredients:
- 5 bananas, peeled
- 6 oz rice flour
- 1 teaspoon vanilla extract
- 1 tablespoon brown sugar
- 1 tablespoon peanut butter
- Cooking spray
- 1 cup water, for cooking

Directions:
Chop the bananas and place them in the mixing bowl. Mash the fruits with the help of the fork. After this, add rice flour, vanilla extract, and brown sugar. Mix up the mixture well. Spray the springform pan with cooking spray and pour banana mixture in it. Pour water in the instant pot, insert trivet; place springform pan on the trivet. Close and seal the lid. Cook the cake for 7 minutes. Then allow natural pressure release for 10 minutes. Spread the cooked cake with peanut butter and cut into slices.

Nutrition value/serving: calories 322, fat 3.1, fiber 5.1, carbs 70.9, protein 5.1

Carambola in Chai Syrup

Prep time: 15 minutes | Cooking time: 6 minutes | Servings: 2

Ingredients:
- 2 cups carambola, sliced
- ½ cup chai syrup
- 1/3 cup water
- ¼ teaspoon ground ginger

Directions:
In the instant pot mix up together chai syrup and water. Add ground ginger. Set Saute mode and cook the liquid for 5 minutes. Then add sliced carambola stir gently and cook for 1 minute more. Switch off the instant pot and let carambola soak the syrup.

Nutrition value/serving: calories 52, fat 0.4, fiber 3.1, carbs 11.9, protein 1.1

Semolina Pudding with Mango

Prep time: 15 minutes | Cooking time: 10 minutes | Servings: 4

Ingredients:
- 2 cups almond milk
- ½ cup semolina
- 4 oz mango puree
- 3 tablespoons brown sugar
- 1 teaspoon vanilla extract
- 1 teaspoon coconut oil

Directions:
Pour almond milk in the instant pot and preheat it on Saute mode. When it starts to boil, add semolina, brown sugar, and vanilla extract. Bring it to boil again. Stir well. Then close the lid and switch off the instant pot. Leave it for 10 minutes. After this, add coconut oil and stir well. Place mango puree in the serving bowls. Add semolina pudding over the puree.

Nutrition value/serving: calories 404, fat 30, fiber 3.7, carbs 32.1, protein 5.5

Conclusion

Presently, the world is divided into people who support veganism and those who are against the complete abandonment of animal products. Hope this book could dispel your stereotypes that vegetarian food is monotonous and not tasty. If you have already read some pages of the cookbook, you know that it includes hundreds of magnificent and very easy to cook recipes. It is possible to say that this vegan recipe guide can be a good gift to everyone who loves delicious food. These days veganism is a sought-after way of life. More often people refuse to consume all types of meat and dairy products and limit yourself with fruits, vegetables, and another produces. It is true that thanks to the vegan lifestyle you can improve your health and feel much better. Scientifically proved that total refusing from any type of meat and dairy products can help fight with Type 2 diabetes, reduce Low-Density Lipoprotein (LDL) level, and helps to decrease blood pressure. Veganism is a good way to raise the level of antioxidant, vitamins, minerals, and dietary fiber in the body. This happens due to increased fruit, vegetable, grains, legumes, and beans consumption.

However, veganism can be harmful to you, cause some inconvenience and make significant changes in your body. Every diet needs a special meal plan that is developed individually for the right saturation of the body with all nutrients. If you have any health problems, a vegan diet can interfere with your health. It is highly recommended to make full medical body examinations and consult the doctor about the possible consequences of changing the diet. The inconveniences can happen while eating out. Single restaurants and cafes can boast a wide range of high-quality vegan meals. There is a solution that is used by a lot of vegans: to take food with yourself. Doing it you won't miss the mealtime and stay full.

Start the vegetarianism diet gradually. This will help you more consciously choose food and reduce the level of stress for your body. Step by step you will figure out the principles of right vegan diet and this cookbook will be a good guide to the world of delicious vegan food recipes!

Recipe Index

ALMOND BUTTER
French Toast Pudding,14
Pot Pancake,15
Morning Muffins,16
Rice with Maple Syrup,18
Tapioca Pudding,21
Soaked Quinoa,21
Breakfast Grits,23
White Couscous with Syrup,25
Baked Oatmeal Cake,25
Granola Bars,27
FlapJacks,29
Chocolate Morning Bars,30
Stuffed Sweet Potato,31
Oatmeal Muffins,36
Tender Tofu Cubes,37
Potato Patties,41
Portobello Burgers,48
Artichoke Burger,51
Wild Rice Burger,52
Sweet Pear Patties,62
Leek Patties,63
Quinoa with Basil and Lemongrass,66
Butter Corn,70
Spiced Okra,72
Soft Kale,72
Buckwheat,83
Amaranth Banana Porridge,88
Green Buckwheat,89
Buckwheat Pasta with Mushroom Sauce,95
Freekeh Tacos,96
Quinoa and Freekeh Mix,96
Taco Pasta,100
Vegan Quinoa Pilaf,105
Lemon Pasta,106
Mexican Pinto Beans,107
Black Beans Chili,111
Chipotle Chili with Hot Sauce,112
Rice and Beans Bowl,118
Buddha Bowl,123
Quinoa Tomato Soup,136
Minestrone,138
African Stew,151
Thai Curry Soup,152
Garden Stew,152
Hot Pepper Chickpea Stew,154
Iranian Stew,156
Jackfruit Curry,159
Posole,160
Spicy Edamame Snack,184
Mushroom Pate,195
Polenta Fries,200
Cacao Spread,207
Pumpkin Butter,209
Mint Filling,217

Coconut Filling,218
Herbed Lemon Sauce,223
Black Beans Cookies,226
Vanilla Custard,231
Pear Pudding,236
Sweet Potato Pie,238
Date Bars,239
Banana Cream Tart,240
Almond Cookies,242
Apple Upside Down Cake,243
Toffee,247

ALMOND FLAKES
Broccoli Soup,144
Pear Pudding,236

ALMOND MILK
French Toast Pudding,14
Pot Pancake,15
Morning Muffins,16
Rice with Maple Syrup,18
Miso Oat Porridge,19
Chia Pudding,22
Breakfast Grits,23
Breakfast Bowl,34
Tofu Omelet,34
Tapioca Porridge,35
Zucchini Frittata,35
Apple Cream of Wheat,36
Quinoa Patties,39
Red Kidney Beans Burger,60
Sweet Pear Patties,62
Pumpkin Puree,65
Red Cabbage with Apples,68
Bang Bang Broccoli,78
Scalloped Potatoes,81
Almond Milk Millet,82
Vanilla Rice Pudding,86
Amaranth Banana Porridge,88
Buckwheat Pasta with Mushroom Sauce,95
Curry Rice,100
Lemon Pasta,106
Creamy Kidney Beans,113
Lentils Shepherd's Pie,126
Masala Lentils,128
Cabbage Rolls with Lentils,131
Kale and Sweet Potato Soup,139
Winter Stew,146
Fennel Soup,151
African Stew,151
Texas Stew,155
Vegetable Gnocchi,172
Polenta Fries,200
Crunchy Artichoke Hearts,203
Mushroom Arancini,204

Vegan Gravy,206
Cauliflower Sauce,208
White Bean Sauce,213
Caramel Pumpkin Sauce,213
Artichoke Sandwich Filling,217
Vegan Buffalo Dip,221
Garlic Dip,225
Vanilla Custard,231
Pumpkin Spice Pie,233
Soda Cake,238
Orange-Pineapple Cake,242
Walnut Sweets,244
Turmeric Loaf,245
Pecan Pie,246
Semolina Pudding with Mango,249

ALMOND YOGURT
Cashew Yogurt with Pomegranate Seeds,26
Corn Burger,54
Cauliflower Rice,73
Tofu Matar,163
Tofu Cubes in Peanut Sauce,164
Korma,166
Hash Brown Omelette,170
Stuffed Mini Pumpkins,179
Beetroot Fold-Overs,193
Vegan French Sauce,208
Cayenne Pepper Filling,210
Ravioli Sauce,213
Guacamole with Broccoli,220
Pizza Sauce,225
Warm Aromatic Lassi,247

ALMONDS
Carrot Cake,232
Gingerbread Pie,243
Breakfast Cookies,30
Superfood Cookies,31
Almond Milk Cocktail,33
Chia Seeds Cookies,241
Almond Cookies,242

AMARANTH
Amaranth Burger,57
Amaranth Banana Porridge,88
Basic Amaranth Recipe,88

APPLE JUICE
Poached Peaches,239
Apple Upside Down Cake,243

APPLES
Apple Cream of Wheat,36
Red Cabbage with Apples,68
Apple Oatmeal,14
Apple Patties,45
Vegan Applesauce,69

Sweet Apple Wedges,194
Apple Crumble,229
Maple Syrup Apples,236
Apple Upside Down Cake,243
Baked Apples,80

APPLESAUCE
Breakfast Banana Bread,26
Caramel Sauce for Vegetables,218
Snickerdoodle Bars,244

AQUAFABA
Breakfast Cookies,30
Superfood Cookies,31
Tofu Omelet,34
Potato Patties,41
Ravioli,174

ARTICHOKES
Artichoke Burger,51
Artichoke Petals,71
Mac with Artichokes,99
Crunchy Artichoke Hearts,203
Spinach Dip,209
Artichoke Sandwich Filling,217
Greek Style Stewed Artichokes,157

ARUGULA
Tomato Farfalle with Arugula,103
Bulgur Salad,104
Eggplant Rolls,190
Arugula Puffs,193
Arugula Hummus,224

ASPARAGUS
Asparagus Burger,64
Garden Stew,152
Asparagus Pastries,192

AVOCADO
Miso Oat Porridge,19
Avocado Sandwiches,38
Beet Burger,48
Green Burgers,49
Red Kidney Beans Burrito,110
Burrito Bowl,111
Edamame Toast,125
Broccoli Soup,144
Crunchwrap Supreme,185
Avocado Pesto,212
Spinach Sauce,218
Green Sauce,223

AVOCADO OIL
Amaranth Burger,57
Mongolian Stir Fry,77
Vegetable En Papillote,79

Classic Vegetable Soup,133
Potato Cream Soup,136
Tuscan Soup,143
Aloo Gobi,165
Nut Loaf,180
Fragrant Spring Onions,180
Cocktail Balls,192
Mushroom Pate,195
Sofritas Tofu,199
Cigar Borek,201
Alfredo Sauce,215

BANANAS
Morning Muffins,16
Chia Pudding,22
Mini Breakfast Carrot Cakes,24
Banana Cream Tart,240
French Toast Pudding,14
Breakfast Banana Bread,26
Banana Pancakes,28
Banana Rolls,33
Banana Patties,55
Amaranth Banana Porridge,88
Apple Upside Down Cake,243
Turmeric Loaf,245
Banana Cake,248

BEANS
Tuscan Sorghum,97
Vegan Black Beans,108
Vaquero Beans Chili with Tempeh,113
Edamame Dip,114

BEANS (BLACK)
Black Beans Burger,42
Tempeh Burger,44
Mexican Style Burger,47
Multi-Grain Porridge,88
Black Beans Chili,111
Chipotle Chili with Hot Sauce,112
Spicy Tacos with Beans,114
Rice and Beans Bowl,118
Frijoles Negros,119
Red Beans Cauliflower Rice,120
Crunchwrap Supreme,185
Mexican Rice Filling,207
Black Beans Cookies,226

BEANS (CANNELLINI)
Tuscan Soup,143
Kuru Fasulye,149
Cassoulet,166

BEANS (EDAMAME)
Edamame Toast,125
Spicy Edamame Snack,184

BEANS (GARBANZO)

Arugula Hummus,224

BEANS (GREEN)
Green Beans with Nuts,74
Vegetable En Papillote,79
Lebanese Lemon and Beans Salad,109
Bean Casserole,119
Chickpea Soup,142
Mediterranean Vegan Stew,148
Garden Stew,152
Tom Yum Soup,153
Turkish Green Beans,157
Broccoli Gnocchi,169
Edamole,225

BEANS (KIDNEY)
Red Kidney Beans Burger,60
Creamy Kidney Beans,113
Bean Enchiladas,118
Texas Stew,155

BEANS (MUNG)
Mung Beans Croquettes,115

BEANS (PINTO)
Breakfast Hash,29
Corn Burger,54
Amaranth Burger,57
Mexican Pinto Beans,107
Pinto Beans Quinoa Salad,116

BEANS (RED)
Japgokbap,84
Multi-Grain Porridge,88
Burrito Bowl,111
Bean Loaf,117
Rainbow Stew,150

BEANS (WHITE)
Baked Beans,107
Curry White Beans,121
White Bean Sauce,213
Bean Cookie Dough,226

BEANS KIDNEY (RED)
Pasta Fagioli,91
Freekeh Tacos,96
Red Kidney Beans Burrito,110
Beanballs,116
Spaghetti Squash Bean Bowl,120
Stuffed Sweet Potato with Beans,121
Kidney Beans Koftas with Mushrooms,122
Stuffed Peppers with Kidney Beans,122
Minestrone,138
Taco Soup,141
Tortilla Soup,144
Winter Stew,146
Iranian Stew ,156

Chipotle Fajitas,171
Red Kidney Beans Sauce,210
Tomato Bean Pate,217

BEETROOT
Samosa Filling,206
Beetroot Garlic Filling,211
Beetroot Fold-Overs,193

BEETS
Beet Soup,140
Beets,71
Beet Steaks,181

BELL PEPPER
Bulgur Salad,104
Red Kidney Beans Burrito,110
Burrito Bowl,111
Chickpea Shakshuka,123
Lentil Bolognese,126
Quinoa Tomato Soup,136
Beet Soup,140
Spinach and Lentils Soup,143
Kuru Fasulye,149
African Stew,151
Lentil Gumbo,161
Stuffed Eggplants,167
Chickpea Slices,197
Red Kidney Beans Sauce,210
Marinara Sauce,216
Mexican Style Burger,47
Chipotle Fajitas,171
Basmati Rague,85
Roasted Pepper Salsa,224
Ratatouille,76
Tofu Scramble,28
Mediterranean Vegan Stew,148
Stuffed Peppers with Kidney Beans,122
Summer Stew,154

BELL PEPPER (GREEN)
Sweet Pepper Patties,56
Tender Sweet Peppers,71
Freekeh Tacos,96
Mung Beans Croquettes,115
Creamy Tomato Soup,141
Spicy Kale Burger,51
Black Beans Chili,111
Celery Patties,58

BELL PEPPER (RED)
Tofu Burger,53
Sweet Pepper Patties,56
Chipotle Chili with Hot Sauce,112
Beta Carotene Booster Soup,139
Vermicelli Bowl,67
Breakfast Potatoes,18

Potato Chaat,32
Spinach and Lentils Soup,143
Egyptian Stew,147
Hash Brown Omelette,170
Breakfast Hash,29
Tender Sweet Peppers,71
Bean Enchiladas,118

BELL PEPPER (YELLOW)
Black Beans Burger,42
Tender Sweet Peppers,71

BLACKBERRIES
Coconut Yogurt with Berries,17
Baked Oatmeal Cake,25

BOK CHOY
Bok Choy Patties,61
Glazed Bok Choy,65
Tom Yum Soup,153
Summer Stew,154

BROCCOLI
Oatmeal Patties,57
Bang Bang Broccoli,78
Broccoli Soup,144
Broccoli Gnocchi,169
Spinach Sauce,218
Broccoli Patties,40
Broccoli Rice,67
Ratsherrenpfanne,156

BRUSSELS SPROUTS
Cilantro Brussels Sprouts,75
Buffalo Brussels Sprouts,195

BUCKWHEAT
Buckwheat with Pecans,20
Buckwheat,83
Buckwheat Groats,104
Pumpkin Spice Pie,233
BUCKWHEAT PASTA
Buckwheat Pasta with Mushroom Sauce,95

BULGUR
Fragrant Bulgur,80
Bulgur Salad,104

BUTTERNUT
Butternut Squash Burger,46
Butternut Squash Ginger Soup,137
Moroccan Stew,147

CABBAGE
Cabbage Patties,54
Cabbage Rolls with Lentils,131
Beet Soup,140

Cabbage Detox Soup,142
Mediterranean Vegan Stew,148

CABBAGE (RED)
Red Cabbage with Apples,68
Spicy Tacos with Beans,114
Spring Rolls,186

CANOLA OIL
Mexican Style Burger,47

CARROTS
Potato Chaat,32
Lentil Burger,42
Tempeh Burger,44
Beet Burger,48
Tofu Burger,53
Oatmeal Patties,57
Semolina-Cilantro Patties,61
Mexican Rice,69
Vegetable En Papillote,79
Pasta Fagioli,91
Buckwheat Groats,104
Baked Beans,107
Lentil Meatballs,110
Lentil Stew with Spinach,117
Lentil Ragout,129
Cabbage Rolls with Lentils,131
Wild Rice Soup,132
Classic Vegetable Soup,133
Quinoa Tomato Soup,136
Carrot Soup,138
Beet Soup,140
Anti-Inflammatory Soup,140
Chickpea Soup,142
Cabbage Detox Soup,142
Tuscan Soup,143
Winter Stew,146
Vegan "Beef" Stew,146
Irish Stew,150
Tom Yum Soup,153
Asian Steamed Dumplings,159
Portobello Roast,160
Cassoulet,166
Bibimbap,171
Mushroom Bourguignon,172
Rainbow Vegetable Pie,179
Nut Loaf,180
Spring Rolls,186
Cayenne Pepper Filling,210
Vegan Cheese Sauce,211
Spaghetti Sauce,216
Tomato Bean Pate,217
Miso Butter,221
Gajar Halwa,229
Carrot Cake,232
Mini Breakfast Carrot Cakes,24

Carrot Patties,50
Sweet Baby Carrots,72
Lentils Shepherd's Pie,126
Sloppy Lentils,128
Noodle Soup,134
Beta Carotene Booster Soup,139
Peas and Carrot Stew,148
Coconut Cream Soup,153
Tempeh Tajine,165
Carrot "Dogs",188

CASHEW
Artichoke Burger,51
Pasta Alfredo,102
Lemon Pasta,106
Nutritious Lasagna,158
Cashew Cheese,173
Queso Sauce,214
Gajar Halwa,229
Cheesecake,235
Cashew Yogurt with Pomegranate Seeds,26
Alfredo Sauce,215

CASHEW BUTTER
Scalloped Potatoes,81
Sweet Rice,84
Stuffed Figs,181
Artichoke Sandwich Filling,217
White Beans Blondies,228
Sweet Potato Pie,238
Cookie Cake,240

CASHEW MILK
Mac'n Cheese,74
Baked Apples,80
Zoodles with Lentils,115
Edamame Toast,125
Cacao Spread,207
Creme Brulee,236
Chocolate Pudding,241
Cream Pie Pudding,248

CAULIFLOWER
Red Kidney Beans Burger,60
Mashed White Potato Patties,63
Tikka Masala with Cauliflower,79
Pasta Alfredo,102
Red Beans Cauliflower Rice,120
Fennel Soup,151
Lentil Gumbo,161
Aloo Gobi,165
Cauliflower Sauce,208
Alfredo Sauce,215
Vegan Buffalo Dip,221
Cauliflower Rice,73
Cauliflower Soup,133
Herbed Cauliflower Head,167

255

Chipotle Fajitas,171
Popcorn Cauliflower,173
BBQ Cauliflower Florets,191
Cauliflower Potato Burgers,40

CAYENNE PEPPER
Sweet Potato Burgers,41
Lentil Burger,42
Jalapeno Burger,47
Spicy Kale Burger,51
Wild Rice Burger,52
Green Peas Burger,56
Spiced Okra,72
Mongolian Stir Fry,77
Mushroom "Bacon",77
Cayenne Pepper Corn,87
Freekeh Tacos,96
Lebanese Lemon and Beans Salad,109
Stuffed Sweet Potato with Beans,121
Stuffed Peppers with Kidney Beans,122
Lentils Shepherd's Pie,126
Cabbage Rolls with Lentils,131
Quinoa Tomato Soup,136
Spinach and Lentils Soup,143
Peas and Carrot Stew,148
Rainbow Stew,150
Hot Pepper Chickpea Stew,154
Herbed Cauliflower Head,167
Boiled Peanuts,182
Spicy Edamame Snack,184
BBQ Cauliflower Florets,191
Sofritas Tofu,199
Cayenne Pepper Filling,210
Avocado Pesto,212
Artichoke Sandwich Filling,217
Kuru Fasulye,149

CELERY
Pasta Fagioli,91
Lentil Ragout,129
Wild Rice Soup,132
Minestrone,138
Celery Patties,58
Bolognese,92
Tuscan Sorghum,97
Lentil Bolognese,126
Noodle Soup,134
Leek Soup,135
Anti-Inflammatory Soup,140
Broccoli Soup,144
Vegan "Beef" Stew,146
Tom Yum Soup,153
Lentil Gumbo,161
Cassoulet,166
Nut Loaf,180

CHEESE (CHEDDAR)

Spaghetti Squash Bean Bowl,120
Lentil Chili,127
Pumpkin Mac and Cheese,94
Pizza Pasta,101
Arugula Puffs,193

CHEESE (PARMESAN)
Mac'n Cheese,74
Mushroom Risotto,76
Arborio Rice,85
Italian Style Pasta,93
Basil Pasta,95
Sorgotto,97
Mac with Artichokes,99
Pesto Pasta,99
Caprese Pasta,101
Tomato Farfalle with Arugula,103
Bean Enchiladas,118
Stuffed Peppers with Kidney Beans,122
French Onion Soup,135
Soybean Stew,155
Broccoli Gnocchi,169
Ravioli,174
Stuffed Spinach Shells,177
Delicious Lettuce Wraps,186
Beetroot Fold-Overs,193
Cigar Borek,201
Mushroom Arancini,204
Spinach Dip,209
White Bean Sauce,213
Artichoke Sandwich Filling,217

CHIA SEEDS
Coconut Yogurt with Berries,17
Chia Pudding,22
Flaked Clusters,201
Chia Seeds Cookies,241

CHICKPEAS
Falafel,23
Butternut Squash Burger,46
Chickpea Burger,46
Beet Burger,48
Carrot Patties,50
Sun Dried Tomato Patties,52
Corn Burger,54
Green Peas Burger,56
Farro Burger,59
Red Kidney Beans Burger,60
Japgokbap,84
Buffalo Chickpea,115
Chickpea Salad,124
Hot Pepper Chickpea Stew,154
Pumpkin Hummus,183
Tofu Omelet,34
Cranberry Patties,62

Chickpea Shakshuka,123
Buddha Bowl,123
Chickpea Curry,124
Buffalo Chickpea,125
Chickpea Soup,142
Moroccan Stew,147
Chana Masala with Spinach,161
Norwegian Style Balls,168
Vegan Sausages,175
Stuffed Mini Pumpkins,179
Vegan Nuggets,185
Crispy Chickpea,187
Chickpea Slices,197
Chickpea Crackers,202
Samosa Filling,206
Vegan Buffalo Dip,221
Chickpea Chocolate Hummus,227

CHILI PEPPER (GREEN)
Texas Stew,155

CHILI PEPPER (RED)
Spiced Okra,72
Tso's Tofu,163
Sriracha Sauce,219
Posole,160

CHIVES
Miso Oat Porridge,19
Potato Pancakes,38
Avocado Sandwiches,38
Sweet Potato Burgers,41
Beet Burger,48
Eggplant Burger,53
Spaghetti Patties,55
Celery Patties,58
Barley Burger,60
Mashed Potato,67
Baked Potato,69
Pumpkin Mac and Cheese,94
Vegan Black Beans,108
Stuffed Sweet Potato with Beans,121
Chickpea Shakshuka,123
Leek Soup,135
Sweet Potato Stew,149
Hash Brown Omelette,170
Bibimbap,171
Tempeh Ribs,178
Delicious Lettuce Wraps,186

CHOCOLATE
Acorn Squash Oats,19
Walnut Sweets,244
Cream Pie Pudding,248
Chocolate Morning Bars,30
Sweet Potato Pie,238

CHOCOLATE (DARK)
Black Beans Cookies,226
Chocolate Cake,230

CHOCOLATE CHIPS
Bean Cookie Dough,226
Cookie Cake,240
Toffee,247

COCONUT
Raspberry Pancake Bites,22
Coconut Cut Oats,24
Breakfast Bowl,34
Spinach Patties,44
Coconut Filling,218

COCONUT BUTTER
Oregano Onion Dip,221
Gingerbread Pie,243
Pecan Pie,246

COCONUT CREAM
Creamed Corn,73
Pineapple Rice,77
Rosemary Creamed Polenta,90
Mushroom Tetrazzini,91
Tofu Spaghetti,94
Basil Pasta,95
Stuffed Peppers with Kidney Beans,122
Wild Rice Soup,132
Pumpkin Cream Soup,132
Cauliflower Soup,133
Potato Chowder with Corn,134
Leek Soup,135
Carrot Soup,138
Beta Carotene Booster Soup,139
Beet Soup,140
Chickpea Soup,142
Mushroom Cream Soup,145
Mediterranean Vegan Stew,148
Irish Stew,150
Ratsherrenpfanne,156
Broccoli Gnocchi,169
Popcorn Cauliflower,173
Mushroom Bruschetta,191
Basil Cream Sauce,214
Creamy Green Peas Filling,214
Tomato Sauce,215
Chocolate Cake,230
Vanilla Caramel Cream,231
Carrot Cake,232
Cookie Cake,240

COCONUT FLAKES
Flaked Clusters,201
Coated Heart of Palm,204
Apple Crumble,229

Soda Cake,238
Turmeric Loaf,245
Cream Pie Pudding,248

COCONUT MILK
Coconut Yogurt with Berries,17
Buckwheat with Pecans,20
Tapioca Pudding,21
Coconut Cut Oats,24
Coconut Cut Oats,24
Chocolate Morning Bars,30
Oatmeal Muffins,36
Jalapeno Burger,47
Onion Patties,49
Spaghetti Patties,55
Farro Burger,59
Mashed Potato,67
Red Cabbage with Apples,68
Polenta,70
Artichoke Petals,71
Sweet Rice,84
Vanilla Rice Pudding,86
Lebanese Lemon and Beans Salad,109
Burrito Bowl,111
Edamame Dip,114
Red Beans Cauliflower Rice,120
Chickpea Curry,124
Potato Cream Soup,136
Butternut Squash Ginger Soup,137
Anti-Inflammatory Soup,140
Tortilla Soup,144
Fennel Soup,151
Thai Curry Soup,152
Coconut Cream Soup,153
Vegan Butter "Chicken",158
Norwegian Style Balls,168
Vegan Nuggets,185
Vegan Cheese Sauce,211
Mushroom Sauce,212
Alfredo Sauce,215
Oregano Onion Dip,221
Bean Cookie Dough,226
Cranberry Cake,228
Gajar Halwa,229
Carrot Cake,232
Lemon Curd,233
Dulce de Leche,234
Pumpkin Pudding,237
Chocolate Pudding,241
Apple Upside Down Cake,243
Cream Pie Pudding,248

COCONUT OIL
Apple Oatmeal,14
Breakfast Quiche,15
Monkey Bread,16
Breakfast Potatoes,18

Breakfast Grits,23
Mini Breakfast Carrot Cakes,24
Breakfast Cookies,30
Avocado Sandwiches,38
Yam Patties,59
Sweet Baby Carrots,72
Glazed White Onions,81
Stir Fried Kale,82
Proso Millet,84
Arborio Rice,85
Oatmeal with Tender Onions,86
Teff in Tomato Paste,87
Rosemary Creamed Polenta,90
Pasta Fagioli,91
Classic Wheat Berries,95
Sorgotto,97
Soba Noodles with Curry Tofu,98
Curry Rice,100
Pasta Alfredo,102
Dill Orzo,103
Creamy Spelt Berries,104
Vegan Black Beans,108
Creamy Kidney Beans,113
Bean Casserole,119
Chickpea Shakshuka,123
Lentil Loaf,127
Red Lentil Dal,130
Leek Soup,135
French Onion Soup,135
Lentil Soup,137
Carrot Soup,138
Beet Soup,140
Spinach and Lentils Soup,143
Broccoli Soup,144
Kuru Fasulye,149
Rainbow Stew,150
Asian Steamed Dumplings,159
Portobello Roast,160
Potato Tamales,162
Tofu Matar,163
Korma,166
Cassoulet,166
Hash Brown Omelette,170
Chipotle Fajitas,171
Deli Slices,176
Mushroom Pie,176
Pumpkin Risotto,177
Rainbow Vegetable Pie,179
Nut Loaf,180
Tempeh Potato Wraps,182
Crunchwrap Supreme,185
Turkish Vegan Borek,188
Lentils Crackers,190
Sweet Apple Wedges,194
Caramel Pumpkin Sauce,213
Tomato Bean Pate,217
Bean Cookie Dough,226

Navy Beans Biscuits,227
Gajar Halwa,229
Pumpkin Muffins,230
Vanilla Caramel Cream,231
Carrot Cake,232
Pumpkin Spice Pie,233
Brownies,234
Cheesecake,235
Rhubarb Bars,237
Soda Cake,238
Chia Seeds Cookies,241
Cinnamon Swirls,245
Semolina Pudding with Mango,249

COCONUT YOGURT
Coconut Yogurt with Berries,17
Tender Tofu Cubes,37
Cauliflower Potato Burgers,40
Spinach Patties,44
Cabbage Patties,54
Mashed Potato,67
Tikka Masala with Cauliflower,79
Italian Style Pasta,93
Taco Pasta,100
Mexican Pinto Beans,107
Lentil Radish Salad,108
Lentil Tacos,109
Bean Casserole,119
Hot Pepper Chickpea Stew,154
Spinach Dip,209

CORN
Mexican Style Burger,47
Creamed Corn,73
Cayenne Pepper Corn,87
PopCorn,87
Quinoa and Freekeh Mix,96
Bean Enchiladas,118
Black Beans Burger,42
Corn Burger,54
Barley Burger,60
Mexican Rice,69
Butter Corn,70
Potato Chowder with Corn,134
Leek Soup,135
Taco Soup,141
Tortilla Soup,144
Mediterranean Vegan Stew,148
Texas Stew,155
Ratsherrenpfanne,156
Potato Tamales,162
Saag Tofu with Spinach,162
Tso's Tofu,163
Tofu Cubes in Peanut Sauce,164
Mexican Rice Filling,207
Red Kidney Beans Sauce,210
Mint Filling,217

Garlic Dip,225

CORN TORTILLAS
Pizza Pasta,101
Lentil Tacos,109
Bean Enchiladas,118
Tortilla Soup,144
Chipotle Fajitas,171
Tempeh Potato Wraps,182
Gyros,189

COUSCOUS (WHITE)
White Couscous with Syrup,25

COUSCOUS (YELLOW)
Tender Yellow Couscous,66

CRANBERRIES
Breakfast Cookies,30
Superfood Cookies,31
Cranberry Patties,62
Cranberry Sauce,209
Cranberry Cake,228
Semolina Halwa,246

CUCUMBER
Rice Garden Salad,105
Bibimbap,171
Delicious Lettuce Wraps,186
Gyros,189

DATES
Chili Sauce,222
Date Bars,239
Chia Seeds Cookies,241
Semolina Halwa,246

EGGPLANTS
Ratatouille,76
Rainbow Stew,150
Summer Stew,154
Iranian Stew ,156
Eggplant Rolls,190
Eggplant Fries,202
Eggplant Burger,53
Stuffed Eggplants,167
Baba Ganoush,222

FENNEL
Fennel Soup,151

FIGS
Stuffed Figs,181

FLAKES (CHILI)
Tempeh Ribs,178
Potato Patties,41

Mushroom Burger,43
Spinach Patties,44
Pumpkin Burger,45
Chickpea Burger,46
Carrot Patties,50
Spicy Kale Burger,51
Corn Burger,54
Amaranth Burger,57
Farro Burger,59
Asparagus Burger,64
Red Cabbage with Apples,68
Garlic Spaghetti Squash,68
Mexican Rice,69
Spiced Okra,72
Creamed Corn,73
Mongolian Stir Fry,77
Spicy Garlic,81
Proso Millet,84
Pasta Puttanesca,90
Pasta Fagioli,91
Bolognese,92
Tomato Spaghetti,93
Mac with Artichokes,99
Rice Garden Salad,105
Vegan Black Beans,108
Red Kidney Beans Burrito,110
Black Beans Chili,111
Zoodles with Lentils,115
Beanballs,116
Kidney Beans Koftas with Mushrooms,122
Edamame Toast,125
Lentils Shepherd's Pie,126
Lentil Chili,127
Lentil Ragout,129
Wild Rice Soup,132
Potato Chowder with Corn,134
Leek Soup,135
Lentil Soup,137
Anti-Inflammatory Soup,140
Tortilla Soup,144
Kuru Fasulye,149
Turkish Green Beans,157
Vegan Butter "Chicken",158
Tempeh Tajine,165
Herbed Cauliflower Head,167
Teriyaki Tofu,169
Chipotle Fajitas,171
Popcorn Cauliflower,173
Stuffed Mini Pumpkins,179
Spring Rolls,186
Appetizer Quinoa Balls,196
Crunchy Oyster Mushrooms,198
Sofritas Tofu,199
Vegan Gravy,206
Mexican Rice Filling,207
Red Kidney Beans Sauce,210
Vegan Cheese Sauce,211

Ravioli Sauce,213
Chimichurri Sauce,220

FREEKEH
Freekeh Tacos,96
Quinoa and Freekeh Mix,96

GARAM MASALA
Potato Chaat,32
Leek Patties,63
Tikka Masala with Cauliflower,79
Lentil Radish Salad,108
Chickpea Salad,124
Masala Lentils,128
Chickpea Soup,142
Vegan Butter "Chicken",158
Tofu Matar,163
Aloo Gobi,165
Korma,166

GNOCCHI
Broccoli Gnocchi,169

HARISSA
Buddha Bowl,123
Moroccan Stew,147
Iranian Stew ,156
Pumpkin Hummus,183
Arugula Hummus,224

HONEY
Baked Oatmeal Cake,25
Cashew Yogurt with Pomegranate Seeds,26
Granola Bars,27
Almond Milk Cocktail,33
Breakfast Bowl,34
Tapioca Porridge,35
Bok Choy Patties,61
Sweet Baby Carrots,72

JACKFRUIT (GREEN)
Jackfruit Curry,159

KALE
Tempeh Bowl,37
Sweet Potato Burgers,41
Green Burgers,49
Spicy Kale Burger,51
Soft Kale,72
Stir Fried Kale,82
Stuffed Peppers with Kidney Beans,122
Lentil Mash,129
Tuscan Soup,143
Garden Stew,152
Saag Tofu with Spinach,162

LEEK

Stuffed Sweet Potato,31
Leek Patties,63
Leek Soup,135
Cassoulet,166

LEMON
Lemon Pasta,106
Lebanese Lemon and Beans Salad,109
Carrot Soup,138
Artichoke Burger,51
Lemon Potatoes,66
Moroccan Stew,147
Herbed Lemon Sauce,223
Lemon Curd,233
Cheesecake,235

LEMON JUICE
Pot Pancake,15
Raspberry Pancake Bites,22
Beet Burger,48
Lemon Potatoes,66
Bang Bang Broccoli,78
Vegetable En Papillote,79
Tofu Spaghetti,94
Cowboy Caviar,112
Stuffed Sweet Potato with Beans,121
Buddha Bowl,123
Lentil Tomato Salad,130
Cauliflower Soup,133
Egyptian Stew,147
Greek Style Stewed Artichokes,157
Nutritious Lasagna,158
Lentil Gumbo,161
Tempeh,164
Herbed Cauliflower Head,167
Chipotle Fajitas,171
Cashew Cheese,173
Tempeh Ribs,178
Fragrant Spring Onions,180
Spring Rolls,186
Vegan Jerky,188
Cardamom Pineapple Sticks,196
Cranberry Sauce,209
Avocado Pesto,212
Caramel Sauce for Vegetables,218
Guacamole with Broccoli,220
Vegan Buffalo Dip,221
Green Sauce,223
Herbed Lemon Sauce,223
Arugula Hummus,224
Black Beans Cookies,226
White Beans Blondies,228
Carrot Cake,232
Lemon Curd,233
Rhubarb Bars,237
Date Bars,239
Banana Cream Tart,240
Apple Upside Down Cake,243

LEMONGRASS
Quinoa with Basil and Lemongrass,66
Tom Yum Soup,153
Saag Tofu with Spinach,162

LENTILS
Lentil Burger,42
Mexican Style Burger,47
Lentil Radish Salad,108
Lentil Tacos,109
Lentil Meatballs,110
Zoodles with Lentils,115
Lentils Shepherd's Pie,126
Lentil Loaf,127
Sloppy Lentils,128
Masala Lentils,128
Lentil Ragout,129
Lentil Mash,129
Lentil Tomato Salad,130
Cabbage Rolls with Lentils,131
Creamy Tomato Soup,141
Egyptian Stew,147
Lentil Gumbo,161
Lentil Steak,174
Nut Loaf,180

LENTILS (GREEN)
Lentil Stew with Spinach,117
Lentil Bolognese,126
Lentil Chili,127
Spinach and Lentils Soup,143
Lentils Crackers,190

LENTILS (RED)
Red Lentil Dal,130
Lentil Soup,137
Beta Carotene Booster Soup,139
Winter Stew,146

LETTUCE
Lentil Radish Salad,108
Gyros,189
Delicious Lettuce Wraps,186

LIME
Iranian Stew ,156
Thai Curry Soup,152
Cashew Cheese,173
Spring Rolls,186
Cardamom Pineapple Sticks,196
Beetroot Garlic Filling,211

LIME JUICE
Chocolate Morning Bars,30
Beta Carotene Booster Soup,139
Vegan Butter "Chicken",158

Chana Masala with Spinach,161
Tempeh Tajine,165
Aloo Gobi,165
Gyros,189
Vegan Cheese Sauce,211
Beetroot Garlic Filling,211
Spinach Sauce,218
Baba Ganoush,222

MANGO
Sweet Rice,84
Semolina Pudding with Mango,249

MAPLE SYRUP
French Toast Pudding,14
Pot Pancake,15
Monkey Bread,16
Rice with Maple Syrup,18
Acorn Squash Oats,19
Buckwheat with Pecans,20
Chia Pudding,22
White Couscous with Syrup,25
Granola Bars,27
Breakfast Cookies,30
Glazed Bok Choy,65
Bang Bang Broccoli,78
Baked Apples,80
Vanilla Rice Pudding,86
Sweet Apple Wedges,194
Candied Pecans,194
Jackfruit Coated Bites,198
Flaked Clusters,201
Coated Heart of Palm,204
Sweet Tofu Cubes,205
Cranberry Sauce,209
Pear Filling,212
Miso Butter,221
Pizza Sauce,225
Chickpea Chocolate Hummus,227
Apple Crumble,229
Carrot Cake,232
Flan Mini Cakes,235
Maple Syrup Apples,236
Pumpkin Pudding,237
Chia Seeds Cookies,241
Orange-Pineapple Cake,242
Gingerbread Pie,243
Snickerdoodle Bars,244

MUSHROOMS
Breakfast Hash,29
Mushroom Tetrazzini,91
Thai Curry Soup,152
Brown Rice Congee,32
Breakfast Quiche,15
Mushroom Burger,43
Mushroom Risotto,76

Mushroom "Bacon",77
Bolognese,92
Buckwheat Pasta with Mushroom Sauce,95
Penne Rigate,102
Chipotle Chili with Hot Sauce,112
Bean Casserole,119
Kidney Beans Koftas with Mushrooms,122
Chickpea Shakshuka,123
Lentil Loaf,127
Potato Chowder with Corn,134
Mushroom Cream Soup,145
Winter Stew,146
Irish Stew,150
Asian Steamed Dumplings,159
Cassoulet,166
Potato Cakes with Filling,168
Mushroom Bourguignon,172
Mushroom Pie,176
Strudel,178
Nut Loaf,180
Spring Rolls,186
Mushroom Bruschetta,191
Mushroom Pate,195
Mushroom Arancini,204
Vegan Gravy,206
Vegan French Sauce,208
Mushroom Sauce,212
Marinara Sauce,216

MUSHROOMS (OYSTER)
Crunchy Oyster Mushrooms,198

MUSHROOMS (PORTOBELLO)
Beet Steaks,181
Portobello Burgers,48
Ratsherrenpfanne,156
Portobello Roast,160
Gyros,189

MUSHROOMS (SHIITAKE)
Bibimbap,171

MUSHROOMS (TRUMPET)
Mushroom "Pulled Pork",170

NAVY BEANS
Navy Beans Biscuits,227

NOODLESSoba Noodles with Curry Tofu,98
Noodle Soup,134

NUTMEG
Baked Oatmeal Cake,25
Breakfast Banana Bread,26
Superfood Cookies,31
Green Burgers,49
Oatmeal Patties,57

Farro Burger,59
Quinoa with Basil and Lemongrass,66
Scalloped Potatoes,81
Vanilla Rice Pudding,86
Chickpea Curry,124
Sloppy Lentils,128
French Onion Soup,135
Butternut Squash Ginger Soup,137
Minestrone,138
Carrot Cake,232

NUTS
Cacao Spread,207

OATMEAL
Acorn Squash Oats,19
Baked Oatmeal Cake,25
Tempeh Burger,44
Jalapeno Burger,47
Vegan Sausages,175

OATS
Apple Oatmeal,14
Miso Oat Porridge,19
Coconut Cut Oats,24
Granola Bars,27
FlapJacks,29
Superfood Cookies,31
Oatmeal Muffins,36
Artichoke Burger,51
Oatmeal Patties,57
Oatmeal with Tender Onions,86
Vegan Nuggets,185
Apple Crumble,229
Date Bars,239

OKRA
Spiced Okra,72
Lentil Gumbo,161

ONION
Tofu Scramble,28
Tender Tofu Cubes,37
Sweet Potato Burgers,41
Mushroom Burger,43
Portobello Burgers,48
Eggplant Burger,53
Green Peas Burger,56
Tikka Masala with Cauliflower,79
Arborio Rice,85
Buckwheat Pasta with Mushroom Sauce,95
Tuscan Sorghum,97
Caprese Pasta,101
Penne Rigate,102
Bulgur Salad,104
Lentil Meatballs,110
Vaquero Beans Chili with Tempeh,113

Spicy Tacos with Beans,114
Kidney Beans Koftas with Mushrooms,122
Lentils Shepherd's Pie,126
Lentil Loaf,127
Lentil Chili,127
Cabbage Rolls with Lentils,131
Wild Rice Soup,132
Cauliflower Soup,133
Potato Chowder with Corn,134
French Onion Soup,135
Quinoa Tomato Soup,136
Lentil Soup,137
Carrot Soup,138
Beet Soup,140
Anti-Inflammatory Soup,140
Taco Soup,141
Mushroom Cream Soup,145
Sweet Potato Stew,149
Kuru Fasulye,149
Coconut Cream Soup,153
Hot Pepper Chickpea Stew,154
Ratsherrenpfanne,156
Turkish Green Beans,157
Nutritious Lasagna,158
Jackfruit Curry,159
Asian Steamed Dumplings,159
Potato Tamales,162
Aloo Gobi,165
Potato Cakes with Filling,168
Hash Brown Omelette,170
Mushroom "Pulled Pork",170
Mushroom Bourguignon,172
Vegan Sausages,175
Stuffed Spinach Shells,177
Strudel,178
Vegan Nuggets,185
Cocktail Balls,192
Appetizer Quinoa Balls,196
Mushroom Arancini,204
Mushroom Sauce,212
Ravioli Sauce,213
Tomato Sauce,215
Marinara Sauce,216
Oregano Onion Dip,221

ONION (RED)
Zucchini Frittata,35
Broccoli Patties,40
Beet Burger,48
Ratatouille,76
Basmati Rague,85
Oatmeal with Tender Onions,86
Freekeh Tacos,96
Black Beans Chili,111
Chickpea Salad,124
Lentil Tomato Salad,130
Minestrone,138

263

Cabbage Detox Soup,142
Summer Stew,154
Posole,160
Saag Tofu with Spinach,162
Herbed Cauliflower Head,167
Rainbow Vegetable Pie,179
Gyros,189
Queso Sauce,214
Guacamole with Broccoli,220

ONION (WHITE)
Breakfast Potatoes,18
Spicy Kale Burger,51
Mushroom Risotto,76
Pasta Fagioli,91
Mushroom Tetrazzini,91
Bolognese,92
Sorgotto,97
Lebanese Lemon and Beans Salad,109
Chickpea Curry,124
Sloppy Lentils,128
African Stew,151
Portobello Roast,160
Chana Masala with Spinach,161
Pumpkin Risotto,177
Spaghetti Sauce,216
Walnut Sauce,222
Glazed White Onions,81
Mushroom Pie,176

ONION (YELLOW)
Artichoke Burger,51
Tofu Burger,53
Vermicelli Bowl,67
Arrabiatta Pasta,92
Bean Enchiladas,118
Bean Casserole,119
Classic Vegetable Soup,133
Winter Stew,146
Vegan "Beef" Stew,146
Tempeh Tajine,165
Nut Loaf,180
Mushroom Bruschetta,191
Vegan Gravy,206
Onion Patties,49

ORANGE
Orange-Pineapple Cake,242
Snickerdoodle Bars,244
Sweet Potato Pie,238

ORANGE JUICE
Pumpkin Butter,209
Tahini Sauce with Orange Juice,219

PASTA
Pasta and Green Peas Side Dish,82

Arrabiatta Pasta,92
Pesto Pasta,99
Taco Pasta,100
Caprese Pasta,101

PASTA (ELBOW)
Minestrone,138

PASTA (PENNE)
Pasta Puttanesca,90
Bolognese,92
Italian Style Pasta,93
Penne Rigate,102
Penne Pasta Soup,145

PASTA (SHELL)
Pasta Fagioli,91

PASTA (SHELLS)
Stuffed Spinach Shells,177

PASTE (CHILI)
Bibimbap,171

PASTE (CURRY)
Soba Noodles with Curry Tofu,98
Curry Rice,100
Curry White Beans,121
Thai Curry Soup,152
Jackfruit Curry,159

PASTE (MISO)
Miso Oat Porridge,19
Carrot Patties,50
Edamame Dip,114
Tofu Strips,197
Vegan Gravy,206
Miso Butter,221

PASTE (TAHINI)
Falafel,23
Beet Burger,48
Carrot Patties,50
Sun Dried Tomato Patties,52
Red Kidney Beans Burger,60
Bean Loaf,117
Tofu Strips,197
Samosa Filling,206
Creamy Green Peas Filling,214
Miso Butter,221

PASTE (TOM YUM)
Tom Yum Soup,153

PEANUT BUTTER
African Stew,151
Tofu Cubes in Peanut Sauce,164

Bean Cookie Dough,226
Banana Cake,248

PEANUTS
African Stew,151
Stuffed Mini Pumpkins,179
Eggplant Rolls,190
Green Croquettes,200
Vegan Cheese Sauce,211
Spinach Sauce,218
White Beans Blondies,228
Chocolate Pudding,241
Semolina Halwa,246
Toffee,247

PEANUTS (GREEN)
Boiled Peanuts,182

PEAR PUREE
Pear Pudding,236

PEARS
Sweet Pear Patties,62
Pear Filling,212
Pear Compote,247

PEAS
Quinoa Patties,39
Cowboy Caviar,112

PEAS (GREEN)
Green Burgers,49
Green Peas Burger,56
Potato Salad,75
Mushroom Risotto,76
Pasta and Green Peas Side Dish,82
Quinoa and Freekeh Mix,96
Rice Garden Salad,105
Quinoa Tomato Soup,136
Vegan "Beef" Stew,146
Peas and Carrot Stew,148
Potato Tamales,162
Tofu Matar,163
Creamy Green Peas Filling,214

PECANS
Buckwheat with Pecans,20
Breakfast Banana Bread,26
Roasted Nuts,184
Candied Pecans,194
Pecan Pie,246

PEPPER (CHILI)
Lebanese Lemon and Beans Salad,109
Beet Soup,140
Fennel Soup,151
Ratsherrenpfanne,156

Lentil Steak,174
Tofu Wraps,183
Vegan Jerky,188
Gyros,189
Mushroom Pate,195
Ravioli Sauce,213
Green Sauce,223
Pizza Sauce,225
Chili Sauce,222
Queso Sauce,214

PEPPER (JALAPENO)
Ratatouille,76
Bean Enchiladas,118
Taco Soup,141
Guacamole with Broccoli,220
Quinoa Patties,39
Jalapeno Burger,47
Vermicelli Bowl,67
Mexican Pinto Beans,107
Cowboy Caviar,112
Spicy Tacos with Beans,114
Lentil Chili,127
Tortilla Soup,144
Soybean Stew,155
Saag Tofu with Spinach,162
Chipotle Fajitas,171
Nut Loaf,180

PINE NUTS
Pesto Pasta,99
Curry Rice,100

PINEAPPLE
Cardamom Pineapple Sticks,196
Orange-Pineapple Cake,242
Pineapple Rice,77

PINEAPPLE JUICE
Pineapple Rice,77

POLENTA
Polenta,70
Rosemary Creamed Polenta,90
Polenta Fries,200

POMEGRANATE
Cashew Yogurt with Pomegranate Seeds,26

POTATOES
Bean Casserole,119
Quinoa Patties,39
Broccoli Patties,40
Cauliflower Potato Burgers,40
Sweet Potato Burgers,41
Bok Choy Patties,61
Bean Loaf,117

Pumpkin Cream Soup,132
Potato Chowder with Corn,134
Lentil Soup,137
Kale and Sweet Potato Soup,139
Broccoli Soup,144
Penne Pasta Soup,145
Mediterranean Vegan Stew,148
Garden Stew,152
Portobello Roast,160
Tempeh Tajine,165
Aloo Gobi,165
Potato Cakes with Filling,168
Tempeh Potato Wraps,182
Cocktail Balls,192
Scallion Pancakes,203
Cayenne Pepper Filling,210
Vegan Cheese Sauce,211
Sweet Potato Pie,238
Potato Tamales,162
Vegan French Sauce,208
Breakfast Potatoes,18
Stuffed Sweet Potato,31
Potato Chaat,32
Tempeh Bowl,37
Potato Pancakes,38
Potato Patties,41
Turnip Patties,58
Celery Patties,58
Mashed White Potato Patties,63
Lemon Potatoes,66
Mashed Potato,67
Sweet Potato Mash,68
Baked Potato,69
Crushed Baby Potatoes,78
Scalloped Potatoes,81
Stuffed Sweet Potato with Beans,121
Classic Vegetable Soup,133
Leek Soup,135
Potato Cream Soup,136
Beet Soup,140
Anti-Inflammatory Soup,140
Mushroom Cream Soup,145
Winter Stew,146
Vegan "Beef" Stew,146
Egyptian Stew,147
Peas and Carrot Stew,148
Sweet Potato Stew,149
Irish Stew,150
Texas Stew,155
Jackfruit Curry,159
Korma,166
Hash Brown Omelette,170
Green Croquettes,200
Breakfast Hash,29
Potato Salad,75
Bean Enchiladas,118

PUMPKIN
Pumpkin Puree,65
Pumpkin Cream Soup,132
Mini Breakfast Carrot Cakes,24
Superfood Cookies,31
Pumpkin Burger,45
Sweet Baby Carrots,72
Pumpkin Mac and Cheese,94
Korma,166
Ravioli,174
Pumpkin Risotto,177
Stuffed Mini Pumpkins,179
Pumpkin Hummus,183
Garlic Pumpkin Seeds,199
Flaked Clusters,201
Pumpkin Butter,209
Pumpkin Butter,209
Caramel Pumpkin Sauce,213
Coconut Filling,218
Pumpkin Muffins,230
Pumpkin Spice Pie,233
Pumpkin Pudding,237

QUINOA
Soaked Quinoa,21
Brown Rice Congee,32
Breakfast Bowl,34
Quinoa Patties,39
Butternut Squash Burger,46
Cranberry Patties,62
Quinoa with Basil and Lemongrass,66
Quinoa and Freekeh Mix,96
Vegan Quinoa Pilaf,105
Burrito Bowl,111
Pinto Beans Quinoa Salad,116
Quinoa Tomato Soup,136
Quinoa Sandwich,187
Appetizer Quinoa Balls,196

RADISH
Lentil Radish Salad,108

RAISINS
Granola Bars,27
Vanilla Rice Pudding,86
Gajar Halwa,229

RASPBERRIES
Raspberry Pancake Bites,22

RICE
Rice with Maple Syrup,18
Rice Pudding,20
Zucchini Patties,50
Mexican Rice,69
Mushroom Risotto,76

Pineapple Rice,77
Sweet Rice,84
Vanilla Rice Pudding,86
Rice Garden Salad,105
Rice and Beans Bowl,118
Wild Rice Soup,132
Summer Stew,154
Stuffed Eggplants,167
Bibimbap,171
Stuffed Mini Pumpkins,179
Mushroom Arancini,204
Mexican Rice Filling,207
Mint Filling,217
Japgokbap,84
Pumpkin Risotto,177
Bok Choy Patties,61
Leek Patties,63

RICE (ARBORIO)
Arborio Rice,85

RICE (BASMATI)
Brown Rice Congee,32
Basmati Rague,85

RICE (BROWN)
Brown Rice Congee,32
Jalapeno Burger,47
Artichoke Burger,51
Brown Rice,80
Multi-Grain Porridge,88
Curry White Beans,121

RICE (JASMINE)
Curry Rice,100

RICE (WILD)
Wild Rice Burger,52

RICE MILK
Rice Pudding,20
Raspberry Pancake Bites,22
Mini Breakfast Carrot Cakes,24
Baked Oatmeal Cake,25
Banana Pancakes,28

SALSA
Freekeh Tacos,96
Lentil Tacos,109
Rice and Beans Bowl,118

SAUCE (ADOBO)
Sofritas Tofu,199

SAUCE (BARBECUE)
Baked Beans,107

SAUCE (BBQ)
Mushroom "Pulled Pork",170
Tempeh Ribs,178
Vegan Jerky,188

SAUCE (BUFFALO)
Buffalo Chickpea,115
Buffalo Chickpea,125
Buffalo Brussels Sprouts,195

SAUCE (ENCHILADA)
Bean Enchiladas,118

SAUCE (FISH)
Thai Curry Soup,152
Asian Steamed Dumplings,159
Tso's Tofu,163
Teriyaki Tofu,169
Tofu Wraps,183
Spring Rolls,186
Carrot "Dogs",188

SAUCE (HOT)
Chipotle Chili with Hot Sauce,112
Vegan Buffalo Dip,221
Edamole,225

SAUCE (MARINARA)
Pasta Marinara,70
Bolognese,92
Italian Style Pasta,93

SAUCE (PASTA)
Pasta Puttanesca,90
Arrabiatta Pasta,92

SAUCE (PIZZA)
Pizza Pasta,101

SAUCE (QUESO)
Crunchwrap Supreme,185

SAUCE (SALSA)
Crunchwrap Supreme,185
SAUCE (TAMARI)
Tempeh Potato Wraps,182
Balsamic Rice Noodles,89
Tempeh Tajine,165

SAUCE (TERIYAKI)
Teriyaki Tofu,169

SCALLIONS
Beetroot Fold-Overs,193
Scallion Pancakes,203
Green Sauce,223

SHALLOT
Chickpea Shakshuka,123
Mushroom Pate,195
SORGHUM
Tuscan Sorghum,97
Sorgotto,97

SOY CREAM
Flan Mini Cakes,235

SOY MILK
Soy Yogurt,17
Breakfast Banana Bread,26
Apple Crumble,229
Pear Pudding,236
Rhubarb Bars,237
Banana Cream Tart,240
Cinnamon Swirls,245

SOYBEANS
Soybean Stew,155
Tofu Cubes in Peanut Sauce,164

SPAGHETTI
Lemon Pasta,106
Spaghetti Squash Bean Bowl,120

SPINACH
Lentil Tomato Salad,130
Breakfast Quiche,15
Stuffed Sweet Potato,31
Tempeh Bowl,37
Spinach Patties,44
Mac with Artichokes,99
Rice Garden Salad,105
Lentil Stew with Spinach,117
Buddha Bowl,123
Minestrone,138
Spinach and Lentils Soup,143
Broccoli Soup,144
Garden Stew,152
Tom Yum Soup,153
Hot Pepper Chickpea Stew,154
Summer Stew,154
Iranian Stew ,156
Chana Masala with Spinach,161
Saag Tofu with Spinach,162
Bibimbap,171
Stuffed Spinach Shells,177
Turkish Vegan Borek,188
Green Croquettes,200
Spinach Dip,209
Avocado Pesto,212
Spinach Sauce,218
Green Sauce,223

SPRING ONIONS
268

Spring Rolls,186
Fragrant Spring Onions,180

SRIRACHA
Tempeh Bowl,37
Portobello Burgers,48
Balsamic Rice Noodles,89
Tofu Spaghetti,94
Spinach Sauce,218

STRAWBERRIES
Soy Yogurt,17

SYRUP (AGAVE)
Jackfruit Coated Bites,198

SYRUP (CHAI)
Carambola in Chai Syrup,249

SYRUP (GOLDEN)
FlapJacks,29
Superfood Cookies,31
Tempeh Burger,44

SYRUP (STRAWBERRY)
Strawberry Gummies,231

TACO
Freekeh Tacos,96
Spicy Tacos with Beans,114

TAHINI
Miso Oat Porridge,19
Pumpkin Hummus,183
Tahini Sauce with Orange Juice,219
Baba Ganoush,222
Arugula Hummus,224
Chickpea Chocolate Hummus,227

TAPIOCA
Tapioca Pudding,21
Tapioca Porridge,35

TEMPEH
Tempeh Bowl,37
Vaquero Beans Chili with Tempeh,113
Tempeh Tajine,165
Tempeh Ribs,178
Tempeh Potato Wraps,182
Delicious Lettuce Wraps,186
Vegan Jerky,188

TOFU
Breakfast Quiche,15
Breakfast Grits,23
Tofu Scramble,28

Tofu Omelet,34
Zucchini Frittata,35
Tender Tofu Cubes,37
Mushroom Burger,43
Jalapeno Burger,47
Tofu Burger,53
Corn Burger,54
Farro Burger,59
Semolina-Cilantro Patties,61
Cranberry Patties,62
Leek Patties,63
Bolognese,92
Tofu Spaghetti,94
Soba Noodles with Curry Tofu,98
Caprese Pasta,101
Pizza Pasta,101
Thai Curry Soup,152
Vegan Butter "Chicken",158
Saag Tofu with Spinach,162
Tofu Matar,163
Tso's Tofu,163
Korma,166
Teriyaki Tofu,169
Bibimbap,171
Deli Slices,176
Tofu Wraps,183
Crunchwrap Supreme,185
Gyros,189
Tofu Strips,197
Sofritas Tofu,199
Sweet Tofu Cubes,205
Vegan French Sauce,208
Cheesecake,235

TOMATO JUICE
Vaquero Beans Chili with Tempeh,113
Cabbage Rolls with Lentils,131
Creamy Tomato Soup,141
Sweet Potato Stew,149
Delicious Lettuce Wraps,186
Ravioli Sauce,213
Pizza Sauce,225

TOMATO PASTE
Tofu Scramble,28
Mexican Rice,69
Ratatouille,76
Fragrant Bulgur,80
Pasta and Green Peas Side Dish,82
Basmati Rague,85
Teff in Tomato Paste,87
Tomato Spaghetti,93
Penne Rigate,102
Bulgur Salad,104
Baked Beans,107
Mexican Pinto Beans,107
Red Kidney Beans Burrito,110

Creamy Kidney Beans,113
Spicy Tacos with Beans,114
Curry White Beans,121
Kidney Beans Koftas with Mushrooms,122
Lentil Loaf,127
Lentil Ragout,129
Lentil Soup,137
Minestrone,138
Beet Soup,140
Tortilla Soup,144
Winter Stew,146
Egyptian Stew,147
Moroccan Stew,147
Peas and Carrot Stew,148
Kuru Fasulye,149
Irish Stew,150
Turkish Green Beans,157
Portobello Roast,160
Tofu Matar,163
Stuffed Eggplants,167
Teriyaki Tofu,169
Chipotle Fajitas,171
Mushroom Bourguignon,172
Vegan Pepperoni,175
Vegan Sausages,175
Stuffed Mini Pumpkins,179
Appetizer Quinoa Balls,196
Red Kidney Beans Sauce,210
Tomato Sauce,215
Spaghetti Sauce,216
Marinara Sauce,216
Tomato Bean Pate,217
Chili Sauce,222

TOMATO PUREE
Chickpea Shakshuka,123
Lentil Bolognese,126
Quinoa Tomato Soup,136

TOMATO SAUCE
Tempeh Burger,44
Lebanese Lemon and Beans Salad,109
Black Beans Chili,111
Chipotle Chili with Hot Sauce,112
Bean Loaf,117
Spaghetti Squash Bean Bowl,120
Sloppy Lentils,128
Lentil Mash,129
Vegan "Beef" Stew,146
Irish Stew,150
Vegan Butter "Chicken",158
Mushroom "Pulled Pork",170
Stuffed Spinach Shells,177
Vegan Nuggets,185
Delicious Lettuce Wraps,186

TOMATOES

Tofu Scramble,28
Avocado Sandwiches,38
Tender Sweet Peppers,71
Arrabiatta Pasta,92
Tuscan Sorghum,97
Dill Orzo,103
Chickpea Shakshuka,123
Lentil Ragout,129
Red Lentil Dal,130
Chickpea Soup,142
Vegan "Beef" Stew,146
Garden Stew,152
Chana Masala with Spinach,161
Tofu Matar,163
Tempeh Tajine,165
Aloo Gobi,165
Stuffed Eggplants,167
Rainbow Vegetable Pie,179
Crunchwrap Supreme,185
Buffalo Chickpea,125
Creamy Tomato Soup,141
Sun Dried Tomato Patties,52
Ratatouille,76
Tikka Masala with Cauliflower,79
Pasta Fagioli,91
Bolognese,92
Tomato Spaghetti,93
Caprese Pasta,101
Bulgur Salad,104
Rice Garden Salad,105
Lebanese Lemon and Beans Salad,109
Black Beans Chili,111
Cowboy Caviar,112
Vaquero Beans Chili with Tempeh,113
Lentil Stew with Spinach,117
Chickpea Curry,124
Lentil Chili,127
Lentil Tomato Salad,130
Classic Vegetable Soup,133
Minestrone,138
Beta Carotene Booster Soup,139
Tuscan Soup,143
Tortilla Soup,144
Mediterranean Vegan Stew,148
Sweet Potato Stew,149
Rainbow Stew,150
Tom Yum Soup,153
Texas Stew,155
Soybean Stew,155
Turkish Green Beans,157
Nutritious Lasagna,158
Lentil Gumbo,161
Cassoulet,166
Herbed Tomato,189
Ravioli Sauce,213

Marinara Sauce,216
Guacamole with Broccoli,220
Chili Sauce,222
Roasted Pepper Salsa,224

TOMATOES (CHERRY)
Tomato Farfalle with Arugula,103
Cabbage Detox Soup,142

WALNUTS
Granola Bars,27
Breakfast Cookies,30
Almond Milk Cocktail,33
Oatmeal Muffins,36
Green Beans with Nuts,74
Tomato Farfalle with Arugula,103
Nut Loaf,180
Walnut Sauce,222
Navy Beans Biscuits,227
Carrot Cake,232
Brownies,234
Cookie Cake,240
Walnut Sweets,244

WINE (RED)
Mushroom Bourguignon,172
Beet Steaks,181
Marinara Sauce,216

WINE (WHITE)
Sorgotto,97
Vegan Gravy,206

YAMS
Buddha Bowl,123
African Stew,151

ZUCCHINI
Breakfast Hash,29
Potato Chaat,32
Zucchini Frittata,35
Beet Burger,48
Zucchini Patties,50
Ratatouille,76
Zoodles,83
Tuscan Sorghum,97
Penne Rigate,102
Zoodles with Lentils,115
Minestrone,138
Rainbow Stew,150
Soybean Stew,155
Nutritious Lasagna,158
Vegetable Gnocchi,172
Rainbow Vegetable Pie,179

Copyright 2020 by Mirra Reddy All rights reserved.

All rights Reserved. No part of this publication or the information in it may be quoted from or reproduced in any form by means such as printing, scanning, photocopying or otherwise without prior written permission of the copyright holder.

Disclaimer and Terms of Use: Effort has been made to ensure that the information in this book is accurate and complete, however, the author and the publisher do not warrant the accuracy of the information, text and graphics contained within the book due to the rapidly changing nature of science, research, known and unknown facts and internet. The Author and the publisher do not hold any responsibility for errors, omissions or contrary interpretation of the subject matter herein. This book is presented solely for motivational and informational purposes only.

Printed in Great Britain
by Amazon